Indigenous Archives

Indigenous Archives

The Maya Diaspora and
Mobile Cultural Production

Floridalma Boj Lopez

Duke University Press
Durham and London

2 0 2 6

© 2026 Duke University Press
This work is licensed under a Creative Commons
Attribution-NonCommercial 4.0 International License,
available at https://creativecommons.org/licenses/by-nc/4.0/.
Project Editor: Ihsan Taylor
Designed by A. Mattson Gallagher
Typeset in Arno Pro by Copperline Book Services

Library of Congress Cataloging-in-Publication Data
Names: Boj Lopez, Floridalma, [date] author.
Title: Indigenous archives : the Maya diaspora and mobile cultural production / Floridalma Boj Lopez.
Description: Durham : Duke University Press, 2026. | Includes bibliographical references and index.
Identifiers: LCCN 2025024289 (print)
LCCN 2025024290 (ebook)
ISBN 9781478033011 (paperback)
ISBN 9781478029564 (hardcover)
ISBN 9781478061755 (ebook)
ISBN 9781478094470 (ebook other)
Subjects: LCSH: Maya youth—California—Los Angeles—Social life and customs. | Maya arts—Social aspects—California—Los Angeles. | Mayas—California—Los Angeles—Ethnic identity. | Mayas—Relocation—California—Los Angeles. | Collective memory—Guatemala. | Politics and culture.
Classification: LCC E99.M433 B65 2026 (print) | LCC E99.M433 (ebook)
LC record available at https://lccn.loc.gov/2025024289
LC ebook record available at https://lccn.loc.gov/2025024290

Cover art: Photograph by Mayán Alvarado Goldberg.

This book is freely available in an open access edition thanks to TOME (Toward an Open Monograph Ecosystem)— a collaboration of the Association of American Universities, the Association of University Presses, and the Association of Research Libraries and the generous support of Arcadia, a charitable fund of Lisbet Rausing and Peter Baldwin, and the UCLA Library. Learn more at the TOME website, available at openmonographs.org.

To the children of the Maya diaspora, especially my daughters Soledad and Luna. You are our collective hope for a today and tomorrow that honors the knowledge, joy, and struggle of our ancestors.

Contents

Foreword ix
Oscar Ubaldo Boj Chojolán

Acknowledgments xiii

Introduction 1

1 Contesting the Logics of Displacement 33
  in the Production of the Indigenous Migrant

2 Weaving Maya Geographies, Textiles, 53
  and Relationality in Diaspora

3 La Comunidad Ixim and Organizing 81
  in the Maya Diaspora

4 Returning the Gaze, Reclaiming the Image: 111
  Contemporary Photography as Archive Making

Conclusion 137

Notes 143
Bibliography 159
Index 175

Foreword

Dialoguing with Dr. Floridalma Boj Lopez, a Guatemalan migrant academic, is important because it allows us to know and understand contexts based on struggles that are invisible to the eyes of the world. *Indigenous Archives* is a relevant dialogue that explores the ways of life of families and extended kinship that gather in the Maya diaspora in Los Angeles. Without a doubt, this dialogue is strengthened by the life story of the author, who migrated to the United States without knowing it due to her young age. It should be noted that the migration of Floridalma Boj and thousands of other migrants is the result of economic, social, and political violence produced by the colonial model that enables the institutional-structural strengthening that rages against the Indigenous population of Guatemala, promoting a racist and exclusionary system in which being Indigenous is one of the worst social positions within Guatemalan society. This historical construction of power in all its spheres spreads, sustains, and reproduces a system that promotes national evils such as exclusion and racism against the Indigenous population of Guatemala.

As Dr. Boj states in her book, arriving in new and unknown territories causes migrants to confront "transnational structures of racism," which in my opinion becomes the dilemma of using culture as a compass that guides those who have little or no experience of their original homeland. This influences migrants to, as the author points out, naturalize settler colonial grammars, which opens the way to accepting the global-consumerist model and leaving aside their original culture. Dr. Boj's proposal is surprising in that it goes against the option of forgetting one's cultural roots and, to the contrary, argues that migrants turn them into strengths to solidly establish their own culture in diaspora.

Dr. Boj proposes that these "Indigenous archives" must be visualized in facts, objects, or things of daily use or contact as well as in other contexts that need a conscious impulse that stirs the seed, that activates the chlorophyll from its roots—but for this it is important to know the structural and systemic context that has caused the migration from its bases in the place of origin. In this sense the book introduces us to conditions that produced migration from the 1960s to the 1990s, through the experiences of Denese Joy Becker/Dominga Sic Ruiz, a survivor of one of the many massacres that were mostly suffered by the Indigenous population of Guatemala, in particular the Río Negro massacre (1982) in the northern department of Baja Verapaz. The book goes on to argue in a remarkable way and, from my point of view, in accordance with its name, that the Maya clothing of migrant women is a tangible example of Indigenous archives, because when we stop to contemplate it, we will find technology, nuances, and designs that at first glance can be conceived as clothing that fulfills the purpose of covering the body. However, when we understand the symbolism of the signs, the colors, and the techniques it contains, it shows the richness revealed by the knowledge of the civilization that sustained it.

The Indigenous archive cannot remain solely a discourse or a static folkloric costume. Instead, these practices are valuable because they emerge from a living culture that not only cares about surviving biologically but fights to gain spaces for "cultural creation" (to use Dr. Boj's term). In this sense, it is necessary to rediscover the basic ethical and aesthetic framework for practicing one's own cultural characteristics as elements of spiritual value. This need flourishes and is concretized in this book, which contains, indeed needs, colors that reveal the racism within "overlapping racial regimes in the United States" (Dr. Boj). Thus, in activating this knowledge, we can give fluidity to culture, activating that torrent which at one time seemed immobile when we did not know that it was the record that has always accompanied us, waiting to mobilize within that body that we recognize as diaspora.

Another of the contributions of the author's academic argument is to promote thinking about extended kinship through the images saved in photographs. It can be observed as distant and immobile memories of ancestors, grandparents, and grandmothers who stayed behind, yet if we dismantle that idea, as proposed by Dr. Boj, and on the contrary we propose them now as Indigenous archives, we can give life to our frozen, forgotten, or buried thoughts. These may have been buried in our memories for one or another reason, but we can now see them as the impulse that shows our strengths and the desire to live again, but now with our own forms, with our colors, flavors, smells, sounds, and textures.

Oscar Ubaldo Boj Chojolán

The discussion is open. If we recognize that our grandparents bequeathed us the values of agreement *and* discernment within the principle of the double gaze, now we must discuss the book which has represented hard work, sleeplessness, enthusiasm, and discipline, but above all the vision of valuing the ancient Maya ancestral culture. I can only express to Dr. Floridalma Boj Lopez my admiration, and to the public my wish for us to reflect on the proposal contained in *Indigenous Archives*. For my part I want to express my gratitude to the author because in this book, I feel her gaze back to the land where she left her Muxu'x (belly button). I allow myself to applaud the call for us to be aware of processes that must give rise to changes, in the direction of regrounding our Maya relationships regardless of the distance or other factors in these challenging historical moments.

Oscar Ubaldo Boj Chojolán
Xelajuj No'j, Ixim Ulew

Acknowledgments

This book would not have been possible without the members of the diaspora who allowed me to interview them. I kept pushing along in my career because I knew that there were members of our community who needed to hear your stories. Much of what is written about our diaspora emphasizes the hardships we face. That is necessary work as we continue to push back against the policies and practices that harm so many of our families. Yet, I also want to honor the truth that when we gather, we share laughter, we share food, we share teachings that have been passed down through generations. We deserve to have space in academia for this love of our culture and history that binds us together. I often imagine a young person, not unlike all of you, who may be assigned this work and might feel that they, too, can gather with other people in the Indigenous diaspora to create community against structures that work to erase and eliminate us. I am so very grateful that, for those few hours, you sat with me and shared a part of your story.

This project was funded in part by the American Association of University Women and an American Council of Learned Societies postdoctoral fellowship. Both fellowships granted me the gift of time to sit, think, write, and revise. The Maya Womxn in L.A. project also received support from the Critical Refugee Studies Collective and was a collaboration with Las Fotos Project, which provided technical equipment, staff support for the exhibit, and hands-on support at every stage of the project.

I also want to thank the editors I worked with at Duke University Press, particularly Alejandra Mejía. From her first reading of my monograph, Ale was an enthusiastic collaborator, and her encouragement helped me find the courage to finish this book. I also thank the reviewers who, through multiple rounds of review, pushed my thinking and helped me take intellectual risks that I hope have paid off. I am also grateful to the production team at DUP that helped get this book completed. All errors are mine and mine alone.

I express my gratitude to my department, Chicana/o and Central American Studies, at the University of California, Los Angeles, whose members have always been supportive of and excited about my work. I especially thank my colleagues Leisy Abrego, Gaye Theresa Johnson, Laura Chavez-Moreno, Karina Alma, Veronica Terriquez, and Charlene Villaseñor Black. At the University of Southern California, Macarena Gómez-Barris, George Lopez, and Laura Serna were instrumental in getting me to the finish line of my PhD. By virtue of being from L.A., I have also been very lucky to connect with critical and committed scholars who have become friends and comrades. My gratitude to Akhila Ananth, Cecilia Caballero, Priscilla Leiva, Maurice Magaña, Steven Osuna, and Gretel Vera-Rosas.

Over time at multiple institutions, I have been fortunate to work with talented and inspiring students like Andy Aleman, Cindy Perez, Paula Ayala, Mario Alvarado Cifuentes, Omar Alvarado, Luis Soltillo, Kristie Valdez-Guillen, Sara Diaz-Montejano, and Madison Garcia. In at least a couple of instances, Kristie Valdez-Guillen supported me with data analysis and Institutional Review Board submissions, and Charlie Navarro helped me fix my citations before I submitted the manuscript. Personally, I try to be mindful of requesting student labor, even when it is compensated, so I am grateful for their support.

I have also benefited from the care and commitment of other Indigenous diaspora scholars whom I have learned from and learned with. Through their own work, they have shown me that, for those of us with ties to our communities on our ancestral homelands, being committed is a responsibility, but really it is a gift. Thank you to Daina Sanchez, Giovanni Batz, Alejandro Villalpando, Brenda Nicolas, Luis Sánchez-López, Gloria Chacón, Genner Llanes-Ortiz, Arce Tecun (Daniel Hernandez), Luis Urrieta, and Lourdes Alberto. Your work and the way you carry yourselves reminds me that academia can be what it is, and still we create space. I especially remember picking up a random book at the library at UC Santa Cruz and being blown away just reading the first couple of pages. The book was *Red Pedagogy*, and since then I have benefited from Sandy Grande's sharp thinking and mentorship.

As someone rooted in community in L.A., I have also had friends along the way who have consistently expressed their encouragement, and the times we have collaborated have been wonderful learning experiences. Thank you to Maricela Lopez Samayoa, Aurora Pedro, Melissa Espiritu,

Cindy Mata, Ron Espiritu, Emily Grijalva, Karla Alvarado Goldberg, and Susie Parras.

I am grateful for the community I have built in Xelajuj No'j. This book is not about the community work I have engaged with in Xela, but you all have provided grounding and care as I turned this project into a book. Willy Barreno and Ixquik Poz, thank you for your kindness; I have learned so much from you, and I enjoy every time our paths cross. To the friends I've met at DESGUA: Jason, Rosita, Ramona, Mildreth, Fabiola, and many others—thank you for helping me build a community there. To EYCEJ, I have continued in academia in part because I have you all as my local community in East Los Angeles to remind me that the struggle toward justice is long, but it is collective.

I am grateful to my in-laws, both the Lopez and Gutierrez families, especially to Gabriel Gutierrez, who let me tag along with him to institutional archives as I was trying to understand what archival methods meant in practical terms. This book would not be possible without the support of my in-laws Gerardo and Elsa, who act as a second set of parents to my girls. I am likewise grateful to my family, the part of the Boj family that migrated to L.A. and faced the reality of loss in a huge urban city; all of us figured out our paths little by little. You all were the inspiration for my intellectual curiosity: I wanted to understand our history to make sense of our realities. I am so glad that many of you have made return trips back to the homeland, something that was not possible decades ago when we arrived, but the experiences of being rooted to Xela will always tie us together.

I also want to express my gratitude to my family in Xela, the Boj family that stayed firmly planted and has opened the door for me to learn and to heal. Every year, at the beginning of November, you go and lay flowers where my grandparents, my auntie, my uncle, and my father have been laid to rest. Every year, that action reminds me that I am loved because my ancestors are loved. Along this path there have been tremendous barriers, but I have always asked my father's spirit especially to guide me, to show me the paths I need to walk, and to help me walk them with integrity. We didn't know each other for very long before borders and death separated us, but it has been in becoming a mother and a scholar that I have felt his guidance. I am grateful to my father, Marlon; to my Tía Flori, my Tíos Fidel and Vinicio, and my grandparents, Fidelio and Paulina; and to the other relatives who have passed away but whose presence I still feel in my life—I remember you often.

And last, but certainly not least, I want to express the sheer joy of belonging to my little family with mark!, Soledad, and Luna. I appreciate your love and kindness every day and, regardless of any struggle, I am so grateful that I get to have you three in my life. You've been very patient as I traveled this journey of being an academic, and I hope that you see the love you give me reflected back to you in this work.

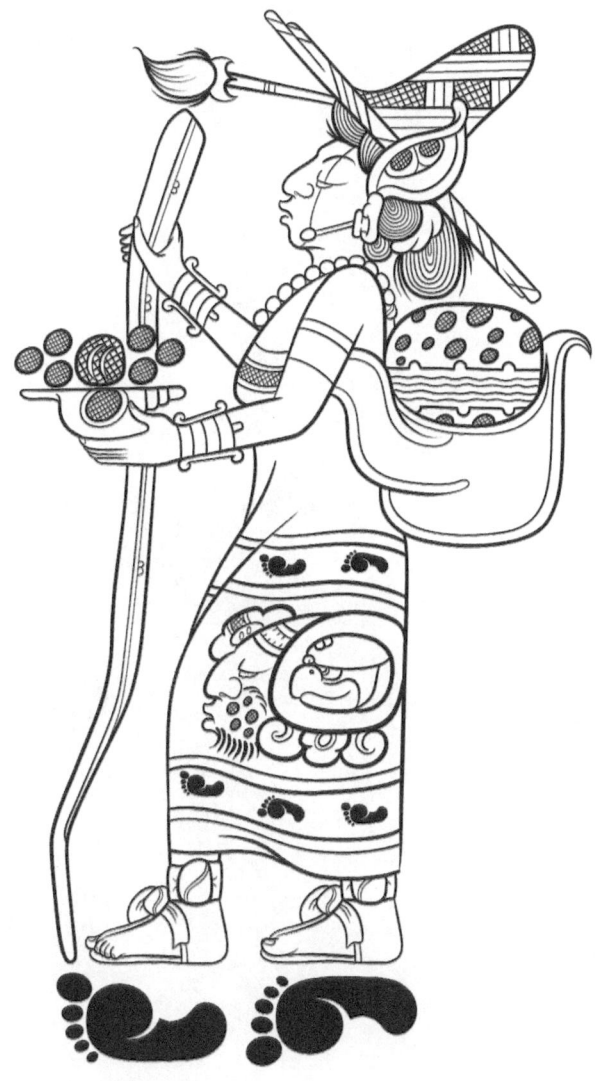

FM. 1 An image created by Walter Amilcar Paz Joj to illustrate the themes of the book and my life experiences.

Introduction

In 2010, Teatro Frida Kahlo in Los Angeles, California, presented *Sentado en un árbol caído*. A play written by Emanuel S. Loarca and performed by Manuel Chitay, it was based on the narrative of one of the survivors of the 1982 Río Negro massacres in Rabinal, Baja Verapaz, Guatemala. In 1993, Jesús Tecú Osorio became a public figure when he submitted an official complaint of an illegal mass grave in his home village. This complaint led to the exhumation of some of his family and other community members whom the military had massacred and buried. Besides the exhumation, Tecú Osorio's testimony and his retelling of the massacre at Pak'oxom were crucial to prosecuting three top-ranking local civilian patrol leaders who had carried out the massacre.[1] Since the initial complaint, documentaries have featured Jesús Tecú Osorio's testimony, and he has written a book that became the basis for *Sentado en un árbol caído*. Centered on the prominent image of an eleven-year-old Jesús sitting on the trunk of a fallen tree as military officers brutalize women and children from the village, this play extends the power of testimony and memory to produce a new archive—one that is visual, audible, and also mobile.[2]

As the 2013 trial of Efraín Ríos Montt and subsequent appeals made painfully clear, seeking justice through juridical structures, especially when top-ranking military officials are involved, is often directly linked to the contest over whose narratives and memories are institutionally legitimate. When official state narratives continue to claim that there was no genocide— that if there were any massacres, they were not tied to the military— cultural productions like *Sentado en un árbol caído* shine light on the need to center Maya experiences to challenge national discourses of forgetting.[3] This type of cultural production directly challenges the layered and transnational anti-Indigenous politics that would have Maya people either disappear or survive solely as an exploited labor force. Cultural productions and practices like this become part of a larger process of organizing the Indigenous diaspora to make political critiques and social demands in a way that centers Maya epistemologies and experiences.

While Tecú Osorio's testimony can be analyzed within a context limited to the territory of Guatemala, the effort to showcase this testimony in Los Angeles demonstrates the power of Maya stories that invoke the armed conflict in Guatemala and use Maya epistemologies to make sense of diasporic life in Los Angeles. As I have seen this play performed across Los Angeles in university spaces, art galleries, and a community theater, it has constantly reminded me that Maya stories unveil the frictions between the necropolitics of state violence and Maya practices of life making. The emotional resonance of the performance is deep sorrow and grief because of the violent massacre, but the power of the performance also lies in audience members witnessing the survival of Tecú Osorio as a Maya person who uses his story to hold the state accountable. That the play was performed in Los Angeles is a testament to the mobility of the medium of performance art *and* to the desire to bear witness for the audience. For me, this bearing witness in the collective is always a powerful experience and reminder that these histories and forms of resistance are indeed carried collectively.

The forms of cultural production I analyze in this book are grounded in Indigenous experiences and critique violence while centering Maya survivance.[4] For instance, the use of Maya clothing in the diaspora, which is the focus of chapter 2, marks Maya bodies as belonging to a living ancestral homeland while simultaneously pointing to the very embodied reality of displacement when worn outside of that homeland. The tension between highlighting the reality of violence while centering Maya perseverance is also present in the cultural production of new space and experiences. For instance, take T-shirts produced by La Comunidad Ixim, the collective I highlight in chapter 3. Their T-shirt reads, "I [heart] L.A.," but the heart symbol usually found on these shirts is replaced with the quetzal, whose red breast is an important identity symbol for Guatemalans in diaspora.[5] The T-shirt becomes a material record of how children raised in the diaspora continue to assert their homelands but intertwine this assertion with their affective attachments to the places in which they have grown up. These cultural productions become artifacts that document longer histories of displacement and belonging and the process of making history while continuing to mark presence for many years to come.

These cultural artifacts and the routes they travel alongside diasporic communities articulate the Maya diasporic experience through multidirectional intergenerational memory around the Guatemalan civil war. The issues of memory extend beyond the boundaries of the Guatemalan nation because so many people have relocated, migrated, and been dispossessed. Mainstream histories and portrayals have depicted diasporic Mayas as victims of brutal genocidal violence in the state of Guatemala and legal violence outside that country as predominantly undocumented immigrants. While these narratives are true, if we extend our analysis of genocidal violence both temporally and geographically, we can also draw connections between these histories to uncover how these systems operate differently across national borders while simultaneously hinging on the elimination of vibrant Indigenous communities.

Mayas represent a paradox of being both rooted in ancestral territory for millennia and hypermobile due to contemporary migration and deportation circuits. As archives move with migrants, Indigeneity travels across national borders and generates disjunctures that can help scholars reconceptualize belonging. Immigrant exclusion is organized around national citizenship, but scholars have highlighted that both historically and in the contemporary moment, the US immigration system is also classed, racialized, and gendered. For Mayas, Indigeneity becomes a critical site of difference in the ways they experience the violence of migration. As migration also represents dispossession from an *ancestral* relationship to specific territories, looking at material artifacts offers a distinct way to conceptualize the continuity that exists alongside deep disruptions. That is to say, Mayas have—and when necessary, create—routes to maintain or establish a relationship to land despite being physically removed from their ancestral territory. An Indigenous migrant identity, being deeply tied to both place *and* mobility, also illuminates a particular nonlinear relationship to racial categories of Latinidad and Indigeneity in the United States.

Mobile Archives of Indigeneity

Historical memory is anchored in Maya epistemologies (ways of knowing) and experiences through materials that move with migrants to support Maya community formation in a diaspora. The journey of migration often requires bringing only what one can carry, and while the things that migrants carry have a story to tell in and of themselves, that story is less about their episteme as Indigenous people and more about their knowledge as migrants attempting to survive an increasingly militarized border landscape that includes all of Mexico.[6] Even just one generation after immigration, the children of migrants do not always have access to family heirlooms or land rights. Within this context of Indigenous dispossession, what materials do Maya migrants keep to tell their stories?

Despite dispossession, Mayas in Los Angeles have changed not only the demographic definition of Latinidad, they have created economic and geographic space to maintain community ties and practices.[7] These include such seemingly contradictory spatial practices as holding Maya ceremonies in the parking lots of churches and open-air markets on the sidewalks of Union Avenue and Sixth Street in Los Angeles. Mobile archives of Indigeneity challenge displacement because they cohere Maya collectives in diaspora and seek to disrupt the way settler colonialism functions to disappear Mayas into a Latinidad defined through mestizaje to the exclusion of Indigenous subjecthood. Mayas in Los Angeles create and add new meaning to cultural materials that engage their experiences and histories. Unpacking these materials and processes through the stories of migrants and their children is critical to expanding how we understand both archives that exist and those that are in formation. The issue is not simply one of being able to access or produce institutionalized archives. The issue is actually much larger, in that the logic that anchors preservation and exhibition has historically relied upon dispossession. It goes beyond collaborating with "culture bearers" and challenges us to understand that mobile archives of Indigeneity are not vested in the preservation and exhibition of artifacts for the general public but instead are meant to retain knowledge of the cultural, spiritual, and political life of Maya migrants in order to build a collective.

Mobile archives of Indigeneity push back against institutionalized archives that consolidate national power by acting as repositories for information that facilitates legibility in the service of governmentality.[8] Given the settler imperative to categorize and organize people and histories in order to create or uphold a national discourse, institutional archives are a particularly difficult place for people who have a long history of being dehumanized. If, however, as María Cotera writes, we must "imagine the archive as both noun and verb,"[9] Black studies and Indigenous studies scholars have done critical work to analyze historical time and archival form creatively to understand diasporic formation. Black feminist historian Saidiya Hartman has powerfully articulated the absence from archives of some descendants of enslaved people brought to the "New World."[10] To combat this seeming absence from official archives, Black scholars—and Black queer scholars in particular—have instead turned to the archives that do exist to provide readings that anchor Black life in its complexity. Paul Gilroy's canonical text, *Black Atlantic,* alongside Omise'eke Natasha Tinsley's interventions in "Black Atlantic, Queer Atlantic," demonstrates that memory and history are stored in even the most fluid places, such as the ocean. These sites of knowing and historical materiality challenge the rigid definition of archives and open possibilities that flow through and outside of the histories valued and produced by institutionalized archives.

For Indigenous peoples, archives also act as a technology of settler colonialism because they naturalize "the righteous fiction of the nation-state and its fundamental desire to disavow the existence and rights of Indigenous peoples and communities."[11] The relationship between Indigenous people and archives is fraught with problematic inequalities, and while institutions hold on to everything, including human remains, Native communities have organized to pass the federal Native American Graves Protection and Repatriation Act (NAGPRA). Despite this federal law, which is meant to return sacred and funerary items back to Native nations, institutions have often fought to maintain their collections, and as a result, ancestral human remains, religious artifacts, and other critical materials have remained in the custody of institutions that do not build meaningful relationships with sovereign Indigenous nations. The historical records that become legitimated in settler institutions of museums and archives represent an attempt to understand objects divorced from their inherently complex relationships to living communities. Museums around the world exhibit everything from archaeological pieces to Maya clothing without acknowledging that acquisition is possible primarily through outright theft, or at best by purchasing materials in a deeply unequal economic reality. Their collections are recognitions of depoliticized art forms beautiful enough to exhibit but not meaningful enough to warrant an understanding of their political context under colonial structures. As a result, it is possible to visit museums that include representations of or focus on Mayas without ever learning about their ongoing struggles and the ways that Maya communities work every day to uphold their epistemologies and care for their ancestral lands and water.

In contrast, Indigenous archival work raises critical questions "such as who ought to own and control Native knowledge, who ought to store this knowledge and for what ends, and, of course, whose knowledge counts as legitimate."[12] Mobile archives of Indigeneity are different from institutional archives in their formation, intention, and audience, and therefore act as embodied sites for transfers of knowledge.[13] They serve as quotidian reminders that history functions differently in the contentious interplay between genocide and Indigenous survivance. Stuart Hall reminds us that cultural identities, "Far from being grounded in a mere 'recovery' of the past, which is waiting to be found, and which, when found, will secure our sense of ourselves into eternity, identities are the names we give to the different ways we are positioned by, and position ourselves within, the narratives of the past."[14] A mobile archive of Indigeneity functions as a practice and process of making a Maya diaspora that is not enclosed by colonial power or defined solely as a permanent Indigenous loss. Rather, the archives I write about allow Mayas to engage with each other in their own cultural vernaculars as they move within societies that benefit from their erasure or silence as Indigenous subjects. When a teenager who is born and raised in Los Angeles wears her great-grandmother's *corte* (skirt), she is literally wearing an archive shaped by her ancestors in the cosmological sense and also by her elders who made decisions throughout their lives to maintain certain practices and keep these textiles—which are instances of vibrant Indigenous social relations.

Beyond the quotidian embodiment of being Maya, there are ways that communities create or use material objects to grapple with this question around the transgenerational transmission of information and knowledge about what it means to be Maya outside of the homeland. The dialogical relationship between the objects themselves and the stories people tell through and with these objects enables us to recognize that this practice is not strictly oral, and that those who enact it make critical choices and thoughtful interventions. Balancing an analysis that looks at the cultural material and the lived experience of the cultural producers allows us to remember that Indigenous archives do not stand alone. Understanding Indigenous archives requires an engagement that fleshes out the nuances of their significance in relation to families and collectives.

The debate over the work of institutional archives and all other forms of documenting and remembering is a struggle over not just the past but also the future. Alternatives to mainstream institutionalized archives exist in multimodal archives, counter-archives, rebel archives, digital archives, unruly archives, and autonomous archives that emerge from communities that have been or continue to be marginalized.[15] These projects and theories are challenging not solely how an archive functions but ultimately reimagine a more expansive public and subvert the role of the expert. Arjun Appadurai's notion that "migrant archives" are a tool for "documentation as intervention" to create forms of collective consciousness is also vital to understanding the mobility of people and archival materials. As Appadurai asserts, "This deep function of the archive has been obscured by that officializing mentality, closely connected to the governmentalities of the nation-state, which rests on seeing the archive as the tomb of the accidental trace, rather than as the material site of the collective will to remember."[16] Appadurai understands the deeply agentic labor and creativity of migrants who, despite their precarious conditions, decide that to maintain their historical memory is meaningful. For Indigenous migrants, the "collective will to remember" also requires a consistent project of refusing assimilation into Mexicanness or Latinidad—in other words into mestizaje. This requires understanding that Maya migrants are not Indigenous to the places they migrate to, but their ongoing commitments to their own places constructed through cultural practice rather than through land tenure or tribal citizenship provides a model for how they contest settler colonialism.

For scholars like Rodrigo Lazo, archives collect artifacts in order to circulate histories, and at times those histories push back against official narratives of the nation. In pushing back or expanding national discourses, archives can participate in the democratization of the nation. These critical conversations between migrant and official narratives clarify that the mobile archive of Indigeneity is distinct from a mainstream archive in that it takes as a primary intervention the (re)production of an Indigenous social and cosmological worldview. For Indigenous diasporas, the archive is less about being included in their receiving country than about maintaining connections to ancestral territories, Indigenous epistemologies, and ties across multiple generations of displacement. As Maurice Magaña writes in his analysis of Oaxacan transborder multimodal archives, "Merely being seen, however, is not enough. Given the hypervisibility that accompanies racialized criminalization, the terms of visibility for Indigenous Latinx and migrant communities are just as important as being seen." This points to the critical function of archives that emerge from Indigenous diasporas. In the face of being physically removed from one's land, relatives, and larger communities there is a need to sustain an Indigenous collectivity rather than to inform the general public. As Appadurai reminds us, "the work of the imagination is not a privilege of elites."[17] The value of mobile archives of Indigeneity does not result from collection or circulation through a settler public, but from the efforts of sustaining ongoing social relations and connections across settler borders.

These mobile archives of Indigeneity are also different from traditional archives in that they do not presume to be specifically about the past. Part of the Maya diasporic archival practice centers on what I understand as archives in formation. As a result, these contemporary archives prevent any single story from standing in for a totalizing view of Maya people. This ambiguity troubles the temporal prescription provided by scholars like Harriet Bradley, who argues that while there are multiple definitions and uses for the archive, it primarily reproduces the following sequence: "archive—memory—the past—narrative."[18] Instead, archives of Indigeneity cross generational divides and require multiple generations of Maya people to be in conversation in order to understand how the cultural materials enact a process of "gathering together signs" and setting "a bundle of limits which have a history."[19] By refusing to stay fixed in space, these sites and archives challenge the ongoing colonial regimes of power that, through various articulations, remain entrenched in positioning Indigenous peoples as disappearing or gone. This is one critical distinction between mobile archives of Indigeneity and migrant archives, which center moving across borders and landing in a new place.

Mobile archives of Indigeneity center Indigenous experiences, but the objects themselves move across borders and are therefore mobile as well. The mobility of the material objects, rather than migrant people, is why I have specifically included *mobile* as a descriptor for the type of archive I focus on. None of these materials remains in a single physical location, yet each contains specific land-based meanings that a migrant population can share across time and space. For instance, in the case of the photo exhibit that is the focus of chapter 4, the photographs are physically present on the walls of a community center in Xelajuj No'j (Quetzaltenango, Guatemala). The center often welcomes returned migrants or the children of migrants who are visiting their ancestral homeland for the first time, and the images become a visual representation of connection across borders and migrant generations. In moving across borders during or after migration, these cultural items acquire added layers of significance in relation to the process of migration, but at their core they are used by Indigenous subjects for the sake of Indigenous collectivity. Through the mobile archives of Indigeneity that Mayas create, all generations engage in cultural production as a site through which to document the process of erasure and the possibilities for intergenerational continuities for themselves, their families, and other Mayas.

Settler Colonialism and the Formation of a Maya Diaspora

The cultural materials in archives of Indigeneity are imbued with political meaning. Before migration, Guatemalans experience the United States as a foreign imperial power. The United States played a key role in destabilizing Guatemala during a democratic and socialist period often termed the Ten Years of Spring, from the October Revolutions of 1944 to the coup that deposed Jacobo Árbenz in 1954. While US interests in Guatemala date to much earlier, it was during this period that the massive landholdings of the United Fruit Company were threatened when President Árbenz attempted to redistribute underutilized land to landless peasants. The agrarian reform prompted the United Fruit Company to leverage its relationships with US government officials to produce a discourse of Guatemala as a communist threat that required US intervention. This began a long-term process of the United States sending millions of dollars in aid to dictators and corrupt administrations, which continues today. While originally provided under the guise of stopping a communist threat, much of that aid is now sent under the pretense that it will deter migration and increase security. As Cecilia Menjívar and Néstor Rodríguez note, to understand the conditions of Guatemala we must acknowledge the role the United States has played and also interrogate how the United States has been able to align itself with a powerful elite in Guatemala who are just as responsible for the everyday precarity poor people in Guatemala face.[20] Examining this alliance between the United States as an imperial power and Guatemala as a settler nation helps us understand that more than one country is responsible for the contemporary repression of Indigenous Maya people. Once Mayas migrate to the imperialist nation, they also experience the United States as a settler colonial power that has its own ongoing project of Indigenous repression, genocide, and control. The normalization of settler technologies in Los Angeles raises the stakes of studying the intentional efforts that Mayas make to document their own histories, struggles, and existence.

Given the context of state violence and dispossession in Guatemala, migration has become a survival strategy against intergenerational precarity. However, migration does not necessarily guarantee that the Maya community will survive geographic displacement from ancestral territories: demographic erasure and a powerful structure of Indigenous elimination await Mayas upon their arrival in Los Angeles. The literature on

Indigenous migrants from Latin America must be put in conversation with critical scholarship on the spatial politics of settler colonialism. These spatial politics include how we conceptualize ancestral territory in relation to coerced migration, the ways that structures of violence may shift across migrant regions, and greater numbers of contemporary arrivals in occupied and unceded Native territory.[21] Settler colonialism has gained wide circulation as an analytical framework because it articulates the ongoing struggle over territory that makes lives disposable.[22] In effect, it connects the violence Indigenous people have faced from the moment of invasion to our present, which is useful in articulating the ongoing power structures Indigenous people confront. While settler colonialism may be applied in various ways, ultimately for my work, settler colonial theory helps us make sense of the horrors Maya people confront today in the context of historical violence that is documented in colonial records. When we read about the burning of hundreds of Maya books by Friar Diego de Landa in 1562 and the co-optation of Maya textiles by fashion designers today, we can understand these as interconnected structures that extract Maya knowledge and make Maya bodies meaningless to settler societies.

Since the formulation of settler colonial theory, there have been questions about its limits when applied to contexts where Indigenous people remain the demographic majority (Were they eliminated?), what their territory was used for (Does use have the same meaning when we deal with extraction as when we think about private property?), and about the intersection of racial capitalism and settler colonialism (Does race matter under settler colonialism?). For this book, I take up settler colonial theory because it offers a set of useful tools that can illuminate the transnational nature of violence against Maya migrants as well as contemplate the complexity of Maya experiences in relation to race and migration.

Settler colonial theory expands the time frame for the study of violence against Maya people: the best-known period of violence is the Guatemalan civil war from 1960 to 1996, which reached its climax in the 1980s. During this time, more than 200,000 people were murdered and 40,000 were disappeared; 83 percent of the victims were Maya, and various branches of the government, military, police, and paramilitaries committed 93 percent of the violence.[23] The coalescing of economic and political elites in Guatemala with the financial and military support of the United States resulted in one of the deadliest epochs of Maya history.[24] Guatemala continues to deal with the material remnants of this violence by exhuming mass graves, archiving police records, and convicting military perpetrators. In this book, however, I want to consider a longer historical context because we cannot understand the precarity migrants flee nor their strategies for survival and resurgence if we consider only the civil war period. Taking a longer and more expansive view of the structures of colonialism in Guatemala is critical to understanding how Maya people themselves understand contemporary violence as interconnected to a racism that persists from the colonial period.

To do this I build on the work of scholars who have provided a critical analysis of settler colonial structures in Central America. Shannon Speed has pointed out that one contribution of settler colonial theory is that it does not take settlement as a permanent and finished project. She challenges frameworks of coloniality and internal colonialism because they "view [power relations] as residual or a legacy of past colony rather than an ongoing settler colonial process."[25] Giovanni Batz illuminates the ongoing settler colonial process in Guatemala by discussing the ways that Maya Ixil communities understand the invasion of their territories by mining and mega projects as a fourth wave of colonialism that falls in line with three previous colonial waves: Spanish colonization, plantation owners, and the 1980s genocide.[26] Each of these invasions has continued the project of colonialism grounded in territorial dispossession, though the time period spans hundreds of years and multiple political economies.

In similar fashion, Juan Castro and Manuela Picq carefully lay out a historiography that threads together colonial, revolutionary, leftist, conservative, and genocidal dictatorships that all rely on the theft of Maya land and the elimination of Maya sovereignty.[27] The spatial relationships between Maya people, the massacres of the 1980s, and territorial dispossession today have been demonstrated through mapping projects that overlay the locations of massacres during the war on the locations of current mining and mega projects. Such mapping demonstrates that both are located in the highlands, where Indigenous people remain the majority.[28] Looking at the ways invasions and settler colonialisms are articulated across centuries is critical in demonstrating that Maya migrants are fleeing deeply precarious situations that have long historical roots beyond the genocide of the 1980s. These connections also help us understand why Mayas continue to migrate despite the signing of peace accords in 1996. The current iteration of settler colonialism revolves around territorial dispossession due to debt, drought, and mega projects, but these are contemporary iterations of a much older logic and structure that have perpetuated the violence experienced by Maya people.

In Guatemala, drought and violent extractive projects result in the dispossession of Maya people at the same time as we continue to see the murder of land defenders and human rights defenders who are organizing to address these systemic issues. Human rights organizations and scholars have documented attacks on campesino and Indigenous collectives that directly challenge the projects disrupting the ecosystems that communities rely on. While this remains a critical issue globally, in Guatemala the assassination or criminalization of organizers, students, academics, and journalists represents an extension of genocidal practices of the 1980s and earlier. Global Witness released a report documenting that the murder of land defenders rose from three in 2017 to sixteen in 2018.[29] These murders and the more widespread issue of threatening social leaders are challenging to document because they occur under suspicious circumstances and at times involve police agents. Leaders from effective change-making organizations like the Comité de Desarrollo Campesino (Committee on Peasant Development, CODECA) have been especially targeted for remaining on the front lines of fighting incursion into and extraction on Indigenous territories. The Alejandro Giammattei administration (2020–24) and the most recent election cycle where Bernardo Arévalo was elected as the next president was an especially tense period. This period saw the manipulation of legal systems to exclude Thelma Cabrera, a Maya Mam organizer and co-founder of CODECA, from running for president. In addition, university students and journalists were also targeted, criminalized, and subjected to police brutality when they contested the corruption occurring within the country and their own institutions. In response, Indigenous ancestral authorities called for a historic level of nationwide organizing that lasted until Arévalo officially took office as president in January 2024. In the context of the genocide of the 1980s, which sought to instill distrust and terror in the general population, it is important to note that there are still many social actors who continue to safeguard the well-being of their communities through their labor, bodies, and organizing.[30] Nonetheless, in the face of these ongoing issues, many Guatemalans find themselves with few alternatives but to migrate to alleviate poverty or simply safeguard their lives from the threats they receive because of their organizing or cultural work.

Settler colonial theories highlight that the nation has always relied on territorial dispossession. The state has never been a site of justice precisely because politicians across the political spectrum have relied on dispossessing Indigenous people of their land and labor. Critical Indigenous studies scholars like Sarah Hunt have also pointed out that structural territorial dispossession is deeply entangled with gendered violence because both effectively limit the social reproduction of Indigenous peoples. Thus, alongside and intersecting with violence against Indigenous people is femicide. Shannon Speed's recent multilayered analysis of Indigenous women in detention looks at the ways individual men, narcotics cartels, and government agencies all participate in making Indigenous women particularly vulnerable to violence—a system she names as neoliberal multicriminality.[31]

The other arm of this violence is the perpetual poverty that Maya families encounter across generations. The loss of land is tied to the widespread poverty within Maya communities, because when pushed out of their original territories the people are coerced into marginal wage labor or into being debt workers. Understanding intergenerational economic poverty as part of a colonial project positions genocide as encompassing not only violent physical deaths, but also the series of social and political deaths that result when Mayas are fundamentally excluded from society or are included only through unequal relationships grounded in multicultural neoliberalism.[32] Speed argues that one iteration of settler colonialism is neoliberalism and the free-market structure that has given rise to the narco state and resulted in a shifting terrain of labor. While migration within Guatemala to work on sugar, coffee, and banana plantations has been a historical reality that constituted brutal violence against Maya people, the current period of migration to the United States has been sparked by unprecedented inflation and a reliance on debt to finance everything from migration to basic everyday survival.[33] The gap produced by multiple waves of settler colonialism now finds its expression among those families who are supported by migrants who have crossed into the United States successfully versus those who have lost what little they did have due to deportation and unsuccessful attempts to cross. In light of the powerful historic, economic, and political forces that Mayas must confront, they have an equally longstanding history of refusal, regeneration, and persistence.

One way that these communities have contested the national project of Indigenous dispossession has been through a turn toward a Maya movement that, while decentralized, operates on the logic that Maya people must push back against these projects of social death.[34] Here, it is critical to understand that the label Maya is not necessarily always used by people we would understand as Maya. The very use of the term *Maya* as an umbrella identity for more than twenty distinct yet related ethnolinguistic groups is part of a strategic move to make Indigeneity legible within national and international forums. As Victor Montejo clarifies, the turn to a Maya identity directly ties to the work of scholars and activists who sought to challenge Ladino discourses claiming that contemporary Mayas are not really connected to precolonial societies.[35] While the international public recognizes Mayas as a civilization with a deep understanding of astronomy and math, elite Ladinos in Guatemala claim that those ancient civilizations are only distant ancestors of the Mayas whom landowners exploit through plantations, mines, and debt peonage today. The supposed distance from the great civilization that "disappeared" has justified the ongoing state violence to which Maya people have been subjected. Maya is a category that exists in relation to older terms signifying Indigeneity that include *naturales, indígenas*, and terms governed by ancestral authorities and identified by local town or *aldea* names. In this sense it is important to remember that the challenge of thinking about Indigenous migrants in relation to their country of origin and country of reception is that although all settler colonialism is rooted in elimination and territorial dispossession, how settler colonists actually accomplish this and manage Indigenous peoples is distinct across local and national scales. R. Aída Hernández Castillo importantly reminds us that "the social, cultural and political processes through which the meaning of being indigenous has been constructed . . . have involved various dialogues of power with national and global discourses."[36] This perspective is critical to thinking about the Maya community as a diasporic, rooted, and migrant experience that is geographically, historically, and culturally constructed.

Maya scholars and activists use the term *Maya* to contest the temporal rupture just discussed, although many continue to identify with their hometown or language group, not necessarily with a Maya identity. One of the complexities involved in analyzing Maya politics is that Maya also represents one way the government of Guatemala promotes one of its major economic streams, the tourism industry. The limitations of Maya identity in relation to a tourism industry operating under a settler colonial imperative to eliminate Maya people as sovereign political subjects opens critical questions around how Maya and Ladino vendors use Maya regional clothing to fulfill international tourists' desire for "authentic" Maya culture.[37] María Jacinta Xón Riquiac notes that Maya men who were doing the work of defining and cohering a Maya identity in the 1990s positioned women as cultural bearers whose function was to reproduce culture, a move that reifies patriarchy and gender norms as essentialist categories at the expense of political subjectivities.[38] Edgar Esquit has also launched an important critique of the way that Maya identity is produced by scholars and activists who ignore the reality of Indigenous people living in poverty who find a sense of belonging and empowerment through religious institutions like the Catholic Church or Evangelical denominations instead of through Maya spirituality. These insightful critiques push back on earlier Maya scholars like Demetrio Cojtí Cuxil and Raxche', who defined political and cultural agendas based on their understandings of Mayaness, which may not resonate for all Mayas.[39] My own choice to use the term *Maya* is in line with a long-standing commitment to acknowledge ourselves as a collective with diverse experiences and perspectives but with millennial roots and ongoing responsibilities relative to our specific territories and each other. In this book, I choose to use *Maya* to signal a political claim to a subjecthood that is not given and must instead be constantly reconstructed generation after generation.

The notion of a Maya diaspora as a purposeful and consciously constructed identity tracks with the repositories of memory I analyze in this book, which do not take for granted that a Maya diaspora already exists. Instead, it is through the archives themselves that Mayas lay out and grapple with the parameters around Maya diaspora. Tensions may exist among those whom the "Maya" identity leaves out, who may struggle internally with questions of cultural authenticity. As a result, the mobile archives emphasize that, rather than forcing a complete rupture or "new alternative," Maya migrants weave in and out of multiple identities and collectives to form a Maya diaspora. Internal diversity generates multiple definitions of Mayaness; generation, geography, gender, queer identity, and class are all important axes of differentiation within the diaspora. While sometimes contradictory, these tensions and frictions also form the basis from which second- and third-generation Mayas in the United States articulate claims to Maya identity that make sense of their lived realities outside of Guatemala.

The Maya Diaspora on Occupied Indigenous Lands

Mayas began coming to the United States as a direct result of either outright genocide or generational poverty resulting from virulent discrimination and exploitation. While Guatemalan Mayas began migrating to escape the civil war and genocide, they have continued to migrate in relatively large numbers even after the official end of the war. However, demographic data that distinguishes between Maya and Ladino Guatemalans is very difficult to find, which makes Maya visibility complicated. In addition, so many Mayas have migrated that, as geographer Juan Herrera documents in his research on day laborers, the terms *Maya* and *Guatemalan* have become conflated.[40] This in some ways obscures the challenges Mayas face as Indigenous immigrants, while also making their culture and Indigenous difference visible as part of Guatemalan folkloric culture. Although quantitative data does not document Ladino–Indigenous distinctions, scholars suggest that Mayas represent a large proportion of Guatemalan migrants to the United States and an even larger proportion of those deported back to Guatemala. Research suggests that Mayas constitute at least 50 percent of the Guatemalan population in the United States, but scholars acknowledge that this may be a severe underestimation.[41] The challenges of obtaining accurate demographic data for this particular population highlight the ongoing need for qualitative work and methods and for those who understand the racial dynamics in Guatemala to support either the creation or disaggregation of data about Mayas.

The contribution of this research to the study of the Maya diaspora is best contextualized by briefly reviewing the literature that exists about Maya migrants in the United States. Early research about the Maya diaspora was largely concerned with language retention; later studies focused on the experience of migration after being targeted by state violence, the transnational economic and cultural practices of migrants in Los Angeles, and the experiences of those people as undocumented migrants.[42] Other research emphasized the notion of diaspora as grounded not only in Mayas' external migration to other parts of the world but also in their internal migration within Guatemala.[43] More recent research on the Maya diaspora has also critically intervened within Latina/o studies to challenge popular notions of what it means to be Latina/o and how this identification often directly contradicts the Maya experience.[44] In particular, this scholarship challenges how the casual lumping together of Mayas with other Latinas/os conceals the direct racism that Maya migrants face from Latinas/os, including Central Americans, who do not identify as Indigenous.[45] This racist discrimination is entrenched and reinscribed in structures of inequality in the countries of origin, and it finds new modes of expression in the diaspora.[46] To distinguish themselves from the Latina/o category, Indigenous migrants often identify as Native American.[47] Pushing Indigenous migrants to the margins actively incentivizes a form of self-policing whereby they may strategically choose to hide their cultural practices or prioritize various forms of acculturation. These "choices" must be understood in the context of ongoing state violence in both Guatemala and the United States. Ultimately, what is clear is that part of the Maya diasporic experience is the difficult project of understanding how and when distinct racial structures (those in Guatemala versus those in the United States) coalesce to produce a politic rooted in the continuous erasure of Indigenous people.

Within the diaspora, youth make sense of their realities through the stories passed down, or at times silenced, by generations of their family in Guatemala and the United States, as well as their own experiences of exclusion from Latinidad due to their Indigenous roots. Maya positionalities in the diaspora create complex linkages between historical family legacies and the political economies of their places of origin, as well as the colonial structures of Guatemala and the United States and how these relationships are configured within Los Angeles, the city in which they live and work. This rich complexity allows Maya collectives to enact an archival practice that searches for commonalities and differences to create materials that embrace multiplicity and a diverse understanding of Maya persistence.

Furthermore, the visible presence of Mayas in parts of Los Angeles like Pico Union–Westlake and South Los Angeles also creates a need to reconsider Latinidad as a category that ostensibly includes all migrants from Latin America. Most research about Maya migrants highlights the ways that Latina/o identity and politics are often premised on notions of Mexican mestizaje. Maya organizers have questioned or outright refused incorporation into Latinidad because it is often defined through an uncritical approximation to whiteness that refuses to engage with Indigeneity and Blackness. Granted, within Chicana/o studies there has been a commitment to Indigeneity due to the movement that led to the formation of the field—much of that discourse, cultural production, and political position rested on a rejection of popular assimilationist projects of Americanization vis-à-vis whiteness in the United States. As a result, Chicanas and Chicanos—deeply informed by Black radical movements, both in the United States and globally—developed key claims to being Indigenous but premised those claims primarily on Mexican national discourses of an ancient Aztec or Nahuatl past. Indigenous scholars like Gloria Chacón and Lourdes Alberto highlight how this identity remains an ongoing tension to which Chicanx subjectivities need to be attuned because these forms of mestizaje, pan-Indigeneity, and generic Indigeneity exist in contradiction to Indigenous diasporas from Mexico and Latin America who have specific and contemporary claims to their territories, communities, Indigenous languages, and cultural practices.[48] A cadre of Indigenous scholars whose territories are in Mexico, including Lourdes Alberto, Luis Urrieta, Luis Sánchez-López, Gabriela Spears-Rico, Brenda Nicolas, Daina Sanchez, and Michelle Vásquez Ruiz, have dedicated themselves to recentering their *pueblos* and demonstrating how their communities have been relegated to the margins by non-Indigenous Mexicans and by Chicana/o discourses. Similarly, because Maya people in Guatemala still have a strong relationship to their territory, language, spiritual beliefs, and political practices, the Aztec-centric, pan-Indigeneity of the Chicana/o movement missed the mark in overlooking the experience of not being Mexican but still laying claim to a specific Indigenous identity. These tensions with Latinidad are also a critical reminder not to reproduce erasure through absorption, but instead to understand that these identities are political projects with historical contexts and collective stakes.

Beyond the limitations of Latinidad and the lack of quantitative data on Indigenous migration is the issue of how we understand places of arrival. Previous research has looked at the ways that Maya migrants make and remake community, but typically without examining the site of arrival through settler colonial frameworks. Los Angeles is a city built through layers of dispossession in which every iteration of Native and Indigenous erasure informs how space is shaped in the city and how race is relationally constructed.[49] From the onset of colonial invasion by Spanish priests, the particularly restricted mobility of Indigenous women has been linked to the economic survival of political institutions that rely on their gendered and racialized labor.[50] Looking at Los Angeles as a site of contested settler occupation rather than just a city of immigrants can help us unpack how systems produced through settler colonialism in the United States come to bear on Maya migrants and their children in particular ways.

Until very recently, generations of Angelenos have been taught to conceptualize Indigenous people as already gone or vanishing through the infamous mission projects. These projects required that children reproduce models of the first European settlements in present-day California and sanitize, ignore, and erase these places as sites of sexual violence and Native genocide. Through an analysis of K–12 curricula and textbooks, Dolores Calderon argues that this instruction produces settler colonial grammars and what Mark Rifkin calls the settler common sense.[51] Consequently, people in Los Angeles are taught to understand the city specifically through histories that normalize and even celebrate the genocide of California Natives both historically and in the present moment. Identifying Los Angeles as a city of immigrants reproduces this erasure and avoids a serious examination of how Indigenous migrants risk perpetuating the same discourses and institutions.

When Indigenous migrants arrive, they step not only onto Native territories, but onto territories that have a vested interest in eliminating Indigenous claims to land, often through the erasure of Indigenous presence in the present. Through entering these structures that actively work to erase Native people, Indigenous migrants are explicitly eliminated as Indigenous people as well. For instance, it is no coincidence that the US Border Patrol recognizes only country of origin, thereby creating structural barriers for scholars and organizers who seek to document the number of Indigenous migrants and their particular needs.[52] The erasures produced through migration actually *reproduce* the Indigenous elimination to which Maya migrants were already subjected in Guatemala. The realities of the Maya diaspora force us to think about Indigenous survivance in the context of arriving in occupied Indigenous territory and the continuities that exist in their receiving country despite their having been displaced from their ancestral territory.[53]

(Un)Mapping Power in the Production of Knowledge

Alongside these conversations about what a Maya diaspora is are critical discussions about what it means for members of these communities and scholars in academia to take up the pen as part of a political commitment to sovereignty. Our choice to become what Dale Turner terms "word warriors" forces us to constantly question our roles, the sites of knowledge that we privilege or reproduce, and the uneven consequences of academic knowledge production.[54] The need to think outside of and with a clear view of the constraints of an academic industry built through settler colonialism and racial capitalism requires us to examine all the ways that Black and Indigenous people survive(d) genocide then live to tell of that survival. The literature on Black and Indigenous methods is built on distinct ontological grounds that run the gamut from using fugitivity to Maya traditional dress as ways to narrate our positions.[55] As Indigenous scholars, we need to walk a line between how we think our work can support our community and what academia requires of us, and in that process we must make critical choices for which many of us do not have a blueprint.

My own methodological choices interweave multiple qualitative methods, including thirty-five interviews alongside cultural analysis, to inform frameworks that bend categories established by academic disciplines. The framework of the mobile archive of Indigeneity emerged from my academic scholarship, but as I worked through the concept, I also began to recognize the ways that it echoed my own lived experience. For instance, upon my undergraduate graduation, I wanted to honor both my elders and my own journey to self-understanding as a young Maya K'iche' woman from Xelajuj No'j. I asked my uncle, Oscar Ubaldo Boj Chojolan, to weave me my very first *po't* for the occasion. Po't are brightly colored blouses, often referred to as *huipiles*, that are handwoven and contain designs related to Maya cosmology, spirituality, geography, and mathematics. Tío Oscar's happy agreement set in motion my first encounter with the complex circuits of diaspora and the travel of cultural objects across settler borders. I had requested my huipil months in advance while visiting my hometown for the first time, but I had to ask an extended relative to pick up and deliver the garments months later. In the hustle and bustle of graduation preparations, three of my aunts helped me put on my traditional clothing for the very first time. While adjusting my skirt, my eldest aunt began to cry: Getting me dressed reminded her of my grandmother. I stood semi-frozen, not knowing how to respond, as my other aunt put her arm around her and shared a funny story about tricks she would use as a little girl to try and put her corte on correctly.

I realized at that moment that wearing my own Maya clothing was also the act of wearing a history of place, defiance, and dispossession across generations. My decision to wear my po't and corte was made based on my excitement over graduating, yet I couldn't deny that this decision reminded my aunts of loss and grief. However, creating a complex emotional space out of my excitement and pride alongside one aunt's grief and another's sense of humor is what makes these cultural objects so special and meaningful. As I have continued to examine the materials that create these spaces of intergenerational engagement, I have realized that what a younger generation chooses to remember and to continue has everything to do with reopening and acknowledging old wounds. An article of clothing that held its own significance in our hometown where it was woven by a relative of mine also acted as a portal to our intergenerational grief and survival as immigrants in the United States. I believe my aunt was reminded in that moment not only of her mother, who had died much too young due to the systemic neglect many Maya people face in Guatemala, but also of everything she had lost because of poverty and migration. I became a living reminder of where we had been, what had been lost, what had remained, and what could be renewed. More than a decade later, my niece Andrea asked to have a corte for her fifteenth-birthday celebration. I happily bought it for her, again asking my uncle to weave it, and gifted it to her. As part of this gift, my uncle traveled to South Los Angeles to conduct a ceremony where we showered Andrea with flowers, as is customary to do for young women in our community. I continue to see in my family and my extended Maya diasporic community the blossoming of these transnational ties that sustain us despite ongoing state violence against Mayas in Central America, Mexico, and the United States.

My own lived reality of belonging to this community grounds my theory and conceptual framework of mobile archives of Indigeneity. Shawn Wilson, in his book *Research Is Ceremony*, articulates an Indigenous research paradigm that acknowledges lived experience as a site of knowledge but extends this notion by stating that as Indigenous people embedded in a collective, our lived experience is not individualistic. He writes, "I think that my entire upbringing, culture, teachers, experiences, and lots of other things (some that I cannot explain) came together to allow me to form a relationship with these ideas."[56] As he continues to articulate an Indigenous research paradigm, he notes that how we understand every part of a research study is saturated with how we exist in the world, and as Indigenous scholars we should embrace the relationality that guides us.

From this vantage point of diasporic Maya relationality, it's clear that there is no one prototypical experience among those who are actively trying to cohere a Maya diasporic community. Hence, I emphasize archives that are contemporary—in formation, continuously engaged in publicly setting boundaries *and* opening spaces. Recognizing the work that goes into spaces that are processing Indigenous migration and responses to state violence, I am compelled to conceptualize this project as an extension of what exists and what may be useful within the Maya community. As a Maya scholar who is trained in an interdisciplinary approach, conceptualizing the mobile archive of Indigeneity has forced me to grapple with disciplinary boundaries and tensions. The mobile archive of Indigeneity as a conceptual tool sits (un)comfortably between social science and humanities. This is rich ground from which to reconsider the place of Indigenous studies in social science and in relation to disciplinary boundaries.

For Indigenous diaspora scholars, our projects force us to confront contradictory modes of being that are often unrecognized in our fields. This is part of a longer project of genocide where accessing formal education made Indigenous people "civilized" and therefore no longer Indigenous.[57] Even in the contemporary moment there are contradictions around what it means to talk about our own stories through our own logics, something that became especially evident in the conflict around Rigoberta Menchú's *testimonio*. David Stoll, an academic anthropologist, argued that, based on his interviews and fieldwork, he identified multiple fallacies in Menchú's account that made her entire testimonio questionable. Published in 1983, Rigoberta Menchú's testimonio contributed to her winning the Nobel Peace Prize in 1992, which some credit as one of the factors that turned the tide toward peace talks in Guatemala. David Stoll's critique of Menchú's testimonio was often taken as an attack on the developing and well-received field of testimonio, but since then, there have been critical contributions to expanding our understanding of the possibilities and limitations of this approach.[58] This controversy may seem old, but as a Maya K'iche' scholar interested in telling our stories and our analysis of these stories, the way academics treated Menchú reminds me of the possible risk in telling our stories in fields and institutions that have often extracted our community's knowledge while reproducing our exclusion from those places.

These conversations remain charged as a new generation of Indigenous diaspora scholars with the knowledge of lived experience and formal academic training have stepped in to write about their own histories and their community's experiences. The advent of scholar activism and the ongoing discussion around insider/outsider positionalities provide important opportunities for us to consider the unintended consequences of our research and the ways our research can support social movement work.[59] However, Black, Indigenous, and People of Color scholars have also discussed critical issues that arise in the process of conducting research with their own community members. Eve Tuck and K. Wayne Yang encourage scholars to reject what they term "inquiry as invasion."[60] In relation to my work, their emphasis that the stories most desired, consumed, and prized in academia are those of vulnerable pain and trauma highlights the need for stories about survivance that center powerful critiques of structures of colonialism. I couch each community-based intervention as existing partially in response to the violence of institutions that ensnare our families and communities but also as a way of pushing back against that violence. I do this work particularly to speak to young Mayas who deserve to learn not just of their community's struggles, but also of its many creative strategies to affirm their dignity.

While outsider scholars of Indigeneity propose frameworks that seem universal, the experiences of Indigenous scholars who write about their own communities are rarely discussed. Even though Indigenous scholars remain a small demographic in academia overall, they offer frameworks that are informed by the knowledge they have beyond their role as researchers. Audra Simpson's critical work on ethnographic refusal is but one way in which we as scholars navigate important tensions in the field. Simpson writes:

> The ethnographic limit then, was reached not just when it would cause harm (or extreme discomfort)—the limit was arrived at when the representation would bite all of us and compromise the *representational* territory that we have gained for ourselves in the past 100 years, in small but deeply influential ways, with a cadre of scholars from Kahnawake whose work has reached beyond the boundaries of the community.[61]

To be part of the community one studies means not only theorizing interviews through transcription and coding procedures but also being responsible for the real-world consequences of those interviews, which some scholars argue is extraction and plunder. The consequence we risk as Indigenous scholars is the potential that our research will have a negative impact on those with whom we hold a collective future. While some sectors of academia still claim that academics should be neutral and objective outsiders, those of us who work within our communities, nations, and pueblos are accountable not just to university standards, but also to our elders, youth, families, and leaders. Unlike outsiders who work with our communities, this accountability is not a choice because who we are informs how the community receives us. For instance, when I decided to begin research with a community space in Xela, leaders of that space had already known my family for years, which I had not realized because I did not grow up in my ancestral territory. Being an Indigenous diasporic scholar means that I am part of social relations that are older than I am, and I am responsible for recognizing how my research may affect those relationships. I have been fortunate to receive both my family's understanding and the organization's permission to do this work, but again, this is an issue that outsiders do not need to contend with. This accountability produces uneven terrains of power that I hope more Indigenous diaspora scholars will take up in their work.

Indigenous scholars like Linda Tuhiwai Smith have been pointing out the limits of these (neo)colonial forms of extractive research for decades, and Native, First Nations, and Indigenous scholars have responded by thinking through their own people's epistemologies to understand land, history, archives, interviews, and research practices. In the process they propose that by looking deeply at their relationships to their nations and people, they can force open a space that acknowledges research as more than data collection. We can take Leanne Betasamosake Simpson's notion of the method of Kwe as one critical example of this. Simpson tells us that Kwe is a refusal to accept and reproduce binaries that divide not only genders but also thinking and doing, the oral and written, the cultural and political.[62] Noelani Arista also uses Koana as a possible methodology.[63] According to Arista, Koana is about the inner meaning of a phrase, chant, or song, which may be obvious or unknowable to outsiders. In looking toward their respective nations' own epistemological pillars, these works point to the scholars' investment in recognizing the limits of research and disciplines as mainstream academia has constructed them. These interventions also depart from others in that they do not seek to present universal concepts, meaning that I as a Maya scholar may not necessarily take up Kwe or Koana as a methodological framework, but instead I can begin by looking to all the ways that my communities understand themselves and, within that conceptual space, begin to build frameworks for what social scientists understand as data collection and analysis.

One example of this practice from a Maya perspective is the work of literary scholar Gloria Chacón in *Indigenous Cosmolectics*. Several of the analytic strategies that Chacón foregrounds in her book speak to possibilities of pushing back on disciplinary norms. For instance, she uses *Mesoamerican* as a contemporary and regional term that allows her to acknowledge Mayas across settler borders and in conversation with Zapotecs. Similarly, she states, "I propose *cosmolectics* for Mesoamerica, tying together the fundamental role that the cosmos and history, sacred writing and poetry, nature and spirituality as well as glyphs and memory play in articulating Maya and Zapotec ontologies."[64] For Indigenous scholars, this process of looking backward even as we examine the present is a form of world building within academia. These concepts are not necessarily new within our communities, but how we use them to ground our academic work, and thereby push back on many of the problematic norms that do not make sense to our communities, opens the possibility for a multiplicity of epistemological frameworks and maneuvers.

The interventions and the embodied tensions Indigenous scholars point to helped me clarify my commitments to intersectional politics within my community. Ultimately, it is important to recognize that for many Indigenous scholars, writing about our communities comes with additional challenges that are unique and rarely articulated in academia.

This requires us to be able to take a step back and articulate the methodological choices we have made.

A Maya Multimethodology

Most academics readily acknowledge that the binaries of social science versus humanities, hard science versus social science, qualitative versus quantitative methods remain entrenched in many disciplines. As a Maya scholar I have to grapple with the reality that many of these divides go against the way we are taught by our elders and cultural teachers.[65] If we take my graduation textile as an example, it is a piece of art, a text that can be read, an ancestral map, an embodied archive, and the outcome of a mathematical process of design and weaving. Similarly, when we are told our ancestors read the stars and tracked the movement of the sun, we mean they calculated large mathematical quantities to track the future movements of the sun or Venus thousands of years in advance, all while sculpting these astral movements and calculations into stelae and visually representing them in codices. How, then, can Maya scholars make sense of being in academia while knowing how contradictory academic boundaries between disciplines are to our own understanding of life?

In this context, a Maya multimethodology crosses disciplinary and methodological limits to be responsive to my own communities. For instance, because of my graduation huipil and many experiences before and after, I continue to look at my and my family's history as a resource that informs how I see and hear other people's experiences and stories. Knowing these embodied histories and witnessing the multiple ways that other Mayas in diaspora and in Guatemala circumvent or outright rebel against the structures that produce and benefit from their precarity has encouraged me to engage multiplicity in my analysis and methodology. The history of genocide and dispossession has also guided my choice to focus on the type of organizing in my community that is thoughtful, hopeful, committed politically, and grounded in our lived and embodied experience. I am primarily interested in telling the stories of a diaspora who do not necessarily have a formal structure yet still find or make space for their experiences with other Mayas. In diaspora, people remain tied to ancestral territories in many ways that have not been analyzed. In each of these spaces and practices of survivance, there is a vibrancy that can be contextualized as an intentional refusal of dispossession and necropolitics.

Such a multimethod approach can center these creative modes of survivance if it can make space for the lived experience and intuition that Indigenous diasporic scholars have.[66] The Maya multimethodology remains committed to being in conversation with academic literature but balances this with a consistent engagement with Maya communities to understand interviews and cultural analysis alongside social movements and ancestral cultural practices. As a result, methodologically speaking there is no rigid definition of what a Maya multimethodology looks like. Instead, the intention here is that we can train in multiple methods so that we can be responsive to what the communities we work with share with us.

As I have begun to work with colleagues and students who are from similar social positions as me, we often acknowledge that most academic training does not necessarily account for what it means to create academic knowledge about your own people when your people are Indigenous *and* deeply impacted by displacement. Reading, writing, teaching, or presenting histories of violence that continue to be relentlessly enacted against our communities today exacts an emotional toll. In my own experience, reading and writing about the Guatemalan civil war and genocide often seeps into my dreams and literally becomes nightmares. Confronting the horrific level of violence, ongoing malnutrition, deaths during migration, territorial dispossession, and gendered violence reminds me of family stories that are hard to share, stories that I live with but that don't necessarily count as part of my formal academic training. These stories are part of a longer legacy that as Indigenous diaspora scholars we must acknowledge is embedded in how we return to our communities and also informs what we hope our knowledge production within the academy will achieve. For instance, Giovanni Batz has honored a steadfast commitment to critically examining powerful institutions in support of the Ixil community's efforts to retain the land they have and, perhaps, one day have the entirety of their land returned.[67] For me, this mindset has meant fashioning projects and writings that acknowledge the deep sorrow and marginalization we experience while remaining committed to a hope that within our relationality we can find spaces of reprieve, love, and joy.

The uncomfortable balance of deciding what we share or how we distinguish what is fieldwork and what is just living is both a practical and an ethical issue that reminds us that academia was not built by those of us who are most often objectified as sites of study. As a result, we often craft our projects with a deeply embodied awareness of ongoing genocide, yet we push ourselves to also recognize and write about what exists despite genocide, like the vibrant, dynamic nature of Indigenous lives. In my own work, a Maya multimethodology allowed me to bring together thirty-five semi-structured interviews and cultural analyses to contour and texturize the traces of Maya social worlds more completely than I could with just one methodological approach.

By training and through further research, I have carved out an approach that relies on qualitative methods in general and semi-structured interviews in particular. This approach is not necessarily new because the Maya diasporic community has been written about in academic projects that have often focused on ethnographic and interview-based data. However, being able to meld cultural analysis with ethnographic data allowed me to consider not just what Maya people told me, but also how these expressions exist in tandem with new and ancestral cultural productions reflecting Maya epistemological principles that do not create divisions between what is spoken or read and other forms of knowledge. The approach Marianna Mora writes about in *Kuxlejal Politics* resonates with my own methodological decisions: While her work with the Zapatistas was meant to be ethnographic and interview-based, members of multiple communities had been given interview questions ahead of time and arrived with or produced written accounts based on community conversations related to her questions. In the process, Mora realized that when we deal with marginalized subjects, we often focus on the oral modality then take it upon ourselves as supposed experts to create the written accounts and the coding schemes we deem appropriate, as if we, "the real scholars," are the only ones with this capacity. With regard to Maya people, overreliance on the oral modality also ignores all the ways in which Maya society depends on layers of textuality in the forms of clothing, textiles, performance, glyphs, poetry, art, and other mediums. Moving away from anthropological research or even strict definitions of archival research allows me to consider the Maya sociological imagination in ways that link the lives of Maya people with a process of creating memory that rejects Indigenous dispossession.

As I have thought about the notion of storytelling, I have also become interested in the afterlives of immigrant narratives beyond the stories we tell and inherit. I began to wonder about the things we use to tell these stories, the objects we hold on to, and the ones that we create. The decision to consider material culture as well as stories became necessary to engage with a community that deals with dispossession, and to assess how we create and use the very objects and materials that are often levied against us. Within this context, I attempted to think about the interviews I conducted alongside the tangible materials present. In other words, this is neither strictly an oral history study nor an interview-based study nor one that looks at, say, Maya clothing as a secondary and supplemental object of analysis. Rather, I seek to understand how stories and material culture have become mirrors for each other. A community member's story about traditional clothing would be limited without an understanding of the clothing's relationship to local Guatemalan landscapes, how it has functioned in relation to gendered state violence, why there is pressure to stop wearing it after migration, and why it may be possible for the second generation to continue finding value in the clothing as "practice, meaning, site, and process."[68]

My interaction with the collectives that feature in the chapters of this book did not actually begin when I took on the researcher role. At no point would I claim to be an objective scholar when writing about my community. Instead, I often participated in or created spaces that I thought were needed, and after years of participation, I decided to write about the collectives. For instance, I was directly involved in forming the Maya Womxn in L.A. youth photo project that is the basis for chapter 4. However, I did not originally conceptualize the project as part of my research, which is why I waited years after the project had ended to conduct interviews and analyze some of the photos. This dual role can be challenging because having boundaries around when you are a researcher versus when you are a community member is still necessary.

In cases where the organized collectives are still active, I shared with them drafts of my work and created formal presentations where I would highlight their direct quotations and my own interpretations of them. I also presented my primary findings, and while there were varying levels of interest in them, making the effort was important. In an ideal world, we would get close reads and notes from our interviewees, but the reality of being a community member is that your interviewees already trust you by the time you sit with them. This trust is not necessarily automatic but is at times premised on the reality that you are raising families together, working in the same spaces, and the like. Most of the community members appear with pseudonyms, but our relationships are so close that they have spent time with my family in Xela without me being present. In another case, I thought I was interviewing a community member I did not know, but when I spoke to her mother she asked me about my last name and went on to tell me how her family had married into my family—something I had no idea about. This is a dynamic that makes a Maya multimethodology unique: A Maya multimethodology acknowledges that we have been and will be part of our community across generations and spaces, and as a result our social relationships exceed the confines of interviews in more ways than traditional methods acknowledge.

Ultimately, I wrote this book for my community—I wanted it to be the book I never had, I wanted more people to experience what I experienced when I first read K'iche' social anthropologist Irma Alicia Velásquez Nimatuj's work: A world opened up in which we as Indigenous scholars could use research and written words to call to task the structures that constantly bring us closer to death, to name them, to denounce them, to link our struggles together, to remember that we are interconnected even when we struggle to understand how. I do not take our future as Indigenous people for granted; it is guaranteed, but not without work—our work, all of our work—to make it so. We maneuver in, out, and around the structures, remembering that they have not always been here, remembering that there are reaches that cannot be known or understood, acknowledging that we each contribute, but we are each limited as individuals and amazingly bountiful as a collective.

Outline of This Book

Chapter 1 offers an analysis of the human rights film *Discovering Dominga* (2003) to argue that Maya intergenerational relationships are disrupted when Indigenous migrants in the United States are folded into the logics of settler colonialism. The documentary follows Denese Joy Becker/Dominga Sic Ruiz, who was adopted by a white family as a child, as she comes to learn that she is a survivor of the 1982 Río Negro massacres committed in Baja Verapaz, Guatemala, against the Maya Achí people. Through a transnational reading of Indigeneity, this chapter argues that the film portrays Indigenous genocide as something that occurs only in foreign countries and not in Denese's/Dominga's US hometown of Algona, Iowa. As a result, the film erases Algona's own history of Indigenous dispossession and absolves everyday white US citizens of extending to Indigenous migrant people the genocidal practices produced through settler colonialism. Nonetheless, the film itself acts as an archive that can be reframed if we consider how various Maya people in it set their own terms for reproducing intergenerational knowledge and historical memory with each other, even when that is not the central narrative of the film. This chapter provides important context around how discourses of Indigenous migrants are produced in relation to their places of arrival.

In order to position the cultural and political commitments that guide my analytical frameworks, in chapter 2 I lay out key tenets that define mobile archives of Indigeneity—especially as they relate to more traditional notions of Indigenous epistemologies—and argue that these archives link historical struggles of Maya people and the contemporary diaspora. Through an analysis of Maya clothing and interviews with people who wear that clothing, I chart how these textiles function as archives because they facilitate the documentation and transmission of geographic, gendered, and classed histories across multiple Maya generations. I use this chapter to argue that mobile archives function through a twofold understanding of mobility: Maya clothing is mobile by its material nature, but it also reflects added layers of meaning in relation to the migrant experience. In Guatemala, scholars and spiritual leaders of the Maya community consider Maya spirituality as an ethical and aesthetic framework for how to be in the world. Building on this notion, I examine how Maya clothing is a relatively traditional cultural practice that migrants utilize to continue claiming their ancestral homelands—in terms of not the country of Guatemala but the local regions of Quetzaltenango and Huehuetenango, among others. I conclude the chapter by contemplating the challenges and possibilities for continuing this practice in diaspora as part of an anti–settler colonial politic.

Chapter 3 builds on the preceding chapter by examining how young adults in the diaspora engage new forms of cultural production to respond to the overlapping racial regimes in the United States. This chapter focuses on La Comunidad Ixim, a young adult group of 1.5- and second-generation Mayas in Los Angeles who produced a children's coloring book. I analyze a series of interviews with organizers in the collective to understand how their family histories and social justice organizing shaped how they created the coloring book. Thinking about the coloring book as the archive they produced, I pay close attention to how queer Maya positionalities, along with investments in social justice, extend the function of these mobile archives outside of the extended kinship networks I laid out in chapter 2. In this extension beyond the settler colonial notion of heteronormative and biological nuclear families, Mayas engage in forming communal notions of what it means to be Maya in diaspora. Family genealogies still play a critical role in how members of La Comunidad Ixim understand being Maya and challenge each other across boundaries of race, citizenship, and sexuality to demonstrate that second-generation Maya organizing positions itself as intersectional and social justice oriented. These first three chapters also establish the importance not just of biological families but of intergenerational relationships within the community. These intergenerational relationships are where the communal is deeply engaged and where these material products take on additional meaning.

Chapter 4 considers how the youth photography project Maya Womxn in L.A. takes up themes of transnational racism, intergenerational dialogue, and the flexible nature of new and old forms of cultural practice. By analyzing interviews with youth participants as well as the exhibit itself, I examine how mobile archives of Indigeneity can use traditionally problematic mediums (like photography) in ways that anchor and expand how we think about consent, reciprocity, and relationality, and actually engage youth and young adults in the formation of mobile archives. Photography has historically been used as a technology of settler colonialism because through its use in the archival process photographs fix Indigenous people as static vestiges of the past. Chapter 4 instead reconsiders how this medium can be used to create archives that can be mobile and even respond to issues of language and literacy as they visually demarcate the wide range of what it means to be a woman in the Maya diaspora.

The conclusion reiterates the primary claims of the book but also meditates on the need for more work on Maya diasporas that attempts to encompass the complexity of our community on our own terms. The works that outsiders have written about the Maya diaspora are useful, but I emphasize the increasing need to engage Latinidad and Indigeneity as categories of power that take on distinct articulations based on the spaces they inhabit.

1
Contesting the Logics of Displacement
in the Production of the Indigenous Migrant

The stories that we highlight about Indigenous migration are critical to how we understand Indigeneity and its elimination within and across settler contexts. In the summer of 2018, US Attorney General Jeff Sessions declared an official zero-tolerance policy around unauthorized immigration that effectively ramped up the separation of asylum-seeking migrant families. In the days and weeks that followed, many watched in horror the development of "tender age" detention centers, videos and photographs depicting family separation, and heated demonstrations protesting the detention of children separated from their caregivers. As more information emerged, it became clear that many of the families were Central American, and many of those were Indigenous Guatemalan families who spoke Indigenous languages. Once separated, some children were sent to group homes or foster homes of those who sought to profit from housing detained children or who simply wanted to create a haven for persecuted children. And while US citizens rushed to donate, organize, and find housing, the fostering and adopting of Indigenous children has historically functioned as a form of Indigenous elimination in many geographic and political contexts. When we examine the narratives around the adoption and fostering of Indigenous children, we can begin to see how erasure is imposed through the normalization of settler logics.

In the case of Guatemala, transnational Indigenous adoption compounds state violence that often targets Indigenous people and impoverished Maya women. The unregulated adoption of Indigenous Guatemalan children from their families began in the 1970s but essentially experienced two peak periods. The first was in the 1980s and the second in the 2000s, until finally in 2008 the United States suspended all adoptions until Guatemala's procedures complied with the Hague Convention on Protection of Children.[1] Silvia Posocco notes that these peaks in transnational adoptions coincide "with the times of most ferocious political repression (early to mid-1980s) and unbridled neoliberalism (mid-1990s and 2000s)."[2] In the context of ongoing Maya elimination in Guatemala, the transnational adoption wave that began in the 1970s and peaked during genocide and neoliberal economic restructuring becomes an additional site through which Maya loss is produced.[3] Karen Rotabi and Nicole Bromfield also begin to formulate how Indigenous structural dispossession makes child trafficking economically profitable and is compounded by an impunity that human rights activists argue ultimately makes "a woman's self-determination to participate in an adoption plan nearly impossible."[4] Multicultural families in the United States became possible and desirable through the unmarked ground of deep loss that was structurally facilitated by Guatemalan elimination and therefore settler colonial logics. To understand why mobile archives of Indigeneity generated by and for Maya diasporas are important, I first examine how the logics used to make Indigenous migrant experiences legible can fall into normalizing the conditions of dispossession.

Adoption can severely interrupt the possibility for intergenerational relationships that anchor a Maya diaspora. As a result, narratives about adoption are a site of cultural production where we can consider how, even under conditions that are entrenched in Indigenous elimination, Mayas seek out material objects that can help them make sense of displacement—or what I term mobile archives of Indigeneity. *Discovering Dominga*, a documentary directed by Patricia Flynn and co-produced by Mary Jo McConahay for the Public Broadcasting System Point of View series, tells the story of Dominga Sic Ruiz, a Maya Achí survivor of the Río Negro massacres of 1982 who was later adopted and renamed Denese Joy Becker.[5] As she recounts in the film, when soldiers arrived in her community and began to round everyone up, Denese/Dominga, then around nine years old, fled into the mountains surrounding Río Negro. With her infant sister on her back, she wandered for weeks and survived on her own in the highlands. Her baby sister eventually passed away, and Denese/Dominga was finally found by her cousin. Because her relatives were still fleeing ongoing military persecution, they decided to hide Denese/Dominga at a local orphanage in the larger town of Rabinal rather than put her life at risk. The nuns at the orphanage then transported her to another orphanage in Guatemala City. Two years later, a white couple from Algona, Iowa, adopted her. The film captures the one- to two-year period when Denese/Dominga—by this time a grown, married woman with two sons of her own—embarks on a journey to recover her past in Guatemala. Cameras follow her as she returns to Guatemala to learn about the politics surrounding the murder of her parents, the multiple massacres of the Achí community of Río Negro, and the genocide that took place nationwide. Over the course of three return trips to Rabinal, we witness Denese/Dominga reunite with her extended family, confront the layers of loss, and pursue courses of justice that make sense within her transnational lived experience.

In this chapter, I frame *Discovering Dominga* as a human rights film that makes violence and Indigenous suffering legible to viewers while normalizing the inclusion of Indigenous migrants through settler-colonial logics.[6] I engage Evelyn Alsultany's concept of simplified complex representations to look beyond the filmic text to read the politics that make such stories desirable.[7] *Discovering Dominga* does not reproduce the negation of the genocide against Mayas in Guatemala. Quite the opposite, it grounds its narrative in the fact that the genocide occurred and even highlights the US role in legitimating and empowering dictators. Thus, the story the filmmakers create seems positioned against the reality that within Guatemala, even decades after the signing of the peace accords that officially ended the armed conflict, the discourse of the Guatemalan nation-state and economic elite is that there was no genocide.[8] In the face of the continuing battle over Guatemala's historical memory, *Discovering Dominga* firmly positions itself as denouncing the state violence of Guatemala and documents the ongoing and precarious struggle for justice. However, in many ways the narratives within the film position the United States as a nation free of genocide, a land of sanctuary provided through a white adoptive family in the beautiful lands of the Midwest. Yet, mobile archives of Indigeneity are about creating processes and sites of memory that refuse easy incorporation into settler colonialism; this framing then allows us to center Maya social relations and their accompanying material culture. By unpacking and challenging the settler gaze, we can glimpse the brief moments when the film centers the need to learn from other Mayas and the ways that Mayas in diaspora must engage with these complexities for the sake of future generations.

This chapter examines the discursive strategies called upon and produced through the documentary to consider these questions: What overarching narrative about Indigeneity and displacement does the film produce or extend through Denese/Dominga's story? How is Indigeneity treated in relation to her migration and the transnational nature of this film? What strategies create the possibility for this documentary to be a part of a mobile archive of Indigeneity? While the film focuses on Denese/Dominga traveling to Guatemala and connecting with her Maya Achí family, I begin my analysis with the scenes that take place in Iowa to examine the way this narrative of an Indigenous adoptee is used to absolve whiteness from settler colonial histories and logics. Doing so allows Denese/Dominga to be claimed as another multicultural citizen within the United States.

The Settler Logics of Transnational Adoption

From the outset, the narrative of *Discovering Dominga* positions the United States and Guatemala in stark and even oppositional contrasts. Alicia Ivonne Estrada's analysis of this film pays particular attention to the visual binary created between Guatemala and the United States and the ways in which it "erases the complexities of both nations in relation to the thirty-six-year Guatemalan civil war."[9] I build on Estrada's analysis with a specific focus on settler colonialism because while the film highlights the role the United States played in the Maya genocide, it also simultaneously positions Indigenous dispossession as something that occurs only in Guatemala.

In part, what lies behind this visual contradiction is an erasure of the parallels that exist between the United States and Guatemala, especially in the way that both settler nations consistently position Indigenous people and Indigenous children as disposable or as assimilable only through conversion and control. In doing so, *Discovering Dominga* extends the project of settler colonialism through the story of a Maya transnational adoptee. This occurs because the film's visual representation of Guatemala as a volatile and violent place relies on representing Iowa as a place of relative security and stability. As a result, without problematizing the longer historical context that centers Indigenous dispossession across borders it is difficult to unpack how US settler colonialism becomes mundane. This film discursively and visually elides the genocide of Native people that enabled Algona, Iowa, to become a predominantly white town.

While Algona, Iowa's, own history of Native American dispossession is not the intended focus of this visual text, this history offers parallels that could have been made to Denese/Dominga's story. The town's name originated from the Algonquian word for waters and lakes, and while Algona itself is a small town with a seemingly untroubled history of open and successful settlement, Iowa is one of the states linked to the Black Hawk War of 1832. This armed resistance to US imperialism was led by Black Hawk and the British Band, a group composed of Sauk, Kickapoo, and Meskwaki people. In the aftermath of the failed attempt to stave off settler colonialism, the Meskwaki Nation of the Mississippi in Iowa was able to purchase land to create a community that enjoys federal recognition but is not part of any reservation.[10] This purchase only occurred in 1857, after a series of failed removals, returns, and relocations supported by the federal Indian Removal Act of 1830. Despite the possibility for more complex historical or contemporary connections around land loss, water rights, and forced removals—all of which would tie the Meskwaki history of dispossession to Denese/Dominga's removal from her ancestral land—the film writes Indigenous genocide as tragic but ultimately foreign.

This film's refusal to engage with the issues of Indigenous dispossession within the United States becomes the ideological terrain upon which it frames the transnational adoption of an Indigenous child into a white family without connecting it to Native child removal. In order to make Denese/Dominga's story accessible to white Western audiences, this documentary reproduces what Mark Rifkin has termed the settler common sense: "the ways the legal and political structures that enable nonnative access to Indigenous territories come to be lived as given, as simply the unmarked, generic conditions of possibility for occupancy, association, history, and personhood."[11] This settler common sense is the unmarked terrain upon which Denese/Dominga's adoption into a white American family is treated as a natural consequence of or even a multicultural solution to the structural issue of Maya genocide. Replicating the familiar trope of feeling out of place in both the United States and Guatemala, the filmmakers never problematize how transnational adoption fails to resolve dispossession for Indigenous peoples in the Americas and further ruptures the possibilities of intergenerational and extended kinship networks among Indigenous people.

To produce this settler common sense, the film positions Guatemala (the genocidal country) and the United States (the safe haven) as opposites. The scenes that tell Denese/Dominga's story about the massacre, her adoption, and her childhood in Algona all follow the opening scenes, where Guatemala and the United States are visually and discursively depicted as opposites. As Estrada argues, against the backdrop of a violent, traditional, and feminized Guatemala, the kind and loving white adoptive family from the modern and civilized world of the United States comes to represent a necessary intervention into the genocidal politics of the Central American country.[12] This trajectory allows viewers to dismiss that Denese/Dominga's story has many parallels to the taking of Native children and the consequent erasure of their realities as Indigenous people. That Algona, Iowa, is never placed into the history of settler colonialism allows Denese/Dominga's story to remain exceptional. The overdramatization and visual production of this difference between the United States and Guatemala hides how Denese/Dominga's story actually illustrates the continuity of Indigenous dispossession beyond territorial borders. Anti-Indigenous politics are not about a single nation and its policies for managing Indigenous peoples within its territorial boundaries. It is imperative to read beyond borders to tease out the continuous violence that allows multiple countries to produce overlapping forms of anti-Indigenous policies that connect along the axis of dispossession.

Unpacking the settler common sense requires that we account for the reproduction of settler logics and desires even in narratives that are not about Native people and sovereignty, precisely because those narratives take Native elimination as normalized. Rifkin argues, "Non-Natives need not function as agents of the state or as conscious purveyors of state aims in order to rematerialize state-effects by drawing on extant geographies, discourses, and normative frames as an anchor in processes of affective sense-making."[13] In the world of the film, erasing Native existence in Algona, Iowa, also ensures that Denese/Dominga's Indigeneity is not accounted for in the United States. In the case of Maya adoptees, their position as Indigenous people has no bearing on the process of adoption, and most literature understands their adoption specifically through frameworks that normalize these children as Guatemalan nationals. This is part of a larger project of erasing Guatemalan racial logics in order to incorporate these populations into US racial logics that are already premised on settler colonialism and Native elimination. When Maya migrants cross the US-Mexico border, they are no longer understood by the state as Indigenous people and instead are categorized as Guatemalans and Latinos, despite the specific challenges they face as Indigenous people, including disproportionate adoption levels. Thinking about Maya migrants from a hemispheric perspective highlights how the settler structure of the United States is extended through white benevolence vis-à-vis the Indigenous child refugee.

The long histories of colonization and nation building premised on Indigenous dispossession are symbolically absolved through the benevolence of Denese/Dominga's adoptive white mother; the white adult citizens of Algona; and Blane, Denese/Dominga's white husband. The scenes that discuss the adoption give as much authority to the adoptive mother, Linda Burk, as they do to Denese/Dominga herself. Set against a backdrop of a sunny outdoor area, the only scene in which Linda Burk appears by herself is when she tearfully states about Denese/Dominga, "She was really excited to have a family again. But many times she would get quiet, she would cry, and so all I could do was put my arms around her. That was the only thing I could do." This scene has the effect of exonerating the figure of the white mother by portraying her as a loving, caring, and innocent woman, perhaps lacking the resources to help Denese/Dominga confront the reality of violence.

Here it is useful to turn to Laura Briggs's work, which directly challenges the dichotomous narratives around adoption as always being either child rescuing or child stealing.[14] For Briggs, this false binary attempts to resolve neatly the complex ways in which both tropes reify transnational macropolitics that do not challenge the very existence or need for transnational adoption. Briggs has elsewhere claimed that images and public support for what becomes federal or international policy are interconnected. While she traces the images of the Madonna and child as a useful trope for visualizing third world poverty, she skillfully argues that these images actually center individual precarity to produce seemingly individual interventions as opposed to thinking about the structural reasons behind poverty, famine, and violence.[15] As a result, we cannot uncouple how the film positions Denese/Dominga's adoptive white family from how it normalizes adoption as a corrective for Guatemalan genocide. In addition, the transnational policy that the film refuses to acknowledge is that Denese/Dominga's adoption occurs in the 1980s, just as the 1978 Indian Child Welfare Act attempts to curb the adoption of Native American children, who in Minnesota had previously been adopted at *five* times the rate of non-Native children.[16] Had the film been connected to a larger conversation about Indigenous dispossession across borders, these links could have helped us question the limitations of transracial adoption and how dispossession continues to function in the lives of Indigenous adoptees.

Indigenous Dispossession, Solidarity, and Moves to Innocence

In order to understand the power of Denese/Dominga's agency and choices within the film, we must first unpack how the film normalizes narratives from the Central American Sanctuary Movement that obscure the power of Maya people within the documentary. Research on the Central American Sanctuary Movement (CASM, also known as one part of the Solidarity Movement or the Central American Peace and Solidarity Movement) has often focused on the intersection of religious organizations and social-movement building. Norma Chinchilla and colleagues state that "what became known as the Central American Sanctuary movement originated in Tucson, Arizona, when Jim Corbett, a Quaker, and John Fife, a Presbyterian minister, were threatened by INS officials for illegally escorting undocumented Salvadoran refugees into the United States from Mexico and providing shelter for them in churches and houses."[17] These authors argue that Central Americans were involved in CASM primarily as recipients of resources and as sources of testimony. While these scholars chose to focus on the US-based religious leaders providing sanctuary, others, including Rossana Pérez and Henry A. J. Ramos, have documented that the larger solidarity movement had a multiethnic and multiracial grassroots base that included Central Americans as leaders both in their country of origin and in diaspora in the United States.[18] These works do locate their analysis around leadership and change in distinct communities, but the tension in this literature reflects larger tensions over centering Central American agency versus white, middle-class US citizens' understandings of the value or role of Central Americans within the movement.

Overall, the Sanctuary Movement was built on the notion that people in the United States had a particular responsibility to hold their government accountable for its interventionist policies in Central America.[19] This objective was accomplished on many fronts, but perhaps the most useful for this analysis is the affective mindset that this type of movement required. As Sharon Nepstad writes, the individuals who participated in this movement required a "moral shock" that would do the emotional work needed to have others support this struggle. This shock ultimately utilized the victimization of Central Americans as a basis for solidarity. Noting that "these dramatizations of US imperialist violence offered a vehicle for redeeming the guilty US nation and its citizens, instantiating a reparative vision of the nation's future as a neoliberal multicultural family," Patricia Stuelke points out two issues in the Sanctuary Movement.[20] The first is that while it visibly stood against the interventionist violence wrought by US President Reagan, among others, it did not necessarily connect that violence to the neoliberal domestic policy being implemented at that time. The second is that it oversimplified the notion that individuals could solve structural issues.[21]

In the context of settler colonialism, the use of stories about Indigenous dispossession and pain as a vehicle to push settlers into action leaves unmarked the possibility of Indigenous futurity and instead utilizes a double move to innocence. "Moves to innocence" is a framework generated by Eve Tuck and Wayne Yang, who argue that "the metaphorization of decolonization makes possible a set of evasions, or 'settler moves to innocence,' that problematically attempt to reconcile settler guilt and complicity, and rescue settler futurity."[22] While they primarily speak about settler colonialism in relation to Native survivance, I extend their analysis to argue that *Discovering Dominga* requires a simultaneous double move to innocence with regard to the United States and Guatemala that enshrines a multicultural, but ultimately settler, futurity. From a lens of Indigenous critique, many of the scenes to which a move to innocence is linked pertain to colonial processes of adoption and missionization. In one scene, for example, Denese/Dominga's husband, Blane, speaks to a group of white Algona citizens inside a church, which gestures to the sanctuary movement. Wearing her Maya clothing, Denese/Dominga discusses her personal experience then steps to the side of the lectern so that Blane can provide a historical context and talk to the congregation, which includes her adoptive parents and her children, about the role of the US government in this conflict. Momentarily, viewers are asked to examine the role of their government in the violence that Denese/Dominga experienced. This scene is followed by one of the church members stating, "If most of the American people had any idea, but they don't know and that's the problem. So education like this is vital. And I'm absolutely astonished to see something like this happening in north Iowa. I think it's absolutely incredible." To which a woman in the congregation responds, "Yes it is, in Algona, Iowa," and the audience breaks into laughter and applause. This scene takes place in a church, linking it to both the Sanctuary Movement and the notion of innocence first heard in the interview with Linda Burk. Both scenes occur in well-lit locations associated with innocence, purity, transparency, and ultimately truth to convey incredulity and, to some extent, the virtue of everyday white citizens in Algona who learn about this story of Indigenous genocide. This trope is extended to nation building when a white man in the audience speaks up from his pew for all Americans to convey not only a sense of disappointment but also an innocence that, when paired with how the story positions Denese/Dominga's white mother, demonstrates that white individuals are simply unaware of the work of their government.

In the context of her adoption and disconnection from her community, Denese/Dominga's white, adoptive cousin is the only exception to the discourse of "not knowing." It is her cousin who ends up asking the survivors of the Río Negro massacre about Denese/Dominga and who, as a missionary who has learned Spanish, serves as her interpreter. Her cousin, however, stands as the single exception to her parents, her husband, and the larger Algona community who justify their inaction as due to not knowing. We are led to conclude that this lack of awareness—rather than the material benefits deriving from settler colonialism and imperialism—is what allows them to remain passive in the face of such violence. Both this scene and the scene with her adoptive mother do the work of cleansing these settler-citizens of responsibility toward Denese/Dominga specifically but also toward the systematic genocide of Indigenous people by US government policies and practices.

This scene reminds us that Denese/Dominga's story is filtered through the popular discourse of CASM. However, Patricia Stuelke and Ana Patricia Rodríguez both provide critical insight into how affective reparative politics also produces a solidarity that co-opts and over-sentimentalizes the narratives of Central American migrants.[23] With few exceptions, most research notes the involvement of Maya refugees but does not consider what the movement has meant for settler colonial imaginaries and politics within the United States. It is this framing of family formation through the transnational adoption of an Indigenous child that requires an analysis beyond sentimentalization, because when placed into the longer history of Native child removal, continuous dispossession is normalized. The audience of *Discovering Dominga* is asked to have sympathy for a white mother and family who, through adoption, facilitate a transborder anti-Indigenous politics by removing Denese/Dominga from her homeland and extended family.[24]

Denese/Dominga herself describes a very different perspective about her adoption and her reception in Algona, Iowa. The sequence that discusses her adoption opens with a photograph of her and her smiling adoptive parents in a newspaper article documenting her adoption by the local couple. We hear the noise of children playing in the background while in a voiceover Denese/Dominga begins to discuss her experience of coming to this small town. As we see images of white children wearing backpacks, we hear Denese/Dominga state, "I tried really hard to fit in. Some of them thought I was Chinese, so they called me [a racial slur]. When I tell my story, they just look at me like I made it up. Yeah, she's ins—yeah, like I was crazy. She has a vivid imagination." Her eyes wide, nodding at someone beyond the camera, Denese/Dominga shares this story with a sense of disbelief that she was accused of lying about her family, her ancestral homeland, and the violence she endured.

As Denese/Dominga describes this experience, the images of white school-age children carrying backpacks, presumably at a school, give the impression that these racist interactions occurred at school with her peers.

However, Denese/Dominga never states that the practice of hostile racism was limited to other children. The stock footage of children, backpacks, and a school bus all allow the racism she experiences to be framed as something that only children would perpetrate. The visual framing ignores the possibility that this behavior was part of a larger project of how Algona, Iowa, is constructed as a white town, where nonwhiteness is read as foreign, and foreign is read as Asian, marked by the use of a racist slur. Against the much more common experiences of Mayas as undocumented migrants that informs other research, the fact that Denese/Dominga arrives in the United States with legal citizenship does not prevent her Maya body from being read as not belonging in Algona, Iowa.

While furthering the discourse that minimizes the discrimination and violence against Denese/Dominga, this scene also does the work of making apparent to the audience the benevolence of her white mother as a way of mediating Denese/Dominga's coercion into silence. This is accomplished in part by what is left out of the narrative of the film. For example, the film never explains why Denese/Dominga was transferred to an orphanage in Guatemala City to begin with. During this period of armed conflict, it was common practice for soldiers and paramilitaries to "adopt" child survivors after their parents had been murdered. Families, even biological parents, often feared for their lives if they were to try and claim their children, who were now living in communities and families who had the authority and power to kill them with impunity. In some cases, the children were brought up as actual members of the family, but more often than not, they were abused and treated as unpaid domestic workers. Many of the child survivors have since become adult organizers who lead calls for justice and accountability and testify firsthand to the treatment they experienced in these new families. In the case of Denese/Dominga, the film itself never clarifies whether her extended relatives had placed her in an orphanage to hide her for fear that she would be targeted as a witness and survivor.[25] In addition to the threat of death, we also have to consider that Denese/Dominga's extended family had just experienced multiple massacres and were still constantly fleeing from the military and struggling to survive in the mountains. These gaps and silences in the film highlight the characterization of Denese/Dominga's adoptive mother as benevolent by hiding away these intimate forms of rupture and, ultimately, displacement.

Transborder Anti-Indigenous Politics

A hemispheric and transborder approach allows us to articulate that Denese/Dominga's narrative is the result of multiple national imaginaries (of both the United States and Guatemala) that objectify her for what she means to the state. In writing about Oaxacans, Stephens argues that transnationalism describes only movements across the US-Mexico border while ignoring the many other borders and boundaries that Indigenous migrants must cross. She states, "Regional systems of racial and ethnic hierarchies within the United States are different from those in Mexico and can also vary within the United States."[26] This means that, while we can understand large categories of identities, we also have to remember that each is produced in relation to local contexts as well. In the case of Guatemala, the anti-Indigenous politics at play positions Maya communities as barriers to progress and development that needed to be eliminated. In the case of the Río Negro community, the military government agreed to build a dam and hydroelectric plant there using foreign funds without considering the communities that had existed along the river for centuries. The dam was intended to deliver electricity to the capital city, and the military responded to various communities' resistance to relocation with massive and brutal repression. The single largest massacre occurred on March 13, 1982, when 178 people were systematically and collectively murdered: 70 women, 107 children, and one man.[27] It was this conflict over the Chixoy Dam that was at the root of Denese/Dominga's orphaning. While part of a longer history of dispossession, the genocide of the 1980s was also connected to a particular economic model of development that operated through funding by international banks and the military regimes of Guatemala. As J. T. Way states, the "epoch of intense modernization in Guatemala culminated in genocide. The period from 1970 to 1985 was one of transformation through terror. Counterinsurgency and development, the army's two missions, are not analytically separate."[28] Not having been eliminated through murder or capture by the paramilitary, Denese/Dominga becomes an adoptable orphan. Brought to Algona, Iowa, as a pastor's daughter, she becomes the object that exemplifies her adoptive father's charity and morals. She is then positioned in this film as a woman who does not know where she belongs and consequently makes it part of her own mission to raise awareness about the violence in Guatemala.

While it is important to recognize that Denese/Dominga's experience is not the same as that of adopted Native American children, positioning her dispossession as something foreign to the United States allows the audience to ignore the adoption of Maya children as a transnational strategy of genocide. By eliminating Iowa's and the United States' history of elimination, we see Denese/Dominga's plight only because of the armed conflict in Guatemala that led to the massacre of her parents. This is of particular concern because it occludes how Indigenous migrants are subject to technologies that are developed under settler colonial societies.[29] Transnational adoption into white families is a technology of erasure: in Denese/Dominga's case, from the time she is adopted until her cousin supports her in finding her community, she is pressured to forget her ties to her native language, family, Maya clothing, and territory. As a result, Denese/Dominga is one less Maya woman who can claim reparations in terms of the land struggle in Guatemala and one more US citizen who can acquire private property in the States.

The film's silence over the long-standing struggles for Native sovereignty allows the United States to absorb displaced Indigenous migrants through citizenship and US racial structures by removing any possibility for Denese/Dominga to exist in relation to Native North America. Viewers are not encouraged to consider her Indigeneity in relation to the Indigenous peoples who are from nearby regions and who may be more capable than the townspeople of Algona of understanding her experience with genocide. Rather than have a discussion about the commonality of dispossession, adoption, and then returning to home communities, the filmmakers instead produce a discourse of difference that creates space for white people to be represented as kind, innocent, and openhearted—but most certainly not as colonizers themselves.

In centering the story of a transnational adoptee, we are also able to sidestep the experience of undocumented migration in Maya communities. While the hundreds of thousands of people affected by the conflict in Guatemala are invoked as victims, the film makes no mention of how common transnational adoption or undocumented migration has been. Among the connections that are left unexplored is that the terror and violence affecting large swaths of Maya communities continues in the United States. The fact that Denese/Dominga entered the US community as a legal citizen and part of a heteronuclear family did little to safeguard her from experiencing a deep sense of exclusion. Much research on Maya migrants in the diaspora exposes the violence and marginalization they experience as a result of not being recognized as refugees and therefore remaining categorized as undocumented and criminalized migrants. Although it is critical to this narrative of not knowing where she belongs, Denese/Dominga's displacement is also never considered to emerge from the racism and exclusion she faces in Algona. Viewers are left believing that Denese/Dominga's experience is a result of the violence of the massacre in Guatemala, as if similar types of violence cannot be traced to places like Algona and are not maintained by normal, everyday white Iowans.

Intergenerational Memory Making

Anti-indigenous politics must be deconstructed to perceive possibilities for forming a diaspora that is not necessarily defined through settler colonial maneuvers of occupation. While the film replicates these politics in how it conceptualizes the Maya experience of genocide, there are also moments that represent different routes for the process and value of historical memory. In the context of Maya organizing and the diversity of responses that have been employed to struggle over the meaning of justice and memory, the film develops a praxis that, while not an overt frame, does important work in providing glimpses into survival strategies that are generated from Maya epistemologies and shared between Maya people. These strategies are not always obvious, but as Kelly Lytle Hernández writes about rebel archives, "the rebel archive found refuge in far-flung boxes and obscure remnants. But it also thrives in plain sight."[30] I would even argue that one of the evasive power relations that this film seems incapable of engaging is how the filter of the white gaze is necessitated through the presumption of Mayas as victims incapable of initiating their own movements for justice. As a result, the film often circumvents the tension by only including scenes around Maya epistemologies and activism in brief and decontextualized moments. Overlooking the possibilities for Maya agency also transforms Maya epistemologies into a trace. While scholars have argued that the trace is the residue of violent structures, I would also argue that in instances where human rights films work so diligently to visually capture and communicate one particular form of violence and atrocity, at times the responses of those directly harmed by state repression become an afterthought. I delve deeper into the moments of connection to highlight the praxis that Mayas have formed to attest to their survival of multiple genocides.

Intergenerational imaginaries, part of the praxis that emerges from a transborder existence, counteract the rupture associated with displacement and state violence. To take one example, one of the underexamined narrative threads in the film is Denese/Dominga's journey as it relates to her own children. In one of the opening scenes of the film, Denese/Dominga lays out a central problem for the diaspora. In reference to her older son she asks, "When he was four he would ask me what I did when I was four. What am I gonna say when he's nine? I can't tell him that my parents were massacred." The politics around intergenerational memory within a context of Indigenous genocide and displacement are critical to thinking about what is remembered and how it is communicated to those who did not live that memory in their lifetime. To some extent, it even begs the question of what it means to "live a memory." Furthermore, it forces us to question whether there are corporeal, temporal, or spatial boundaries for memories of genocide. The very critical question Denese/Dominga poses forces us to reconceptualize how our visions of the future must simultaneously embrace that the past is more than historical fact; it remains a formative force in our everyday lives in diaspora. The moments that highlight the tensions and possibilities around intergenerational imaginaries or Indigenous social relations extend beyond the generational schema of migration studies that focus on immigrant/first generation, 1.5 generation, and second generation by making these connections less about assimilation and more about Indigenous continuity. This makes the film a critical mobile archive for the Maya diaspora despite its primary framing being tied to the white gaze. The narrative frame of *Discovering Dominga* that positions Guatemala and the United States as inherently different in relation to Indigeneity also obscures the critical ways in which Denese/Dominga mobilizes her own agency to create bridges to her extended family in Guatemala and to extend those intergenerational relationships to her children in the United States and to generations that have passed away.

One of the challenges to thinking about the intergenerational nature of memory is that doing so can lead to an analysis that romanticizes the discourse of recovery. Recovery assumes that there is an authentic Indigenous experience or a specific form of Indigenous consciousness that was fully ruptured by genocide and colonization and which must somehow be recuperated.[31] Such an analysis can be problematic because it assumes that Indigeneity is not complex enough to include the realities that someone like Denese/Dominga experiences. It also does not account for how Indigeneity shifts. As noted in the introduction, before the 1980s it may have made sense for Denese/Dominga's story to be highly localized within an Achí experience of Río Negro; however, the advent of the Maya movement and the international recognition it has garnered also open the possibility for a pan-Maya identity to be claimed, especially in relation to challenging the discourses and actions of the genocide. As the film focuses on Denese/Dominga, we only vaguely remember that the story is not just about her but also about the narrative she will construct for her sons. Rather than revolving around the generational gains that are measured in immigrant integration research—such as intermarriage, homeownership, and higher education—the question she poses in the film is about Maya historical memory and how we maintain the memories of those so brutally eliminated precisely because they were deeply connected to their ancestral territories. The intergenerational imaginaries that she creates throughout the film extend temporally beyond her migrant experience and that of her children to include generations as far forward as back. That is, her Indigenous descendants will all have to engage the same questions if they wish to continue understanding themselves as part of Maya social worlds anchored in ontologies that emerge from their ancestral territories.

While her children are peripheral characters in the film, part of her concern is about how to transmit her experience to her children. Her children appear on camera in only a handful of scenes, and only twice are they speaking with Denese/Dominga. Toward the beginning of the film, we see Denese/Dominga reading a book to her children about Mr. and Mrs. Porcupine attempting to name their child. Her children sit on a couch in a cozy home and engage with their mother and the book. Both the scene and the book itself are about family, identity, naming, and sharing narratives. We see the three of them again toward the end of the film, after we learn that she and her husband have separated. She and her sons are sitting on their beige couch when we see her showing her two sons a sahumador (incense burner) and attempting to explain to them that her grandfather was a "Maya priest," or what is known as an ajq'ij'ab in K'iche', a spiritual guide and daykeeper who leads ceremonies.

This is something Denese/Dominga learns when she attends a ceremony during her first trip back to Guatemala. In the documentary the center frame is the fire of the ceremony as we hear a voiceover of Denese/Dominga stating, "The smells brought a lot of memories to me. I just kept thinking how my mom and dad when they would go mourn their dead, they would do the same thing. I kept thinking, is this what it's like to be part of these people? And if it is, I think I like it." In an article reflecting on the documentary, the director, Patricia Flynn, noted that it was when Denese/Dominga saw the ceremony leaders wearing red headscarves that she remembered her grandfather would do the same. Although this was not the filmmakers' direct intention, the ceremony plays a critical role in jogging

Denese/Dominga's sensory-based memories and helping her identify the role that her grandfather played in the community. This allows Denese/Dominga to extend her narrative beyond the violence of the genocide to something much larger, which is Maya spirituality or cosmovision. The sensory remembrance of smelling incense and seeing the headscarf and candles creates a critical space from which Denese/Dominga begins to question and affirm a connection with Maya people. Given the violent circumstances surrounding her parents' death and the power of Maya ceremony in communicating Maya epistemologies, it is spiritual practice that becomes the connection she wants to share with her children. Memory is a critical aspect of diasporas produced out of state violence and dispossession. It becomes critical in articulating visions of both the past and the future and locating sites from which to generate political intentions. Within the context of her original question, "What will I tell him when he is nine, I can't tell him my parents were massacred," the film moves toward a place where she does indeed tell both sons about the massacre but with a commitment to tell them much more, to root them in Maya spirituality briefly, perhaps fleetingly, but to do it nonetheless.

It is important then to recognize that theorizing intergenerational relationships for Mayas must center the notion that generations are not restricted to categories often employed in traditional immigrant integration studies. Rather than disaggregating migrants as the first generation and their US-citizen children as the second generation and so on, centering the reality that these generations do not always fall into clear categories or patterns is critical to understanding the Maya experience. For Mayas, there is also an intergenerational imaginary that extends beyond the physical and temporal realm of the here and now. Spiritual ceremony becomes a critical avenue through which this intergenerational imaginary is produced and, as such, these relationships become difficult to measure in sociological metrics, but they nonetheless have important spiritual and memory resonances. In addition to naming your specific grandparents across generations during spiritual practices, it is common to speak of *abuelas/abuelos* (grandparents) with the understanding that these ancestors are collectively all of our grandparents and can include the mountains, rivers, and other nonhuman entities as part of the ancestral genealogy that shapes who you are.

In the scene where Denese/Dominga shows her sons the sahumador, one asks about her Maya cousins who died. Denese/Dominga affirms that when her children's grandma and grandpa were killed, a lot of her cousins were indeed also murdered. Her son responds by asking how many cousins she has left, and Denese/Dominga responds that she probably has about fifty cousins still alive and that one cousin actually looks just like him. The scene ends in quiet contemplation. The importance and power of the discursive practice through which an intergenerational imaginary occurs is critical to how we conceptualize Maya cultural production and continuity in the face of displacement. Hence, mobile archives of Indigeneity use our cultural materials (like the *sahumador* used for ceremony) to tell stories about our ancestors that tie us together as a community. I want to stress again that, while these scenes are not central to the documentary overall, they are important because they intervene against the notion that displacement is the ultimate rupture and always equates to insurmountable loss. For both Denese/Dominga and her sons, mobile archives of Indigeneity are found in the moments and exchanges that center continuity, attachment, and genealogy.

These intergenerational imaginaries are also not necessarily anthropocentric or bound by time or physical space. At the beginning of the film, we see Denese/Dominga as she embarks on her journey; as she sits silently on the plane, staring out the window with a pensive expression, we hear her voiceover: "I just wanted to step on the land, to complete my memories, to make sure I was not insane." As we see her in the airport in the capital city and as her van travels on paved roads through the mountainside, we also hear her say, "I could see the valleys and the mountains and the hills. I could see the little children dressed in Mayan clothing, and all I could see was me as a little child and my mother. And that was when I knew I was home." Through her tearful words, we remember that the trip back to Guatemala is what will allow Denese/Dominga to make sense of the memories she has carried for years. We are introduced to land as a site of memory while we also begin to sense that her journey is about returning to a reality she was violently cut off from. However, land is not solely positioned as a site of home. During her second trip back to Río Negro for the commemoration of the massacre in which her parents were killed, she takes a small boat to reach the site of the massacre. As she silently rides in this boat across what appears to be a lake, we hear her state in a voiceover, "The river—the river's gone, it's a lake now. I don't even want to touch the water, my home is gone." The dam that precipitated the conflict in Río Negro forever marks the literal loss of her home, which is now completely inundated under the reservoir behind the dam. This lake is a site of pain and disgust for Denese/Dominga because its creation marks the loss of her parents and the life that she knew as a child. In this sense, land is a site of memory and does not always equate to "home."

However, land also plays a critical role in memory making that gives it a unique position in the creation of the intergenerational imaginary. As we see in the film, Denese/Dominga meets Jesús Tecú Osorio during this trip for the commemoration of the massacre at Pak'oxom, and he recounts for her in gruesome detail what he saw during the massacre. As described in the introduction, Tecú Osorio has been a key and courageous leader in advocating for exhumations in the communities that were targeted during this conflict. While the film does not position him in this way, he plays one of the most important roles in it. As Denese/Dominga stands silently, she asks her interpreter not to translate Tecú Osorio's stories because she understands them despite the language barrier. As she cries and thanks him for sharing painful memories, he responds, "Like I said earlier, sometimes it's hard for us humans to bear seeing such things, like the day of the massacre. But like I was saying, these trees have more memories than we do because they, the trees, saw everything, and so did Mother Earth." In this sense Tecú Osorio extends the role of land beyond just being the physical place on which things occur to serving as an archive itself, a holder of memories. Land is the oldest relative, which has borne witness to everything that has occurred and, according to Tecú Osorio, it provides a model for resilience and continuity despite violence. Land, then, is not simply an inert site whose value is understood only in what it produces for human sustenance. Instead, land remains and spans across multiple generations, continuously bearing witness.

Conclusion: What Remains

Analyzing how cultural productions can miss the nuances that connect Indigenous dispossession across borders alerts us to a larger historical, legal, and social process that is the context within which the Maya diaspora intervenes. As I consider what remains after this film is seen and analyzed, I return to what Denese/Dominga shares after the mass grave that holds the men of Río Negro is exhumed. In the film we see the exhumation, and the material remains in the grave include clothing and fragments that point to who these men were and what happened. As I consider how in these scenes the viewer is asked to bear witness to an incredibly painful moment for those present, I am reminded that even in this moment the emphasis can also be on what remains for the Achí survivors and for Denese/Dominga.

What remains is the process of rebuilding, of creating stability and harmony, of creating narratives of consciousness and continuity. This necessarily includes the exhumation, so that the remains can be reburied with dignity and in alignment with the community's spiritual practices. Contrary to the lingering in-betweenness of the Guatemalan Dominga and American Denese that the film leaves us with, Denese/Dominga states after the exhumation, "The community will bury the bodies that have been exhumed. I'd love to be there, to say good-bye to my dad. I really do hope that he knows that I am fighting for him. That he didn't die for no reason." For Denese/Dominga what remains is the will to continue extending the intergenerational bonds that supersede transnational anti-Indigenous politics.

These intergenerational bonds include oral histories like those shared with Denese/Dominga as well as the material objects that she will use to convey Maya belonging to her children. For Maya diasporas, it becomes critical to use the objects we can access to maintain our own historical memory, which includes but reaches beyond the borders of the nation and even beyond the memory of the 1980s genocide. These can be sahumadores like the one Denese/Dominga uses to talk to her children or, as noted in the following chapters, may take the form of cultural productions created by young people who are living and growing up in the United States. These cultural productions make sense of mobility because the people and the objects themselves are mobile and acquire new significance through that mobility.

2

Weaving Maya Geographies, Textiles, and Relationality in Diaspora

In Guatemala, wearing Maya clothing is one of the markers that the government officially recognizes as making someone Indigenous. Yet, often absent from this "acknowledgment" is the ways the state has utilized war, laws, sexual violence, and systemic racism to make it difficult to wear Maya clothing and thereby be officially counted as Indigenous. While Maya clothing can mark belonging to a Maya people, it can also mark Maya women as targets for structural violence. This anti-Indigenous structural violence shifts across settler borders but remains constant in acknowledging Indigeneity only in ways that normalize the power of the nation. As a result of this targeting, the impetus to continue the practice of wearing Maya clothing, transmit its significance, and use it as a medium for storytelling all make this act a critical site of community making between generations of Maya women and femmes, who are the primary wearers of the clothes. For the diaspora, Maya clothing is therefore one of the material ways that Maya people reproduce their social norms through Indigenous geography and kinship making across time and space. In this chapter, I continue this line of argumentation through interviews with Maya women. But I ground my analysis in the expansive concept of a mobile archive of Indigeneity to (1) unpack the continuation or creation of Maya cultural practices despite state violence and displacement that threaten cultural memory, and (2) explore an ongoing process of engaging Maya epistemologies.

In addition, the wearing of regional clothing by young, second-generation Maya women in Los Angeles disrupts social and political hierarchies that exist around Indigenous practices, beliefs, and people in Guatemala and the United States.[1] In the diaspora, the use of Maya clothing requires an intergenerational transmission of knowledge that centers Maya women. Beyond the actual textiles are the relationships embedded in the wearing of them and the opportunity that the clothing provides to share stories of Maya life. The process of learning to wear Maya clothing and understanding its function allows specific family histories to be maintained despite the experience of crossing multiple borders, which then allows for the second generation to continue claiming and transforming traditions.

Unlike normative archives that seek to categorize and organize in order to control difference and consolidate national projects, Maya clothing acts as a mobile archive of Indigeneity that anchors localized Indigenous geographies even as those geographies remain attached to a broader Maya collective. In line with most of Maya cosmovision, each part of the Maya dress has its own significance. The po't (blouse) has images woven into it, but in the act of putting it on, a woman's body also becomes a central part of the cosmos. This relationship is on the scale of the cosmos but directly reflects local geographies through the fabric's many designs and styles that incorporate the immediate landscape. If a family does not weave the cloth, it is expensive to purchase, costing anywhere from $150 to $700 depending on the piece, the thread used, and the quality of the design. The garments are incredibly long-lasting; they can be used as everyday clothes for years or, if reserved for special occasions, can be passed down across multiple generations. The longevity of the actual material is critical for maintaining place-based relationships across vast geographies and time periods.

The ontological and geographic significance of textiles can best be understood by providing a glimpse into how they hold or produce meaning that coheres Maya social worlds. This practice embeds local specificities into the textile, and it does so as part of a practice of history, archive, and territory. Maya textiles could be lumped together as beautiful, colorful textiles, but they actually represent a wide range of localized histories and epistemologies: towns or areas near prominent bodies of water may feature predominantly blue tones in their dress; places near volcanoes may feature red; and in Xelajuj No'j (Quetzaltenango), a valley surrounded by volcanoes and mountains, weavers incorporate images of mountains. In the case of Quetzaltenango, or Xelajuj No'j, the weaving of the local mountain range manifests the ontological understanding that the people and the mountains are interwoven and are part of each other. We understand the mountain range as a source of spiritual life and a place where we go to be happy; we also see the mountains as elders who, through their physical presence, protected us from immediate colonial invasion by making it difficult for Spanish invaders to reach us as they marched from Teotihuacan. This produces a longer historical consciousness about Xelajuj No'j (Quetzaltenango) in which the mountains are part of the imagined possibility of Indigenous resistance because they are the site of deep knowledge and care. The textiles from Xelajuj No'j (Quetzaltenango), then, are one way this community actively works to maintain and pass on a relationship to that place and history.

One possibility that this practice generates is for Maya belonging to exceed the boundaries of the settler colonial nation-state. Investigating how regional Maya clothing is attached to specific towns, and not the Guatemalan nation, helps us understand these practices as part of building diasporic communities through Indigenous geographies. Migration is an ongoing process rather than a one-time event, which informs how second-generation Mayas participate in the structures and meanings of the multiple local places they consider home. While this is true for many migrants, Indigeneity also plays a key role in the attachment not to a national homeland, but to specific towns and places that are understood as ancestral.[2]

Maya regional dress is significant because of what is woven into the textile, but it also speaks to the social, political, and economic lives of Maya women. The materials used to create the clothing reflect gendered histories of labor and colonial conditions. While in Xelajuj No'j (Quetzaltenango), I visited Museo Ixkik', which at that point was a grassroots effort to document the history of the po't for Maya people in Guatemala. Located in an abandoned train station that had been used to torture students during the war, the museum is part of an effort to reclaim such spaces of terror.[3] The physical location of this museum represents the ways in which mobile archives are layered between, on top of, or under legacies of violence. While I was visiting the museum, its director, Raquel García, told me that in some regions women used lace in their regional clothing not just because it was available, but because they actively resisted having to manufacture cotton. Specifically, so much of women's labor during the colonial period was exploited to produce dyed cottons for export that they vowed no longer to use it in their weavings. In this way, Maya women sought to protect younger generations of girls from coerced labor by using lace in their huipiles. This dynamic relationship to textiles is one of the ways that Maya women subverted colonial gendered conditions.

Alongside these political and economic layers is the discursive violence that positions Maya (and Indigenous people in general) as inherently inferior, lazy, and uneducated and casts individuals who organize for collective rights as communists or terrorists. In 2021, the lead vocalist of the Guatemalan rock band El Tambor de la Tribu, Ale Puga Ortiz, commented on a podcast that Maya women should not wear their Maya dress to "formal" events and galas but should instead follow the fashion norms expected for the event. Regarding whether Indigenous women could or should enter formal spaces, he claimed they could if they were to change their dress: "If you grab an Indigenous woman and you dress her well, and you take her to buy clothes, she could probably enter."[4] His public comments represent a much wider, persisting belief about Maya dress and Maya women as dirty and backward that is unfortunately more common than many outside the Maya community comprehend.

The settler colonial structure of the United States operates to similar ends, but functions discursively through the widespread notion that Native people are gone or disappearing.[5] For instance, few people in Los Angeles know who the Tongva, Kizh, and Gabrielino are, and more emphasis is placed on the historical period of the missions than on the contemporary struggles and issues that these communities experience today. Understanding this distinction between settler colonial structures and their respective discursive violence is critical in thinking about multiple diasporic generations. Unlike Mayas who migrate as adults, those who migrate as children or are born in the United States experience life through social spaces like public education that naturalize settler colonialism.[6] Like their older migrant counterparts, US-born or -raised Mayas continue wearing Maya clothing. However, despite or perhaps because of their experiences in spaces that naturalize settler colonialism, Maya youth strive to analyze more deeply how they actively engage in this practice and the significance it holds for them as part of the larger Maya community.

Maya Dress as a Site of Gendered Dispossession

The context of genocide, colonialism, and ongoing gender-based violence has been and continues to be central to understanding that the use of Maya textiles has broad political significance everywhere, but especially in Guatemala. To understand the continued use of corte in the diaspora as an act of refusal, the practice of using Maya clothing must first be analyzed in the political context of Guatemala. It is there that we can understand the violence against and exclusion of Indigenous women and clarify why, despite this violence, Maya women actively mobilize to defend their right to continue to wear traditional clothing. Tracing the meaning of Maya clothing back to Guatemala is also necessary because the use of Maya clothing in the diaspora does not occur in a vacuum but requires ongoing transnational connections.

Maya clothing has served multiple functions in Guatemalan history and has often marked Maya womanhood as outside of, yet central to, the formation and the economy of the nation-state. According to Irma Otzoy and Greg Grandin, Maya men were forced to discontinue the use of regional clothing to enter mainstream institutions of politics, government, education, and trade. Writing about Quetzaltenango specifically, Grandin asserts that the historical production of Maya clothing as a predominantly feminine cultural practice was an essential way for K'iche' patriarchs in the early twentieth century to participate in public positions while maintaining their ethnic identity through their wives' and daughters' continued wearing of Maya clothing.[7] This means that while Maya women were left out of mainstream institutions that defined what it meant to be Guatemalan, their exclusion was also the foundation for Ladino and K'iche' elite men to lay claim to the masculine national subject. The gendering of this cultural practice is especially significant because, unlike other cultural markers, it literally imprints Maya identity upon the body, making it a highly visible act.

As many scholars have demonstrated, and as the sweeping tide of femicide shows, discrimination against Maya women has persisted in Guatemala. Analysis of femicide in Guatemala has been linked to the global issue of gender-based violence that centers on the murder and disappearance of Maya women. Yet, in addition to physical violence, Maya women are dispossessed of their labor because economically precarious conditions often relegate them to agricultural work, domestic labor, street vending, or other forms of informal labor. The Sepur Zarco trials of 2016 shone a spotlight on sexual violence against Q'eqchi' women who, under threat of violence and death, were forced to complete three-day shifts as slave laborers who cooked, did laundry, and cleaned the military outpost in Sepur Zarco. Regarding the Sepur Zarco trial, Patricia Arroyo Calderón writes that the theft of reproductive labor through coerced domestic work indicates that physical assault is accompanied by other forms of theft and dispossession that may seem innocuous but are actually forms of labor that would have been integral to the social reproduction of Maya lives and communities.[8] Scholars of Guatemala have also meticulously documented the growth of this violence because a context of impunity remains a barrier to justice in the aftermath of the armed conflict and genocide. The freedom to act violently without fear of legal accountability makes impoverished and Indigenous women especially vulnerable because, as Rosa-Linda Fregoso and Cynthia Bejarano note in their introduction to *Terrorizing Women*, femicide implicates larger institutions and individual perpetrators who, regardless of intention, act in tandem to subject women to gender-based violence. Femicide in Guatemala has risen to the level of international concern, but as scholars have pointed out, this violence operates in Guatemala for a multitude of reasons that make women particularly disposable.[9]

In addition to the types of violence noted above, Maya women also face exclusion directly tied to their use of regional clothing. Maya scholar and activist Irma Alicia Velásquez Nimatuj, for example, publicly denounced the discrimination she encountered because of her wearing of regional clothing. In one instance, she sued the exclusive restaurant El Tarro Dorado in Guatemala for denying her entrance because she was wearing Maya clothing. After detailing this situation in her article, Velásquez Nimatuj explains the politics at issue: "Whenever we are seen in regional *traje*, the ruling classes are reminded of the failure of their efforts to make us disappear, which have ranged from genocide to ideological coercion. Five centuries of humiliation have not succeeded in bringing the Maya people to their knees."[10] In addition, in 2015, Lina Eugenia Barrios Escobar and Lilia Irene Cap Sir published a report on discrimination faced by Maya women studying at public universities. While the authors addressed several factors, Maya women noted that wearing Maya clothing marked them for exclusion before they even opened their mouth or engaged in interpersonal interactions. Of the twenty-eight women interviewed, 70 percent faced discrimination based on their clothing, and of those only one filed a discrimination claim with the university.[11] These forms of exclusion enact an embodied form of gendered discrimination that mirrors the more extreme violence of femicide.

Indeed, the foundational struggle of enduring colonial structures is expressed in how we understand textiles. Velásquez Nimatuj adds that neoliberal changes in the global market have resulted in an increased national economic dependency on tourism in Guatemala that has exacerbated the folklorization of Maya textiles in ways often completely divorced from the lived realities of Maya people.[12] Maya clothing cannot be bought or analyzed as a simple folkloric tradition since it is used by the state to exclude Maya women and yet is used by communities to make themselves and their epistemologies present. Literary critic Gloria Chacón writes, "In Western art systems, [textiles] are treated as expressions of folklore or ethnic materials existing in the public domain. Indigenous poets, however, insist weavings represent a type of writing because they communicate information that can be read at various levels and are unique individual and collective ancestral expressions."[13] Chacón points out that this distinction between

Western and Indigenous definitions of textiles results in a lack of legal protection for weavers and communities.

This lack of legal protection creates a series of questions often discussed in relation to appropriation. Underneath these egregious forms of appropriation, however, rest questions about economics. In a deeply unequitable country like Guatemala, where economic opportunities are scarce, entrepreneurship becomes one of the sites where Indigenous people can sustain themselves and their families. In a country where 49 percent of the population lives in poverty and child malnutrition rates are among the highest in Latin America, any available economic opportunity must be considered in the context of survival.[14] This, then, must be part of the conversation: appropriation is a symptom of a deeply racist and economically unjust society that makes entrepreneurship one of the very few pathways to economic survival. A recent example of this form of appropriation is Caroline Fuss's designer line, Harare, which used textiles woven by Maya women from Atitlán, Sololá, as part of its New York Fashion Week show in 2014. Unlike other forms of appropriation in which designs and patterns from Indigenous material culture are essentially copied and used by designers, Fuss utilized textiles produced *by* Maya women, keeping the method of backstrap loom weaving but changing the colors and design.[15] Products manufactured by designers like Fuss retail for hundreds of US dollars under the free market's consumption patterns, yet the free market does little to change or even acknowledge the structural marginalization that creates and constantly reproduces the inequality most Maya women live with.

Harare and projects like it often portray themselves as conscious producers, creating high-end material commodities for a niche market of wealthy individuals who want to purchase goods made through global cooperatives. While Harare does attempt to pay Maya women weavers a better wage, it also effectively divorces the material product from the histories and epistemologies of the weavers and their communities. It ignores that, as Chacón reminds us, weaving and textiles are "a constant world-making, both individual and communal, ancestral and modern."[16] This divorce occurs by engaging Maya women solely as artisanal wageworkers and requiring them to produce textiles that are appealing to a Western market and trendy in mainstream fashion. In projects like this, Maya women become the backdrop for a designer line that again centers the white neoliberal gaze and reinforces Maya communities as desirable because they are folkloric.[17] This appropriation by designers has also led to outcries against the notion of legal ownership, as some Western designers have gone so far as to try and copyright exact replicas of clothing that Indigenous communities have used for centuries.[18]

Alongside the struggle to maintain *collective* intellectual and cultural property over Maya textiles, there are also moments when Maya clothing informs collective resistance to injustices like systemic gendered violence. The Sepur Zarco trials highlighted sexual violence as a strategy of war during the genocide. It was not until 2016 that the women who were enslaved and assaulted were able to find justice in a courtroom when two men were convicted of several charges, including crimes against humanity. One of the most visually stunning images during the court case occurred when Maya women covered their faces using a *peraje* (shawl). The brightly colored textiles served to protect the testifying women from public stigma and victim blaming. The sexual assaults that took place during the genocide were facilitated by the fact that Maya women could be identified as being from certain places through their clothing, yet in this case the clothing served as a shield from further marginalization.[19] Regional clothing functions as a material object that is deeply embedded in and celebrated by Maya communities even though it places Maya women at particular risk for state-sanctioned and systemic forms of violence.

The issues around how, when, and who has access to Maya clothing are deeply embedded within larger political and economic concerns around Maya communities being able to sustain themselves not just as individual people or organizations, but as a collective. Maya clothing remains a terrain of political struggle under neoliberalism and against necropolitics where Indigenous culture represents a break with settler colonial structures that would have communities define themselves through notions of individual national citizenship. Instead, the practice of weaving and wearing regional clothing marks Indigenous belonging and active refusal of the erasure of Maya people. Maya women who use Maya clothing are engaging in a political praxis founded on Maya worldviews because they contest discrimination by using their labor to refuse erasure.

In the diaspora, Maya clothing takes on added meanings that contribute to its function as a mobile archive. It is in diaspora that the clothing creates the possibility to challenge settler colonial frameworks by recognizing Native Americans in a nation-to-nation relationship that respects Native American survivance. As Mayas form enclaves in places that are not their ancestral homes, Maya clothing becomes a critical and dynamic mechanism through which they can tap into longer historical trajectories of what it means to be Maya and claim forms of being that include the experience of migration in the twentieth and twenty-first centuries. In this chapter, I explore how interview participants respond to the colonial legacy of Guatemala and highlight the experiences young adult and older women have with Maya clothing.

Maya Clothing and Migration

If an archive is a collection of material objects that documents the experiences of people at any given time or place, then Maya clothing and the stories around those clothes can be considered a form of family-based archive. While some museum collections include Maya clothing, it is individual families that hold on to either the practice of wearing these clothes or the stories around why they no longer wear them. In essence, textiles facilitate the process of reproducing relationships to ancestral territories which, in the face of displacement, take on additional layers of storytelling that revolve around the experience of moving through new spaces. This is not just to say that the clothing itself can be transported across borders, but that the narratives about this practice also act like documents that explain the experience of displacement. Maya clothing therefore illustrates how mobile archives are deeply anchored in Indigenous geographies, and their production and use in the diaspora expand this geography beyond settler borders.

When thinking about Maya clothing as a mobile archive, we must also consider that previous migrations shape how migrants in the United States presently engage in the use of Maya clothing. I have chosen to interview older migrants, some of whom are the parents of the young adults I interviewed, to formulate the intergenerational connections or ruptures that occur around traditional clothing in the context of diaspora. For example, youth at times transform how the clothing is used and, while elders and activists may oppose these changes, it is important to remember that such changes are often how young adults negotiate both their relationships to elders and their homeland *and* the context of their lived experiences in Los Angeles. Mobile archives therefore do not solely memorialize the crossing of national borders but also attach meaning to displacement from ancestral communities to urban centers. The historical and contemporary movement from home communities to other places within Guatemala is primarily analyzed in the context of labor and displacement during the war; however, most research about the Maya diaspora does not connect a history of internal relocations to transnational migration to the United States. In the interviews I conducted, many interviewees described their family experiences through migration from a hometown or village to a bigger city, then to Guatemala City. These movements happened when they were children or even a couple of generations before they were born, often preceding the final decision to cross the US-Mexico border.

Esperanza, who was sixty-five at the time of the interview and migrated to the United States for the first time at the age of twenty-four, shared that she did not use traditional clothing as an infant and toddler. During her first years of life, her K'iche' parents made the decision to migrate from their hometown in Xelajuj No'j (Quetzaltenango) to the capital city to escape poverty and, perhaps more importantly, avoid dealing with the issue that they were from different socioeconomic classes. Esperanza's mother was raised as a domestic worker; her father was skilled in shoemaking, and his family owned land. Esperanza's paternal grandmother objected to the marriage for this reason, so the young couple decided to try living independently in the city. It was in Guatemala City that Esperanza and her older siblings were born. When Esperanza was eight, her paternal grandmother became ill and invited Esperanza's family to live at her house. Under the economic support of communal living, Esperanza and her sisters began to use Maya clothing as an everyday practice. However, her grandmother died a few years later, and soon thereafter her father unexpectedly passed away. Esperanza's mother was left widowed with six children and without a formal education or a high-paying trade to support them. Hence, the family left for the capital city once again. Upon arriving, Esperanza's mother could no longer afford to keep Esperanza in Maya clothing, and Esperanza at the age of twelve had to find work as a live-in domestic worker to help support her siblings. Since her time of living with extended family in Xelajuj No'j (Quetzaltenango), Esperanza has not owned her own set of Maya clothing.

This narrative demonstrates that dispossession around Indigeneity goes beyond territorial displacement from ancestral territory to include the loss of material objects that do critical place- and community-making work among Maya people. It is not a coincidence that the period when Esperanza could wear her regional dress was when her family was embedded within her community, among relatives who owned land and practiced skilled trades. Some level of economic stability is necessary to enable the choice to wear regional clothing, as economic precarity makes engaging in this practice challenging. In addition, because Guatemala has reduced Indigeneity to speaking an Indigenous language or wearing Indigenous dress, economic precarity combined with internal displacement to major cities becomes an avenue through which the settler nation denies Maya subjecthood and limits possibilities for establishing kinship networks through the practice of weaving and wearing Maya clothing. Extending the analysis of migration back through generations can place the experiences of the second generation born in the United States in conversation with those of the first people to leave their home communities, like Esperanza's parents. The first generation to leave the original community may not necessarily be the same generation that migrates to the United States. Textiles, then, can become an interesting way to understand complex histories of internal displacement and international migration together as we begin to examine how migration shapes whether a particular woman continues to wear Maya clothing. The inability to own and use Maya clothing in Guatemala can shape the narrative around multiple generations of a family across settler borders. In Esperanza's case, her children are the first generation that has not worn Maya clothing as an everyday practice.

Esperanza's ongoing struggle to escape poverty remained a salient barrier in being able to claim Maya clothing as her own practice, even though she remembers fondly her time in Xelajuj No'j (Quetzaltenango) when she was able to do so. Attached to these memories are also stories of the discrimination her mother faced in the capital city, including racial slurs, because she wore a corte. Esperanza was well aware that her family was poor and Indigenous, or as she termed it, *naturales*, and when it came time for her to begin dating, she purposefully sought young men of a similar background because she did not want her mother to be discriminated against. She stated, "I didn't want them to treat her badly, so I knew it was better to be with someone like us. Someone who was poor like us." So, while popular understandings of what it means to be Maya in Guatemala would no longer count Esperanza and her children as Maya, the abject poverty produced by their displacement—alongside their acute awareness of the anti-Indigenous discrimination they faced—were deeply entrenched and undeniable realities.

Esperanza understood clearly that, while she was not wearing Maya clothing as an everyday practice anymore, the fact that her mother did meant that she had to choose a partner who she believed would have no reason to be discriminatory. She linked poverty and Indigeneity in a way that made sense in her lived experience because she loved her mother and did not want her to continue suffering. This connection between poverty or extreme poverty and Indigeneity in the Maya context remains high even today.[20] As a result, many Maya and non-Maya people link economic precarity with Indigeneity, and this link does not disappear as a result of migration. In Esperanza's case, it was by pawning her mother's Maya dress that she was able to gather enough funds to migrate to the United States. While some Maya migrants are able to use property as collateral for loans, in Esperanza's case, as part of an already territorially dispossessed family, the clothing was the most valuable asset her family owned. It was enough—along with a small savings—to make her journey.

Esperanza's story highlights the multiple ways to think about the function of Maya clothing across generations of people who are displaced from their ancestral places. The narrow definition of Mayas as those who speak a Maya language or wear Maya clothing creates simplified notions that support a project of ethnocide in which the state rigidly defines communities in ways that make it easier to demographically shrink the Indigenous population. However, the stories about when and how people stop wearing Maya clothing also hold important insights into how embodied epistemologies extend beyond single bodies. In other words, the embodied experience of wearing Maya clothing holds communal and familial significance, and therefore individuals who do not wear the clothing themselves still connect their ancestors' use of the clothing to a meaningful relationship with Maya people. In Esperanza's story, it is her mother's and grandmother's use of Maya clothing that continues to bring her family back to Maya cultural practices. Decades after migrating, Esperanza was able to return to her hometown with her granddaughter and borrow Maya clothing from relatives to attend a family wedding. Her pride as she shared photographs of the wedding—in which she and her granddaughter are wearing corte and beaming with happiness—demonstrates that loss is never quite permanent. The sharing of oral histories within the diaspora also creates an opportunity for following generations to understand the value of artifacts like the corte that do critical work to establish and maintain relationships to land and kin based on Indigenous ontologies.

Therefore, while these clothes are material objects, it is the particular histories of struggle, displacement, and even discrimination associated with them that make them an archive. They record individual stories, but those stories reflect upon and engage with larger policies of anti-Indigenous hatred that can inform subaltern histories of what it means to be Maya in Guatemala and through multiple migrations. In addition, robbing Maya migrants of their ability to wear their Indigenous clothing is an issue of ongoing cultural genocide that only compounds the racism Maya women face in Guatemala. While the rupture of this practice may not involve the literal death of breathing bodies that occurred during the genocide, it perpetuates a type of social death since it restricts the ability of migrant Maya women to maintain ties to their ancestral communities and also limits what is in turn possible for second-generation Mayas in diaspora. In addition, it renders Maya women and their cultural practices as contradictory to their legal status, marking them as "illegals" and therefore criminals.[21] When Maya women refuse to accept these conditions as permanent, and instead demonstrate the will to regain and retain these knowledge systems, they also archive their own will and determination against settler projects of elimination.

Like Esperanza, another interviewee, Anabel, shared that her grandparents had migrated from Xelajuj No'j (Quetzaltenango) because of poverty and a lack of economic means to sustain a family. While her grandfather made a living from weaving textiles on looms, he produced tablecloth-like textiles rather than clothing. When I asked Anabel why she did not grow up wearing traditional clothing, she responded that her family just did not have enough money. Surprisingly, Anabel first wore the traditional clothing of Xelajuj No'j (Quetzaltenango) in Los Angeles when she was in her thirties. Her mother obtained a visitation visa about ten years after Anabel migrated, and Anabel was able to borrow one of her mother's outfits to wear. Her inability to return to her hometown also meant that Anabel would be in her forties when she could finally possess her own set of clothes. Within the diaspora, the migrant generation uses Maya clothing to transmit family and community history in Guatemala and the experience of being undocumented to the second generation.

In most cases, the ability to own or even borrow Maya clothing depends on having an extended family network, in part because the cost of the clothing is still prohibitive for migrants and, for many, the lack of legal citizenship inhibits travel back to Guatemala to purchase or retrieve the clothing. Another migrant woman, Valentina from Xelajuj No'j (Quetzaltenango), stated that her daughter's godmother in Guatemala first gifted the young girl both a corte and a huipil. Valentina said that it was important for her that her daughter have the connection to their hometown, but she on her own would not have been able to afford the outfit. Some women also prefer to purchase Maya clothing from Guatemala because they are aware of economic exploitation. Anabel, for example, was especially adamant about not buying traditional clothing in Los Angeles because her mother had told her that it was part of an unjust cycle where US merchants acquired the clothing from impoverished families at very low prices and sold them for much higher prices in the United States. As Maya migration has continued to increase, the ways migrants acquire the clothing and the impact they have on its circulation changes. More recently, in trips back to Guatemala I have heard community members note that migrant demand has driven the cost for the clothes higher. Still, intergenerational poverty across borders shapes the conditions under which migrants are or are not able to obtain Maya clothing. Conditions of economic precarity result in difficult choices for Mayas who migrate and cannot freely choose to wear Maya clothing, thereby interrupting the continuation of ancestral place- and kin-making practices.

For some migrants, not wearing Maya clothing is a choice rooted not in the cost or origin of the clothes, but in how the clothing can mark an individual as undocumented, a fact noted in previous research. Xóchitl Castañeda, Beatriz Manz, and Allison Davenport found that Guatemalan Mayas identify as Mexican to minimize the negative consequences of being marked as an undocumented migrant, an Indigenous person, and a Guatemalan in California, a state where the majority of Latinas/os are of Mexican origin or descent.[22] In addition, Giovanni Batz found, "For undocumented Maya, wearing traditional dress may represent an increased risk of being deported or being discriminated against while crossing Mexico and settling in the United States."[23] Within the context of displacement and migration, Maya dress marks a difference that some migrants fear will be read as "illegal" status.

The stories of Anabel, Esperanza, and others collectively illustrate that the decision to use Maya clothing often involves stories of sorrow and loss because intergenerational poverty and migration deeply fracture this practice of belonging. The clothing is so deeply related to a person's home village, town, or region that it fulfills a connection to ancestral territories that are worn on the body. When this practice is prohibited for any reason, it adds to a process of ethnocide that literally erases Indigenous people in terms of state recognition in Guatemala. However, as the women I interviewed have noted, the rupture is not necessarily permanent. The narratives and histories linked to the clothing itself continuously open the possibility of reclaiming this practice. The ability for cloth or textiles to serve as not just a space for targeting Maya women but also a place of resistance to national projects of elimination in both the United States and Guatemala has deep implications for how migrants can lay claim to their epistemological sites as a process of archive making and collective consciousness.

A young second-generation Acateca woman, Camila, shared the following about her identity:

Author Do you feel like, outside of language, there was anything else that really—even, for example growing up—where you were really conscious of being Acateca, you know what I mean? Or was it just something like, it was just what we spoke and how we did things.

Camila Conscious? Maybe not at that level that I am now. I did know I was different in a sense because, I don't even know how I identified myself when I was younger. I might have said I was Indian or Native American, because I do have memories of being younger and my mom sewing me skirts from the material of the cortes, and I do have a memory of my mom running into, like, when we were at the corner store, and then she randomly met another Acateco man.

Author Aw, she was probably like, oh my God! [Laughter]

Camila Yeah, and she was wearing her skirt, too, and that's how he recognized her. That's such a big identifier, and I just remember seeing that and I'm just like, Why are they so excited to see each other? [Laughter] And then I just remember him specifically pointing out her skirt and I was like, oh, that's something different.

To this point in the interview, we had not explicitly discussed Maya clothing. Yet aside from language, it was what Camila specifically remembered as part of her growing understanding of a collective difference that had significance for her mother and others in Los Angeles. The clothing marked not just a Maya practice, but one from the Acateco community. Camila later shared that she has and wears huipiles from other areas in Guatemala, although her mother's encounter illustrates the existence of one unique to their hometown. This exchange also emphasizes that, for both of us, as diasporic Maya people, there is joy in sharing these moments of recognition that our textiles create. Our laughter during the interview was shared as we understood the excitement of recognition and the ways these moments offer a reprieve from living at the margins in the public sphere. Grounded in connection, this exchange stands in stark contrast to the history highlighted at the beginning of this chapter and is an important reminder that clothing continues to be a site of kinship making not only among those from specific towns but even among those of us who are Guatemalan Maya from different towns.

The role of Maya clothing in producing belonging and community cannot be understated as a key aspect to building intergenerational sites of meaning within the diaspora. Despite displacement, transnational networks of extended community, issues related to lack of legal status, and the ongoing poverty many migrants find themselves in before and after migration, there is nonetheless a possibility to engage with traditional clothing in meaningful ways. And while migrants often treat wearing traditional clothing as a normative practice, evidence shows that even after one or two generations have stopped using the clothing, it remains an artifact that facilitates oral history.[24] This possibility requires ongoing dialogue among multiple generations to engage in a practice that is constantly thwarted by settler nations that seek to eradicate any form of Indigeneity that does not work to consolidate the power of the state.

Intergenerational Archive Making

As a site through which migrant Maya women can document and transmit their own histories of displacement, violence, and resistance, clothing also becomes a source of oral history available to 1.5- and second-generation young people in the diaspora. The clothing itself presents an opportunity to discuss family history in relation to major issues of intergenerational poverty, Indigenous exclusion, and gendered violence, while the process of donning the clothing also centers the knowledge of women elders in relation to youth in diaspora. In the context of discrimination, the ability for an elder to occupy the position of teacher and historian to young Mayas is part of what makes regional clothing a mobile archive that functions across generations. Using Maya clothes becomes an avenue to engage Maya geographies, not to reproduce state-defined notions of authenticity, but for the sake of promoting belonging and understanding.

Part of this sense of belonging involves women elders encouraging and instructing young Mayas in how to wear the clothing. As Brenda Nicolas notes, a sense of belonging in the diaspora also relies on "pueblo pedagogy" or what Luis Urrieta has called "diasporic community knowledge."[25] In both cases, there is an epistemological anchor that involves learning through the embodied practice of everyday life in relation to one's community. This process of learning and sharing information can occur through very many avenues, which I would argue includes mobile archives of Indigeneity like Maya clothing, precisely because the clothes require connections between Maya women. When I asked Araceli, a young woman in Los Angeles, if she had ever worn her clothing in the diaspora, she responded, "Yes! Right when I came back from Guatemala, it was like two years ago. We came back early in the morning, and we went to visit my tíos and my tías because it was the first time both my great-grandma and my grandma came [to Los Angeles]. So, it was a really, really big deal." Araceli's grandmother's visit motivated her to wear regional clothing during her trip back to the United States. In addition to providing the inspiration to wear Maya clothing, women elders also play an important role in teaching younger women how to wear it.[26] For second-generation young women who are not raised wearing region-specific clothing as an everyday practice, the support and skills provided by elders are essential to their participation. Camila shared that when she was a child, her mother would sew zippers onto her cortes to facilitate her use of the clothing, even though this is not typically done:

> **Author** Who taught you how to wear it, now that you're older? How to wear it in the traditional way without the zippers?
>
> **Camila** I kind of just looked at how they put it on and then I was like, oh, this is how you do it, and then any little things I didn't know, I asked my mom. I was like, "How do you actually tie the belt?" Or like, "How do you tuck it in so it actually looks like I know how to put it on?" Because I've heard my mom say before, like, "Oh, she didn't tie it tight enough. You can tell because it's falling down on the inside, or if you put it on properly or if you know how to put it on, at the back it doesn't crinkle up when you tighten the belt." I guess constantly hearing it from my mom, I was like, Does it look like I know how to put it on? Like, double-checking with her. [Laughter] My mom is such a perfectionist when it comes to that.

The clothing is made entirely of fabric, held together by a fabric belt. Fasteners such as hooks, zippers, or buttons are usually absent or are used very minimally in more contemporary designs. As a result, choosing the correct length of fabric, folding it appropriately, and fastening the belt tightly so you can go about your day requires specific, Indigenous knowledge. It is this distinctive use of textiles that makes the clothing unique and part of an Indigenous ontology.

As she grew older, Camila began to use the corte without zippers. Even though she had learned the basics from years of observing her mother and older relatives, she still needed her mother's verbal and physical guidance to make sure she fastened the garment properly. It is not uncommon during gatherings and fiestas (community celebrations) to hear young women ask older women if their corte is on correctly or to help them tighten the *faja* (belt). This is an important point because, contrary to research that emphasizes intergenerational conflict among the Maya diaspora, dialogue and transmission between generations is crucial for the continued use of Maya clothing by young women in Los Angeles.[27] Wearing Maya clothing is a cultural practice that involves the oral transmission of information and the gifting of the actual outfit. It is also a practice that allows elders to share oral histories that can help second-generation youth learn about the economic and sociopolitical hierarchies that exist in Guatemala.[28]

Moreover, second-generation women employ dynamic clothing practices that transform the traditional use of Maya clothing. In a follow-up conversation, Araceli shared that sometimes she uses her corte as a blanket and continued, "Actually I just wore my rebozo (shawl) on Friday for school. . . . I do wear them, not the corte like the dress, the skirt, [but] I do wear the shirts and my morrales, my bags." Another participant, Jasmine, an eighteen-year-old being raised by her Mexican and Guatemalan Maya maternal grandparents, shared similar experiences. During the interview, I asked her about Maya regional clothing. Jasmine commented, "I like wearing the camisa [blouse] with jeans, and I think that looks nice. You can still show who you are with a different look to it." Such innovation can be a point of contention, given that the traditional clothing is meant to be an entire outfit, and each piece has its own function and significance within the whole. As Morna Macleod writes, "Mayan dress has a deep significance for those versed in the Mayan worldview who can read and interpret the symbols represented in the weavings. Such depth of knowledge is not shared by all community members; different people have different levels of ethnic consciousness."[29] However, it is important to consider that young women, especially those in diaspora, are typically a minority whose Indigenous practices are often invisible and uncommon in most places in diaspora. In this context, the fact that they still wear regional clothing, albeit in an altered way, is a critical opportunity for the community as a whole to retain this practice.

Despite the fact that Maya dress varies regionally, each garment represents an aspect of Maya cosmovision. Whether it is the sacred numerical values of significance in the Maya calendar, which are present in the technique of weaving, or the figures and designs, which speak to important landmarks in the area (lakes, mountain ranges, or volcanoes), the regional clothing is, as Macleod has noted, a crucial form through which not only identity but spirituality is engaged. For instance, in the clothing of Xelajuj

No'j (Quetzaltenango), there are thick embroidered lines that unite the three sections of the blouse and the two ends of the skirt. Essentially this line traverses the entire outfit and visually connects the various pieces together. When I have spoken to weavers in my family, they say that this line or cord represents the snake, which corresponds to a day in our calendar that represents fertility and is considered the protector of women. Given such layers of meaning in the traditional garments, the decisions of second-generation Mayas to adapt the wearing of regional clothing in ways that make sense to them can lead to a slippery slope that involves questions of tradition and authenticity. Rather than consider this difference a rupture, however, we can see it as an extension of regional dress; since second-generation youth want to connect their cultural practices to their everyday realities, those practices must be flexible.

Perhaps the most unusual use of the corte textile that I have witnessed was a handmade tube-top dress worn by the daughter of one of the leaders of a national Maya organization. When I asked her where she had gotten her dress, she replied that she had made it herself. There is also a cross-gender aspect to the shifting use of textiles. At the same conference, I saw a young man wearing a similar textile in the form of a men's dress shirt. In the context of displacement, we cannot determine whether these changes are representative of cultural loss or an attempt to continue identifying as Maya in a new environment. Notably, with few exceptions, it is uncommon to see women wearing traditional Maya clothing in Los Angeles public spaces.[30] Family or community celebrations, like the ones I attended, are where many women wear their Maya clothing. These spaces are a far cry from the everyday context of public school or the workplace. Thus, young Mayas are negotiating a desire to embrace their distinctive culture, knowing that to do so will mark them as different from their peers. This fear of difference needs to be understood in the framework of settler colonial perceptions of Native people as extinct or disappearing. In a US settler colonial context, Indigenous difference is refracted through elimination, which is distinct from the forms of exclusion that occur in Guatemala. Consequently, how young Mayas in Los Angeles engage with traditional clothing carries the layers of their migrant families as well as layers of what it means to be Indigenous in the settler colonial nation of the United States.

These diasporic experiences and uses of Maya textiles become an intervention against systematic erasure. As noted previously, Indigenous Los Angeles is Tongva, Kizh, and Gabrielino territory and is home to millions of displaced Indigenous people from other parts of Turtle Island and Abya

Yala. Despite this physical presence, many children and youth continue to be taught in public schools that Mayas no longer exist, or that the most interesting aspect of their history is that they practiced human sacrifice. It is precisely because of these discourses and their accompanying policies that it becomes necessary to focus on the strategies that Maya young people use to remain connected to their communities, including new and creative uses of textiles. While respect for our elders and their teachings around the deep significance of these textiles remains a priority, we also must acknowledge that young people who make these shifts are engaging with Maya cosmovision despite the fractures the collective has survived. These textiles become the tangible archive that holds their family and communal experiences and speaks to the diasporic condition.

Maya clothing is a visible marker not just of difference, but of being rooted in a Maya worldview. As Macleod mentions, being able to read the spiritual and historical meanings embedded within regional clothing is linked to the knowledge one has access to.[31] For example, when I directly asked some of the young Maya women if they knew the significance of their clothing, they responded that they did not. They wore it because it represented a connection to older generations, to Maya identity, and to a homeland, but they were not necessarily able to articulate what each textile meant. However, it is ultimately unhelpful to write off how subsequent generations in the United States understand Maya clothing. Instead, we should understand that the whole signifying world of Maya clothing is augmented by young people's creativity in integrating textiles as blankets, as shirts to be worn with jeans, or as fabric for new silhouettes. At the very least, their transformations continue to make these textiles and the clothing an active process of cultural production. Irma Otzoy rightly argues that "the incorporation of new symbols into the Maya meaning system permits textiles to serve as a dynamic expression of the Maya experience."[32] In response to the specific charge that changes in the colors and designs used in huipiles make some of them less authentic than others, Otzoy claims that what makes these textiles authentically Maya is that members of the Maya community are integrating these new designs. I propose that, in a similar fashion, the experiences and perspectives presented here demonstrate that traditional clothing continues to be a dynamic space in which young Maya women (as well as femmes, men, and nonbinary people) in Los Angeles negotiate their sense of belonging to diaspora.

The ability to engage the shifting terrains of Maya clothing is also partly informed by how elders understand this practice. I asked Lila, a young, second-generation Maya K'anjob'al originally from Los Angeles who at the time of the interview was working in Houston, Texas, if she ever experienced negative reactions while using the clothing. At first, Lila stated that she hadn't because she typically wore the clothing in community and family spaces where doing so was common. However, toward the end of interview she backtracked:

> Well, actually, going back to the negative experiences, this might be an important thing. I haven't heard people state this about me, but I've heard, like, even my own mom has said when she sees other women wearing corte out on the street on a regular Monday or Tuesday. A lot of times, she'll say, "Why are they wearing that. Why are they dressed up like that?" Like, "We're not in Guatemala anymore." . . . Like it's a negative thing. It hasn't been to me, but she said it, which is weird because I'm like, "Okay, but you wear it, too." I guess she doesn't see it like an everyday thing anymore.

This was a point of confusion for Lila since her mother had encouraged her to participate in community events and had facilitated her use of traditional Maya clothing. However, her mother had also decided that this use of clothing had to be practiced differently in diaspora and had attempted to pass that message on to Lila. I include this experience because, while much of what has been written focuses on discriminatory actions by non-Maya people, Lila's comment shows that Maya people also have important internal conversations around cultural practices in diaspora. Regardless of why Lila's mother made this comment, it reinforced for Lila that the wearing of traditional clothing is an occasional practice. Lila also stated that she had never really reflected on this remark and what it meant, but that she would talk to her mother about it more. This demonstrates the layers that second-generation Mayas must navigate given that the clothes are a site of attachment to homelands that some of them have never visited and that the use of Maya clothing has different meanings for older generations. Ultimately, it is a hopeful sign that Lila is able to reflect on this as somewhat of a confusing contradiction and is willing to continue a conversation with her own elders.

These generational distinctions are also not uniform. I interviewed one family with two generations of migrants. At the time of our interview, Valentina was in her early forties and living in Arizona. She had migrated in her late twenties to complete her doctoral degree in the United States.

Her mother, María Rosario, had recently begun making trips to the United States and happened to be visiting at the time of Valentina's interview, so she agreed to be interviewed. When I asked Valentina whether she had ever had any negative reactions to her use of the clothing, she stated, "The clothes are beautiful, so why would anyone have anything negative to say?" In contrast, María Rosario, who spent the majority of her life in Xelajuj No'j (Quetzaltenango), responded, "Of course. People say things all the time, it's to be expected, but my husband always tells me that I should be proud and be who I am and to not be bothered by what others have to say." I interpreted these diverging responses as indicating both women were acutely aware of prevalent discrimination in Guatemala, but each responded in a very different manner based on the position she held. Valentina had studied in private schools and universities in Guatemala and came to the United States to attain an advanced degree, while her mother was from different class origins. In addition, María Rosario shared that her husband had told her not to raise Valentina to wear traditional garments, reflecting a perspective within the household that Indigenous cultural practices could be a hindrance. María Rosario completely disregarded her husband's opinions and continued with her choice to raise Valentina with Maya clothing. It was perhaps her mother's defiance to include her daughter in this ancestral practice that in turn enabled Valentina to be adamant in her defense of the clothing and to wonder why anyone would ever say anything discriminatory when they saw her wearing Maya clothes.

Lila's, Valentina's, and María Rosario's experiences illustrate that, in a given context, a textile may hold similar significance but elicit different perspectives. This contextual engagement is distinct from engaging with textiles held by museums. María Rosario's textiles are more than fifty years old, but she has had to actively refuse her husband's initial eliminatory logic to continue the practice for herself and her daughters. Mainstream and well-funded institutions that hold massive collections of Maya textiles do not often engage in conversations around the ways Maya women are profoundly discriminated against. Instead, in the mobile archive of Indigeneity that these personally owned textiles represent, the materials are held by women who use them and have affection and respect for the depth of cosmological, epistemological, and ontological meaning they represent. This understanding is deeply integrated into who we are as Maya women, and the mobile archive requires both an understanding and a refusal of the politics of exclusion that exist around the clothing. For both Lila and Valentina, challenging or reaffirming their mothers' perspectives is precisely what informs their own practice. In addition, unlike heirlooms that get tucked away in private homes, Maya dress becomes an archive that unites communities when it is worn publicly. For me, when I see Maya women wearing Maya dress, I appreciate the time, labor, and wisdom that exists generationally in that act—meaning that, for Mayas, even bearing witness to this ongoing embodied practice in private and public spaces holds a significance that traverses borders and histories and is a recognizable testament to what Anishinaabe scholar Gerald Vizenor rightly terms survivance.[33] The use of Maya clothing demonstrates a life that transcends victimhood and even surviving solely as a passive object to include the active agency of Indigenous people in continuing critical Indigenous practices.

Rather than view Maya epistemologies or worldviews as static and rigid, mobile archives of Indigeneity recognize the ways in which these aspects shift and change depending on the needs and views of Maya people themselves. The experience of existing at the intersection of multiple, dynamic worldviews highlights what autonomy looks like in practice. To acknowledge the critical role of elder knowledge while leaving space for migrants and second-generation Mayas to play with and create new modes is part of what will allow us to understand the ways in which Indigenous sovereignty is rooted in long, vibrant histories. No matter what boundaries Mayas choose to break or enforce, they make choices while entrenched in the lived experience that puts youth at risk for discrimination and direct physical violence. Despite the potential risk, the use of regional clothing continues to visibly affirm Maya migrants' and their children's relationship to their ancestral places and communities. Despite anti-Indigenous politics that cross borders, coalesce, and morph to produce ongoing marginalization, Maya women engage with the clothing as a site of oral history, thereby creating a mobile archive that allows their practices and stories to cross borders.

Oral history isn't the only way that Maya clothing functions as a mobile archive; migration and Maya clothing are also intertwined through the return trips that Mayas born in the diaspora make back to Guatemala. I conducted a follow-up interview with Araceli ten years after the first. In that interview she shared that she had recently returned to Guatemala for a relative's wedding. This experience taught her about the ongoing reality of discrimination in Guatemala because her Maya cousin was marrying a Ladina from a wealthier family. She shared the following about the wedding day:

> All the women [in my family] wore corte and we looked fly, we looked good, makeup was done, our hair was done, we were wearing heels, and her family is Ladinos.... I just kept thinking, I wonder what their family is thinking of us, they're just sitting down. These were Ladinos with money, I'm sure they're not around many Maya folk. In my head I was like, damn, I wonder what they're thinking of us, but I also felt really proud, like, I look beautiful, and I'm wearing my corte, and I'm happy to wear it. It was an interesting moment. The clothes meant so much to me that day.

This interview highlights how second-generation Mayas born and raised in the United States learn about racial hierarchies in Guatemala on return visits. These racial differences become pronounced and embodied when wearing Maya dress in multiethnic contexts in Guatemala, where even now intermarriage between Mayas and Ladinos can be uneasy and is at times outright forbidden.

Araceli also highlighted how she struggled to understand her own use of corte in relation to her privilege as a light-skinned woman with a Maya father and Ladina mother:

> People tell me, "You look so pretty, and it looks nice on you," and stuff like that. But I wonder how much of that comes with me being [pause] I'm pretty sure a lot of it comes with me being light-skinned in comparison to, let's say, one of my cousins who's darker-skinned than me. And what does it mean for her to wear it? What do people tell her, I wonder?

In a US racial context, colorism helps us understand that white privilege can be bestowed upon people of color and Indigenous people if they have some proximity to whiteness and also when they enact anti-Blackness. However, this interviewee is expanding the discourse on colorism to consider her own privilege as a light-skinned Maya woman in relation to her darker-skinned Maya relatives in the United States and Guatemala.

How the intersection of race, colorism, migration, and Indigeneity shapes the experience of this respondent extends to larger conversations around settler colonialism and racial capitalism. Native scholars have had ongoing conversations about distinguishing race from Indigeneity, in part because to be integrated as a racial group in the United States is also to ignore Native sovereignty.[34] At the same time, part of what is emerging is a need to think about how, despite Indigenous belonging, race is also made by how people are perceived. The perceptions of others, whether in terms of interpersonal interactions or legal structures, also contours the level of discrimination or privilege faced by Indigenous people. Ultimately, when someone like Araceli states this, she is not necessarily accepting whiteness and its eliminatory logic but rather attempting to honor the struggles of her relatives who are more easily targeted, whether that be because of phenotype, language ability, accent, or documentation status. None of these factors contradict being Maya, but they are nonetheless hierarchies that the outside world uses to target and marginalize Maya people around a logic of white supremacy and its counterpart (or core) of anti-Blackness.

Maya clothing marks Indigeneity within racial hierarchies in both Guatemala and the United States. When these experiences are bridged through the embodied practice of wearing Maya clothing, we can pose questions that cross those settler borders to clarify how race and Indigeneity are being operationalized. Maya dress, therefore, can be an archive that considers these experiences across space and generation. As is clear in Araceli's interview, even for young Mayas born and raised in Los Angeles, thinking about their relatives' experiences and learning from those relatives are processes intertwined with the clothing itself. As a result, for young Mayas in the diaspora, how they think about, learn through, and continue to use Maya clothing is a collective process of memory making anchored in a material archive.

Settler Colonialism and Mobile Archives of Indigeneity

In thinking about the role of Asian Americans in settler structures that attempt to eliminate Kanaka Maoli people in Hawai'i, Dean Saranillio poignantly states, "Perhaps until we become multilingual in each other's histories, we will continue to renew a system of imperial violence and capitalist exploitation."[35] Mobility is one historical reality that needs to be unpacked in relation to Indigenous people lumped into the Latina/o category. Maya clothing is a material object that allows for thinking about mobility, oral histories, Indigenous geographies, gender, and migration. It marks the subject as Indigenous and often as femme, and therefore shapes an intersectional precarity in the context of settler violence. However, it is the fact that Maya women continue to wear the clothing in diaspora and add new understandings of race and migration to it that makes it a mobile archive of

Indigeneity. The clothing, much like the people who wear it, moves across settler borders, and along with both the clothes and the people come new stories of experiencing settler colonialism and anti-indigenous politics.

The Maya experience exists somewhere in between Latina/o and Native American experiences, so it is critical to think about how Mayas enter a settler colonial political project that is premised on elimination. Alliances with Native communities would force us always to be aware that we (Mayas) are visitors, and that in order not to become settlers and reproduce Native dispossession, we must always refute the notion that we are occupying emptied land and instead work actively and concretely to build solidarity networks with Native nations and communities. However, given the vast geographies and multiple specificities of Indigeneity, there are a multitude of ways and time periods in which this relationality could be built. The persistence of Maya clothing among the diaspora in Los Angeles will remain one of the critical avenues through which Mayas can contest these problematic logics. That is, Maya cultural practices such as wearing regional clothing blur the boundaries among settler, Native, and migrant in ways that challenge what it means to be an Indigenous migrant in a settler society. By marking Mayas as outsiders to the US nation-state and Indigenous to specific towns or regions in Guatemala, Maya clothing has the potential to be a practice through which geographies of belonging, identity, history, and spirituality can simultaneously (1) be retained through intergenerational dialogue, and (2) be the foundation for an Indigenous anti-settler colonial politics.

In her work on the ways in which Native women produce decolonial spatial logics through narrative, Mishuana Goeman challenges the idea that mobility and Native subjectivity are often considered oppositional. She writes, "I contend that instead of ingesting the norm of immobile Native women, we open up the possibility of (re)mapping the Americas as Indigenous land, not only by rethinking dominant disciplining narratives but also critically examining how we become a self-disciplining colonial subject."[36] While this demarcates the hemisphere as Indigenous land, it also shifts how we conceptualize migration for Indigenous people. Goeman's work primarily focuses on Native American migration within Turtle Island; however, her writing pushes us to reconsider what Indigenous migration across US and Canadian borders means. Thinking across these settler borders has been central to transnational work, but it also holds value for thinking about Indigeneity beyond national boundaries and recognition politics.

As noted earlier, in Guatemala, Maya people are marked as those who speak a Maya language or wear Maya dress, but part of what it means to be Maya in Los Angeles is, or should be, to disavow the dispossession of the Indigenous peoples on whose lands we maintain our own cultural practices. Native communities are inherently complex and diverse, and they face a series of challenges. However, understanding the multiple geographies of Maya identity that exist in regional clothing may help us move toward a common politics that challenges settler colonialism by making Indigenous communities visible and accountable to one another in a nation-to-nation structure (or people-to-people, since some of us do not use the terminology of *nation* and *citizenship* to define belonging). If settler colonialism is dependent on the elimination of contemporary Native struggles for the sake of territorial appropriation, then embracing a migrant or mobile positionality that can be reflected in Maya dress allows Mayas to continue denouncing the politics that led to their displacement without necessarily laying claim to other Indigenous territories.

Part of what makes a nation-to-nation approach useful is that it creates space for the Maya diaspora to be accountable in a settler colonial structure that seeks to incorporate them in order to further the dispossession of Native people. In this context, rather than presume that a connection to Indigeneity is automatically resistant to all forms of colonialism, I posit that this remains an ongoing conversation that should take place between Maya communities and specific Native communities. I position Maya clothing as a site of this possibility without prescribing an automatic notion of "decolonization."[37] As Tuck and Yang are careful to remind us, "decolonization is not a metaphor," and "decolonization specifically requires the repatriation of Indigenous land and life. Decolonization is not a metonym for social justice."[38] Nor does this possibility assume that all Native nations or peoples will respond in the same ways to Maya people. Instead, I highlight that the process of diaspora making requires an ongoing engagement with local geographies of Maya ancestral homes while also accounting for Indigenous sovereignty in Native North America.

Conclusion: Threads That Bind

The collective work of Maya migrants and second-generation Mayas to navigate and negotiate traditional Maya clothing practices highlights that this tradition remains a dynamic terrain through which Mayas respond to mobility by transforming cultural practice when necessary. These shifts across time, geography, and generation are anchored in the actual clothing and in the oral histories that surround the wearing of clothes. In this sense, mobile archives of Indigeneity do not cohere around a single, stringent definition imposed by a national government that seeks to accumulate wealth through territorial dispossession. Rather, the mobile archive relies on centering the voices of Maya people to create avenues through which their experiences of discrimination and struggle are documented alongside stories of joy and celebration. These diverse experiences are expressed through the use and circulation of textiles that continue to bind Maya people to an ancestral practice despite historic and ongoing discrimination. Whether that discrimination takes place in relation to their displacement from their hometowns or their inability to wear their regional clothing due to being undocumented in the United States, Maya women interweave political and historical critique into an Indigenous practice that contests their erasure. They rupture the normalization of Indigenous dispossession in Guatemala and create opportunities for second-generation young people through one of the most visible markers of their ancestral homelands. Furthermore, the use of Maya clothing in diaspora also opens the opportunity for contesting settler colonialism by ensuring that Maya geographies remain rooted in their homelands and local places of belonging, therefore acting as an intervention against making newly arrived Mayas into settlers.

3

La Comunidad Ixim and Organizing in the Maya Diaspora

Formed in 2010, La Comunidad Ixim is a grassroots collective led by a group of Maya, Xinca, and Guatemalan people raised in Los Angeles, California. The members are primarily young adults who have found each other through informal networks within the social justice organizing community in Los Angeles. La Comunidad Ixim chose its name to reflect an engagement with Maya cosmovision and culture, since *ixim* (maize) is considered the basis of creation and life within the Pop Wuj, one of the Maya creation stories. The founding of this collective is unique because it has primarily developed out of the experiences of the members themselves, the majority of whom were not raised as active participants in spaces that centered the Maya experience. La Comunidad Ixim adds to previous academic research about the Maya diaspora by presenting perspectives that do not focus on hometown associations (HTAs) or community-based organizations created through religious networks.[1] Through individual friendships or participation in other organizations, members found each other and built on their common understandings of organizing and Maya identity to create a collective that centers the experience of 1.5- and second-generation Maya migrants.

I have participated as a member of the collective since its formation, and during the period when it was most active—from 2010 to 2020—I watched it develop to include and reflect a growing diversity of Maya experiences in Los Angeles. Members are from various parts of the city, including East Los Angeles, Culver City, Huntington Park, and Boyle Heights, so La Comunidad Ixim meets all over Los Angeles. This geographically diffuse political formation is also reflected in the fact that members are from various regions within Guatemala—including the departments of Huehuetenango, Quetzaltenango, and Sololá—and belong to a variety of ethnic groups: K'iche', Kaqchikel, K'anjob'al, and Acateco. Since the decision to name the group La Comunidad Ixim in 2011, a non-Maya Xinca individual has also joined the collective. As discussed in this chapter, some of the members can trace their migration only to areas within or around Guatemala City. In addition, because they connected with each other through other social justice organizations, the diversity of geographic areas and ethnic groups represented stands in contrast to most civil and religious Maya organizations, which are organized around specific towns or close-knit families that have known each other since they were in Guatemala. Family genealogies continue to play a critical role in how members participate in La Comunidad Ixim, but these genealogies are layered on a critical orientation toward intersectional politics and social justice. While in the previous chapter I discussed how Maya women are vital to upholding Maya epistemologies through the use of regional clothing, in this chapter I extend the work that mobile archives of Indigeneity can do by examining its function in spaces where young people directly grapple with what links them together when the process of migration has created various ruptures. As a result, they bring a variety of definitions and experiences of the Maya community to the children's book the collective published, *The Colors of Guatemala: Las aventuras de Gaby*.

This chapter examines how second-generation Maya youth organizing draws from both familial genealogies and intersectional relationships to develop a mobile archive of Indigeneity that grapples with multiple racial structures. I read the children's book that the organization collectively created as a mobile archive of Indigeneity to demonstrate that while members document and center common struggles, they do so with an understanding that there is no totalizing narrative of the Maya diaspora experience. Because these young adults have experienced life in their ancestral communities through temporary visits or primarily as children, their cultural production presents an opportunity to think about Maya Indigeneity in relation to migration for youth who have lived most of their lives in the diaspora. As I examine how these kinship ties operate in conjunction with experiences in social justice organizing, I ask the following: How do second-generation Mayas make sense of the overlap and differences in Guatemalan and US racial hierarchies? How does La Comunidad Ixim challenge heteronormative and patriarchal conceptions of kinship? What types of common experiences do they document in their cultural production as they attempt to produce or engage with a Maya community?

Maya identity is often defined through state-driven identifications that reproduce erasure.[2] I highlight how, in the absence of regulated identifications, Maya youth in Los Angeles have formed Maya collectivity through other means. I first analyze the familial genealogies of various members, not as a practice of authentication but as a set of histories that help trace the intergenerational impact of colonialism that mobile archives of Indigeneity can speak back to. I then move to how the group grapples with what it means to be Maya within the collective where they interact with others who may have different experiences, definitions, or practices that anchor their sense of belonging. To varying degrees, all the members grew up with diasporic linguistic or cultural practices normalized within their homes, and La Comunidad Ixim becomes one of the few spaces in which they can begin to understand these experiences in relation to people who are not their biological relatives. In other words, La Comunidad Ixim is also about building a network of kinship outside of the constraints of heteronormative notions of nuclear families that often work in the service of settler colonialism.[3]

The key to this process in La Comunidad Ixim is that, in addition to being part of the Guatemalan and/or Maya diaspora, all group members have participated in social justice organizations that consider justice and liberation expansively. This creates a secondary context that allows La Comunidad Ixim to lay out parameters around Maya identity that include queer and genderqueer possibilities. While this was not a goal in the initial formation of the group, as more members joined who identified as queer, it became something that the collective sought to prioritize as part of their Indigenous organizing. This choice is especially important given that much Maya organizing has been through institutions that rely on patriarchal and heteronormative hierarchies, so to have a youth group state outright that they were also a queer space represents an important intervention and possibility for the landscape of Maya organizing in Los Angeles. La Comunidad Ixim is a space that makes Indigeneity legible outside of family structures, and even in moments when an individual's family members reproduce heteronormativity, members of La Comunidad Ixim support each other in challenging the notion that Indigeneity and queerness are contradictory. This is most apparent in the combination of their familial histories and intersectional politics to create a children's book that centers critical orientations toward queer experiences, intergenerational dialogues, and the second-generation Maya experience.

In addition, I foreground La Comunidad Ixim's organizing and cultural production to redefine the Maya experience through intergenerational memory that does not always flow from parents to children. For members in this collective, family histories and community memories must at times jump generations because of the experience of migration. As one generation is forced to migrate and struggle for economic survival, the bonds between grandparents and grandchildren may fill the gaps in memory left by these pressures. This also produces nonlinear relationships to categories of Latinidad and Indigeneity in the United States. As multiple generations collectively share information, youth are left to piece together these narratives in ways that make sense within their lived experiences in Los Angeles. In the process of understanding and filling these gaps, young Mayas in diaspora then generate materials that also function as mobile archives of Indigeneity and can serve to create new routes and understanding of Indigenous diaspora.

Embracing Fragmentation and Expansiveness

One aspect of complexity and multiplicity among Maya youth is their strategic and fluid forms of identification. These ever-shifting identities challenge notions of ethnic categories because they force us to recognize that the diaspora includes young people who cannot claim a Maya identity but do not claim a Ladino Guatemalan ancestry either. As scholars have noted, the contemporary racial structure of Guatemala pivots around the Ladino-Indigenous binary, with Ladinidad defined as the cultural absence or outright denial of Indigeneity.[4] For US scholars this makes Ladinidad an ethnic category; however, what they often fail to recognize is that the settler logics that underpin Ladino identities also perceive Indigenous people as inherently, and at times biologically, inferior.[5] These anti-Indigenous discourses and policies have softened since neoliberal multiculturalism has symbolically embraced Indigeneity, yet in many spaces racial projects continue to do the work of racist exclusion that materializes in the ongoing neglect and violent physical displacement of Maya communities. As noted in the introduction, this overarching racial structure gives rise to localized understandings of Indigeneity, but with the emergence of the Maya movement in the 1980s, Maya identity in particular became critical to publicly and globally contesting the violence of the Guatemalan civil war.[6] Ladino identity, on the other hand, has historically been tied to race and class and articulates privilege relative to Black, Indigenous, and Black Indigenous people; it simultaneously operates through a racist structure by defining itself as superior to Black and Indigenous culture or heritage. The consequence is a national structure that absorbs individuals as long as they articulate Indigeneity as inferior, obscure any Indigenous genealogy they may have, and act in accordance with a neocolonialist national culture. It is this racial structure that then authenticates Indigeneity through language and dress because while Indigeneity is highly visible and characterizes the majority of the population, it must be confined to support the settler nation.

Understanding this dichotomy as a historical construction is incredibly difficult for youth in the diaspora when they and their families become submerged under a Guatemalan identity that, in the United States, also becomes categorically Latino. Ladino identity is hard to trace in migration, at times leaving youth confused about their heritage. Rather than interpret this point of ambiguity as a form of cultural loss, I examine these fragments to analyze the impact of the (neo)colonial legacy of Guatemala on youth who have been primarily raised outside Guatemala.

These longer trajectories of family history also create an opportunity to think about Maya kinship networks and ideas of belonging in relation to the larger landscape of Indigenous political subjecthood. Indigenous belonging is complicated terrain because settler nations have sought to manage and constrict Indigeneity while Indigenous people often struggled to resist encroachment and refuse incorporation in whatever ways were possible, including using the language of legal/political sovereignty, citizenship, and nationhood.[7] What becomes clear in many of these discussions is that the settler colonial structure has ensnared many Indigenous collectives even as they do the important political work of defending themselves. I situate my writing alongside scholars who consider belonging not as the choice of an individual but as part of a collective struggle. However, one of the challenges for Mayas is that, even though they practice their own governance and observe their own customs, they are not articulated as politically sovereign in relation to the Guatemalan nation.

One of the La Comunidad Ixim participants, Miguel, acknowledged that his parents might identify as Ladino. Miguel does not claim to be Maya, but his experience can help us understand how youth in the diaspora contend with multigenerational dispossession that has been happening in Guatemala for centuries before the official beginning of the armed conflict in the 1960s. This intergenerational dispossession informs how youth in the diaspora understand themselves, and it obligates La Comunidad Ixim to constantly reexamine its definitions of Maya identity with an eye to who is excluded. Miguel recounted that his maternal great-grandfather was a railroad worker who raised Miguel's grandfather in tenement housing. Miguel's grandfather was orphaned by the age of six, and soon thereafter, Miguel's great-great grandmother, who had become his caretaker, passed away as well. As a result, Miguel's grandfather became homeless as a very young man and was recruited to join the military. The strictest commander in his unit was Indigenous and especially hard on Indigenous recruits. His grandfather was often confused as to why the commander treated him with similar harshness. His grandfather then decided to leave the military and join the labor force building the railroads. Subsequently, his family traveled to different parts of Guatemala and lived in tenement housing. This narrative spans more than a century and points to the fact that youth have many unknowns in their family history, but nonlinear genealogies place them in the Ladino category by virtue of the absence of Indigenous language and dress.

Like many other youth, Miguel has few if any material family heirlooms to create a sense of connection and belonging to a particular community. As an orphaned, homeless young man, his grandfather became hypermobile within Guatemala as he traveled building the railroad, and while he did not necessarily have the anchor of a family genealogy, he was discriminated against for his perceived Indigeneity. Lisa, another organizer in the group, recounts similar dynamics of discrimination in that her paternal family disparaged her maternal family as darker, inferior, of a lower status, and Indigenous. Based on what Lisa's mother has told her, Lisa's great-grandmother died in childbirth and her great-grandfather died when Lisa's grandmother was a very small toddler. Until the age of four or five, it was Lisa's great-great grandmother who raised the young child, but she passed away. At that time, Lisa's grandmother was left completely orphaned, and someone who claimed to be her grandmother's aunt took her in and made her a household servant. When that woman's husband sexually assaulted Lisa's grandmother, the grandmother escaped and became homeless. Lisa isn't sure what her grandmother did between that time and the time she met Lisa's grandfather, who was much older and an organizer in Guatemala. They eventually married, but Lisa's mother and her uncles are all convinced that Mama Julia (Lisa's grandmother) most likely made up her surname and her birthdate. Her uncles did once try to find birth records for their mother but were told that all the records had been destroyed in an earthquake. Archival records in Guatemala are not only neglected but at times are also changed, disappeared, or withheld. Communities and organizers in Guatemala have documented that archival records showing ancestral ties to territories have been changed or destroyed to facilitate land theft against Indigenous families and communities.[8] In this context of intergenerational orphanhood and utter state neglect for both children and official records, discrimination is often based on phenotype and class that mark a proximity to Indigeneity, but actual Indigenous bonds are foreclosed for following generations. Many cases of child abandonment and lack of access to historical archives continue to take place today.

Even within families there can be tensions around Indigeneity that are informed by larger structural racism but ultimately impact diasporic generations. When I asked Carlos if he identified as Maya, he said that after feeling insecure about whether he was Maya he was finally understanding that he was. He noted that his paternal aunt would often say that they were Ladino, but his dad would always challenge her and ask her how she could say that when their older siblings and their parents all spoke *lengua* (tongue or language, meaning a Mayan language). Even at the time of the interview, however, he remained somewhat hesitant as he struggled to understand why his aunt would want to claim Ladino identity. In other words, the Ladino-Maya or Ladino-Indigenous binary that has operated in Guatemala for centuries is especially challenging for youth who are raised outside of that everyday context to understand. It is even more difficult for those whose grandparents and great-grandparents lived the neglect of settler colonialism and did not survive long enough to name that state violence or pass down stories of Indigenous survival.

I have begun with stories of uncertainty and fragmentation because they reflect what Maya and Guatemalan youth must grapple with. Both Miguel and Lisa choose to identify as Chapina/Chapin (someone from the capital city) because so much remains unknown within their family histories. The indefinite information is in part due to the silence among and loss of older generations, but it is also reflective of a longer trajectory of dispossessing poor and Indigenous people as part of the Guatemalan national project. Within Guatemala, Chapines from the city are associated with being Ladino and enacting Ladinidad by believing they are better than those from other departments, *aldeas* (villages), or from the highlands. In the context of transnational research, however, it is important to note how the term *Chapin* also shifts in the context of migration: it becomes a label applied to all Guatemalans, and for these youth it becomes an identity marker linked to a clear understanding and acceptance of ambiguity about their ethnic heritage. La Comunidad Ixim directly grapples with the ongoing question of whether youth like Lisa and Miguel should be active participants in a space that is for Maya youth in part because *everyone* has experienced the process of learning about and making sense of these longer and at times incomplete or contradictory genealogies.

Making sense of these genealogical ties or ruptures to places and people also points to the limitations of thinking about "the family" as the primary organizing institution of diaspora belonging. That is, invoking family as the site of belonging limits our understanding of how one engages in community building in the face of genocide. The human rights report *Guatemala, Never Again!* notes that one result of the armed conflict was a wave of orphans who lost one or both parents and were subsequently raised by nonbiological kin or extended relatives.[9] Given that conceptualizations of family often uphold exclusionary politics that relegate undocumented, Indigenous, queer, immigrant, and other subjects to the margin, it is necessary to think about Indigenous belonging apart from solely biological claims to family lineage. I address how mobile archives of Indigeneity are useful in confronting these intergenerational disruptions in chapter 4, but for now it is important to understand the issues that intersectional collectives like La Comunidad Ixim are grappling with as they create their own sites of connection.

In this sense, understanding genealogical histories and nonbiological ties that create Maya belonging in diaspora begins with recognizing these fractures and the nonlinear process of racialization for youth who must make sense of long(er) histories of displacement across settler borders. As Julianne Pidduck writes, "against hegemonic kinship narratives of continuity across space and time, of heredity and progress, the motifs of displacement, illness, death, and loss . . . produce fractured and affectively ambivalent kinship documents characterized by disruptions, silences, traumas, and gaps."[10] It is also critical to note what Gretel Vera-Rosas argues: "While it is easier to blame family break-up on migration, family separation is a historical legacy for colonized peoples: it is the result of structural conditions and regimes of racial violence that propel our scattering in the first place and make displacement the order of the day."[11] Rather than attempt to piece historical realities together, I make fragmentation useful to understanding 1.5- and second-generation youth. The more expansive notion of kinship and genealogy that I employ adds to the literature contesting the role of the normative nuclear family by extending this concept to diasporas created out of anti-Indigenous state violence.

Other members of the collective, though, have a strong awareness of their families' connections to the Maya communities of Guatemala. For example, one of the organizers, Camila, was born in Los Angeles and is a fluent speaker of Acateco and English, but she does not speak Spanish. Camila shared in the collective that the 1980s genocide forced her family to leave their hometown and relocate to refugee camps in southern Mexico. Her family then hid in Chiapas, Mexico, for three years before eventually deciding to complete the migration to the United States, a two-part journey that mirrors findings in previous research.[12] Some parts of the family went to Indiantown, Florida, while others remained in Los Angeles. While Camila's family strongly advocated for language maintenance, they equated language loss with the loss of culture and identity. Camila shared that it was not until her participation in La Comunidad Ixim that she realized how many people are erased through this belief that language equals culture. This is precisely why spaces outside of nuclear families are critical in expanding community belonging and kinship beyond the social institution of the family. If one family is especially concerned with language retention but another is more concerned with the use of traditional dress, the space where these family-based ideas come together must have an expansive definition of Indigenous belonging. In the case of the collective, this also requires going beyond dress and language to consider those who practice neither and to embrace those whose personal notions of Indigeneity are still in flux.

Multigenerational Observations

In addition to sharing stories about migrating to the United States, La Comunidad Ixim members are very familiar with the preceding migrations their families made within Guatemala. While scholars have examined the historical nature of Maya displacement within Guatemala, few have examined these displacements and migrations through the perspective of young people primarily raised in the United States.[13] For 1.5- and second-generation youth, acknowledging and building a genealogy that casts migration not as an irreparable loss but as a process embedded within longer historical trajectories creates the opportunity for them also to look for and build continuities—or at least acknowledge that the loss is rooted in larger structures of power.

This is why it is critical to think about Indigeneity in relation to immigration. As Shannan Mattiace and Patricia Loret de Mola write, "While first-generation migrants tend to focus their organizational activity on transnational issues, much like the HTA leaders we observed, second generation and '1.5 generation' migrants tend to focus more on ethnic discrimination in the United States."¹⁴ Part of what this literature has missed, however, is that for Indigenous migrants, creating community in diaspora includes encountering spaces where people may be forced to move away from a localized Indigenous identity (like K'iche' or being specifically from Santa Eulalia, a predominantly K'anjob'al town) toward an immigrant identity and then to a US-based ethnic label. In addition, for La Comunidad Ixim members, identity formation is not a linear process premised on Indigenous loss. Instead, they are forced to maneuver important contradictions, and the archives they create point to how they hold multiple identities together in a way that still makes space for Indigenous relationality.

For those I interviewed, the deeper history of internal displacement was often premised upon knowing their grandparents' experiences. For example, in Mateo's story, their grandmother's migration is pivotal to understanding why their parents migrated when their extended family did not. They shared that his grandmother was their maternal figure during their childhood because both their parents had migrated to the United States. Their grandmother told them that she left Quetzaltenango due to political turmoil that had caused her parents to lose their land. When their grandmother and all of her five siblings fled Quetzaltenango to different places, she was captured by a military general and forced into marriage, giving birth to two children. Unbeknownst to the rest of her family, she lived with her captor for years until she managed to escape and decided to work to raise her children.

Furthermore, as a single mother with an additional two children from another relationship, she ended up being the poorest member of her family. Mateo stated, "There is a photo where [my grandmother is] with her sisters and even with the huipil and the corte, you could tell that hers is the most used while her sisters are wearing newer ones. Even by the shoes you can tell that my grandmother was poor." The end result is that only Mateo's branch of the family has migrated. These fractured familial relationships demonstrate that the migration of one generation can directly trigger the migration of the next generation. Facing intense poverty, Mateo's grandmother did not have any wealth to pass down, and this informed Mateo's parents' perspective that migration to the United States was the most viable option. It is important that researchers on migration understand that, for Indigenous people, displacement and dispossession can occur within their country of origin before they cross settler borders.

Other family migration stories point to important gaps in our understandings of Indigeneity. For the participants and organizers of La Comunidad Ixim, it has been important to bend and blur categories as it makes sense to their organizing. For example, they created registration forms to reach out to participants for a workshop series. That the members wanted Maya participants was explicit from the outset, but they also all understood that they themselves were not necessarily raised identifying with the umbrella term *Maya* because they were more closely tied to their parents' hometown or language. They knew through their own experiences that family history becomes colored by the experience of displacement and migration, and for many members this resulted in not coming to a concrete understanding of Indigeneity until they were adolescents or young adults. As a result, when they were discussing who should be invited to participate in La Comunidad Ixim, they were open to participants who were unsure what Maya community their family was from. Members collectively understood that they had not always had the vocabulary and historical context to actively claim a clearly defined identity and that developing a process for sharing this knowledge was critical.

For the members who did have close connections with Maya identity, those ties were often a result of grandparents who transmitted Maya epistemologies and encouraged the youths to see themselves as members of particular ethnolinguistic groups and places. Their parents generally did not emphasize Maya cultural, linguistic, and spiritual practices during their childhood in part because they were the generation who struggled to support their families as undocumented migrants in Los Angeles. Outside of a Maya social network of support, the concern for Maya spiritual and cultural practices took a backseat to the very urgent material concerns around providing for their children. In some cases, the grandparent generation had experienced similar obstacles due to internal migration. As a result, though they spoke a Maya language, they saw no concrete economic, political, or social benefit to passing down those language skills. However, even though the grandparents may not have passed down Maya social and cultural practices to their children, they were often much more open about their Indigenous heritage and supportive of their grandchildren's desire to connect with it.

For example, in Araceli's case, her desire to learn her language now that she is in her twenties is arguably more supported by her K'anjob'al grandparents than her father. When Araceli has asked her parents to teach her K'anjob'al, her father has often joked that she will not learn the language because she is too old. Her grandmother, on the other hand, teaches Araceli K'anjob'al words and, in return Araceli teaches her grandmother words in

English. More importantly, her grandmother also validates Araceli's desire to participate in their culture. On a recent occasion when her family gathered to celebrate Araceli's birthday, her grandmother asked Araceli permission to pray for her in K'anjob'al. Araceli was extremely moved by her grandmother's offering to say not just a prayer, but a prayer in their own language.

For many of the members of La Comunidad Ixim, their relationship to matriarchal elders, especially grandmothers or great-aunts, roots them in their Maya identity. This represents a very interesting generational relationship because multiple members of the collective describe being the only ones in their families, especially among their siblings and parents, that actively embrace Maya cultural and spiritual practices in a collective outside of the family. Sometimes, parents feel emboldened by their children to begin to challenge their own conceptions of being Indigenous. For example, when I interviewed Mateo, they shared that they were not sure why their mother never communicated very much about her experiences growing up with her grandparents in Xelajuj No'j (Quetzaltenango), especially since her grandfather was an *ajq'ij'ab* (spiritual guide and daykeeper) who conducted ceremonies and rituals at home. Instead, Mateo's grandmother was instrumental in teaching Mateo that they were Kaqchikel. When she first told them that they were Indigenous, Mateo asked if they were K'iche' because the international Maya K'iche' leader Rigoberta Menchú was all they knew of Maya groups. Their grandmother laughed and told them that they were actually Kaqchikel. They believe their grandmother told them stories that she had not shared with their mother. As a result of the grandmother's stories, Mateo encouraged their mother to celebrate her Maya heritage for her fiftieth birthday party. With support from their family, his mother decided to wear corte, have marimba at the celebration, and dance *el son* as it is done in Xelajuj No'j (Quetzaltenango).

These critical opportunities to create multigenerational exchanges about Maya cultural, spiritual, and linguistic practices allow families to create the intergenerational imaginaries that sustain Maya life in the diaspora, even if those practices are relatively muted during certain phases of the migrant experience in the United States. The fact that it is youth and children who encourage their parents to embrace Maya practices directly challenges the notion that memory flows solely from older to younger generations, further demonstrating the multidirectional flow of memory in the Maya diaspora. The youth who become aware of the historical context of displacement and who participate in community spaces also represent important opportunities for healing for their parents who were unable to name these structural issues at the time they were in the process of surviving them. This flow of knowledge across generations creates the basis for a dynamic mobile archive that invites or requires multiple generations to participate in reclaiming and upholding ancestral practices that orient Maya people in their relationship to the cosmos and to each other.

Intersectional Politics and Queering Kinship

Aside from their various family-based genealogies, the members of La Comunidad Ixim build on their family histories by connecting them to political understandings and practices gained in non-Maya-specific spaces. Members' varied prior experiences in these non-Maya spaces have strengthened La Comunidad Ixim in many ways, including laying the foundation upon which the group operates. For example, the very structure of the collective calls upon everyone to use their assets to coordinate projects without necessarily having a director. The members rotate facilitation, note-taking, and task delegation to each other as necessary. In the case of the workshop series, for example, each session had two organizers who were responsible for the bulk of the curriculum work. Their other responsibility was to determine what they needed for the workshop and contact other members to help with necessary tasks. Such an organizing culture based on consensus and mutual support reflects two values found in social justice organizing but also practiced in a variety of ways in Indigenous families and nations. It is important to recognize that group members acquired this operational method through their participation in various spaces where they recognized each other's labor without overburdening any single person. Rather than taking a vote, their method is to address concerns that arise and have the collective adapt as needed. While this can be tied to an ancestral practice of discussion and consensus that is recorded in the K'iche' story of the Pop Wuj, for La Comunidad Ixim, it is also informed by the notion of shared power and facilitation that they have found or wanted in other organizing spaces.

The members of La Comunidad Ixim took many routes to Maya youth organizing, and participants' history in relation to political organizing demonstrates that there is no uniform and linear trajectory to a Maya identity. At the same time, it is critical to note that most participants in La Comunidad Ixim are college graduates, and a few have advanced degrees. As students, many participated in student or community organizations that do not center Maya issues. It was through Chicana/o studies courses, Chicana/o organizations, and Latina/o organizations that many members began to participate in social justice organizing.

Miguel, for example, first experienced organizing as a graduate student at Columbia University, where he ran for president of the Latin American Student Organization. His decision was informed by early politicization through reading Oscar Zeta Acosta's *The Revolt of the Cockroach People* for an undergraduate course. Not only did he feel that the story reflected an aspect of his life, but for the first time he knew more about the topic than his peers, who in other courses could expound on European, Greek, or literary knowledge while he sat confused and unsure of himself. In another instance, Lisa noted that it was through MEChA (Movimiento Estudiantil Chicana/o de Aztlán) that she became a youth leader in high school and continued to organize in college. For her part, while she was in college, Araceli joined Xinachtli, an organization whose "purpose is to serve as a circle of growth and support for the empowerment of the Xican@/Latin@ community."[15] As a member of Xinachtli, she was able to build on a consciousness that initially emerged from her interest in punk and ska music and her high school participation in environmental justice organizing. While for most collective members, a Maya consciousness emerged in high school or afterward, they mobilized the cultural wealth of organizing they had gained in other types of organizations to form and sustain La Comunidad Ixim.

Given their varied prior organizing experiences, members have nuanced discussions that consider Maya identity from new angles. For example, Mateo's recruitment into an environmental justice organization as a high school student led them to work with the Southern California Library and Q-Team, a queer trans youth of color collective. Their political activity on behalf of the environmental justice issues facing their Southeast Los Angeles community, along with their growing consciousness around a politicized queer of color identity, has informed their La Comunidad Ixim participation in multiple ways. During one planning meeting, group members were discussing how to understand their migration as Indigenous people. They had chosen to term their place of origin their ancestral home, but they were stuck on how to label their arrival and creation of community within the United States.

I suggested that terming Los Angeles our "new homeland" could reproduce erasures of the original peoples of Los Angeles, the Gabrielino, Tongva, Kizh, Tataviam, and Fernandino, who are still very much present in the area and struggling to have their sovereignty recognized by the millions of residents who occupy their territory. Mateo, who stated that through their activism they had learned to denaturalize the criminalization of migration, countered my argument. They proposed that migration was a natural process that many species engage in when their homes are no longer able to sustain them. For decades youth involved in organizing for immigrant rights have worked to enact this paradigm with slogans of "Undocumented and Unafraid."[16] Mateo's and my positions mirrored a critical tension that exists for Indigenous migrants who have been dispossessed and contend with the possibility of enacting similar Indigenous dispossessions.

As a result of our conversation, when Mateo and Camila led the workshop on migration they discussed the conceptualization of migration as a natural process but also noted that the migration of Mayas was generated by other humans in service of capitalism. They also gave space to the idea that that the use of "new homelands" erases the struggles of Native people in Los Angeles and instead suggested that we were producing a kind of "Native hub," following the work of Renya Ramirez.[17] While we did not necessarily create a new vocabulary to name this experience for Mayas, we were at least able to interrupt a settler colonial imaginary by discussing the notion that, as in Guatemala, wherever we go there are Indigenous people who more often than not are struggling for political, economic, and cultural survival. Ultimately, their prior investments in social justice spaces allow La Comunidad Ixim participants to form and shift how they understand their own personal experiences and the Maya diaspora in general.

The experiences of second-generation youth illustrate that just as the path to Maya relationality is not linear, neither does it always emerge through Maya organizations. While for some organizations, HTAs and churches have been sites of gathering, sources of support networks, and spaces of engagement in Maya spiritual and cultural practices, I would argue that gaining skills and knowledge through non-Maya-specific organizations also strengthens the formation of Maya relationality in the diaspora. Such spaces have allowed Maya youth to engage with notions of heteronormativity, patriarchy, and homophobia in particular. For example, during the first workshop series, Araceli structured the introductions using a method that she had learned through her participation in Xinachtli. She asked each person to state their name, something about themselves, and their preferred gender pronoun. Normalizing the experience of people who are trans or gender nonconforming is critical to acknowledging that members of this group and of the larger Maya community are queer.

The group has often been frank about being a queer-friendly space, something that makes it unique among Maya organizations. About a third of those who participated in the workshop series identified as queer and discussed how being both queer and Maya created challenges and opportunities for them. One such moment occurred during an exercise in the first workshop. Participants and organizers were each asked to bring an item from home that they felt connected them to Guatemala and to being Maya. Carlos, one of the participants, brought his morral, which he carries with him to most places, and stated that he appreciated how the bag was gender neutral. Unlike most Maya clothing, which is conceptualized through gender binaries, a morral is a common item that is used by Mayas of all genders. This can also be read in terms of what Mario Alvarado Cifuentes has termed "critical Maya aesthetics," which "looks at how Maya peoples from diverse genders and sexualities have showcased their resistance through critical aesthetics. These forms of aesthetics by Maya peoples center their resistance to the imposition of binaries."[18] This concept highlights that while colonial understandings of gender, sex, and sexuality have been powerful tools of domination, Maya youth can point to an ancestral practice that continues today and which is not circumscribed by European binaries.

At a later workshop, a different participant, who is K'iche', mentioned that he often felt conflicted and saddened because he had stopped going back to Guatemala. He had not come out to his family there and felt that it was best for him to avoid seeing them so that he would not have to address their heteronormative questions about why he did not have a girlfriend. As a result of his willingness to discuss how heteronormativity spurred his detachment from biological relatives in Guatemala, members reached out to him and shared YouTube videos of transgender festivals in Xelajuj No'j (Quetzaltenango), where people of various genders use women's Maya clothing. Mobile materials like digital videos have value for informing and strengthening Maya diasporic belonging alongside, but also beyond, family or biological ancestry. Part of this strengthening comes from the power of diasporic youth to share the challenges they face with their nuclear families or biological relatives. These may be small acts under the weight of settler colonialism and racial capitalism, but they are important interventions that create the possibility for contesting exclusions often premised on values from violently imposed colonial religions.

These youth collectively share and build queer Maya possibilities through an intersectional politics that does not position queerness as a contradiction to Indigeneity. As Chris Finley notes, settler colonialism reproduces itself through patriarchy and heteronormativity. However, she also reminds us, "Purposeful deconstruction of the logics of power rather than an explosion of identity politics will help end colonial domination for Native peoples."[19] In other words, (settler) colonialism reorders kinship to privilege not only men, but heterosexual formations that become sanctioned through legal and economic practices and (re)produce settler societies. La Comunidad Ixim challenges this logic not solely by contesting heteronormativity, but by doing so through Maya cultural practices and epistemologies. They make space for queerness in Maya cultural practice as a direct challenge to heteronormative and homophobic attitudes among some of the members' families. The youth members instead point out and affirm that cultural practices like the use of morrales or Maya clothing can defy gender binaries that align themselves with heteronormativity. As Jodi Byrd notes, we consider Indigeneity and queerness as contradictory because of politics "that extend from genocide and the loss of languages and worlds those languages contained to the masculinist heteronormativity of some modes of Indigenous resurgence that has tried to overwrite, silence, and then speak for queer and feminist voices through homophobic gestures of liberalism."[20] In this context the members of La Comunidad Ixim are building a collective that works to expand and reposition gender and sexual multiplicity in the face of institutions like families that seek to constrict those realities. These dynamic understandings also influence how La Comunidad Ixim members form mobile archives of Indigeneity that center the experience of Maya youth in Los Angeles. Given the wide array of experiences present in the collective, their determination to produce a material archive that reflects some of their commonalities required them to think and work through intersections in order not to reproduce a single, normative, and uniform understanding of Maya diasporic lives.

Las Aventuras de Gaby

Maya collectivity in diaspora is rooted in Maya epistemologies and engages Maya people in the creation of their own sites of memory. In the face of institutional violence and the limits of normative conceptions of archives, Maya people in diaspora seek out and create sites of memory that account for the legacy of genocide in Guatemala, as well as the experience of migration and diaspora. In the form of a coloring book titled *The Colors of Guatemala: Las aventuras de Gaby*, La Comunidad Ixim created a mobile archive that grapples with these layered experiences. It would be possible to analyze this text outside of its connection to the members' stories, but doing so would arguably miss the political context for the book's narrative and stylistic challenges. Rather than ignore tensions, the collective used the creation of this coloring book to dialogue about them, at times presenting adamant positions and at other times leaving open-ended possibilities that reflect the group's inability to create a singular narrative about what it means to be second-generation Maya.

The coloring book itself follows an ethics of DIY (do-it-yourself) printing that sidesteps the mainstream publishing industry. DIY printing made sense for the members given their backgrounds with working-class experiences, intersectional organizing that centers marginalized people, or punk and ska music scenes—all social realms where being self-reliant when neglected by industries and systems is part of everyday life. In relation to documenting the existence/erasure of punks of color, Mimi Thi Nguyen writes that through her DIY zine *Race Riot* she "sought to establish an informal record of our presence and a critique of those practices of absenting us, through neglect or through violence."[21] DIY has been part of various subcultures, including punk, because it documents the creativity and struggles that are invisible in mainstream representations. This practice focuses on sharing work for the sake of the work; in other words, it refuses to anchor its production in consumption for profit. Because multiple members felt that it was best to share their work on their own terms, DIY printing became a necessity that, more often than not, meant people had to come to physical events and locations to acquire a copy of *Las aventuras de Gaby*.

Importantly, all members had input into the book's creation. The general storyline emerged from one conversation, and one member took up the task of writing part of the story. By the following meeting, no matter how incomplete the story was, it was passed on to another member to continue writing, and so on. Once the story was finished, the group gathered again to reread, edit, and question the content and direct revisions. As a result, it is nearly impossible to attribute the story to any individual or even a set of members. As members wrote the storyline, they also began to verbally describe the images that could accompany each page. The images were created once most of the story was finalized, and they went through a similar process of revisions. Two members, Lisa and Miguel, drew most of the images for the interior and front cover.

Las aventuras de Gaby, which took approximately six years to complete, centers on Gaby, a young, gender-neutral child who experiences memories in the form of dreams. In the mobile archive of Indigeneity that La Comunidad Ixim produced, Gaby's gender neutrality reflects the group's notion that some ambiguity can offer a space for possibility. Every night, after saying good night and kissing Nan (Mom), Gaby has a dream. Sometimes the dream is a nightmare about a familiar place where familiar homes are destroyed. Other dreams are about food: Nan cooking black beans or *plátanos* (fried plantains) and *echando tortillas* (making tortillas). Through the story, the reader discovers that Gaby's dreams are actually a form of remembering. That is, the act of dreaming reflects memories that may or may not be Gaby's lived experience, and the dreams are also an expression of Gaby's desires. I would argue that the use of multiple dreams as part of the narrative and visual structure of the coloring book reflects the multiplicity of experiences of growing up as part of a diaspora. For example, the way in which a dream blurs temporal moments, transcends physicality, and embraces ambiguity reflects how many La Comunidad Ixim participants felt about the multiple migration stories of their families: nonlinear family histories tell who left what part of Guatemala when and why, and perhaps the book even reflects their own mixed emotions about what it means to grow up Maya. In addition, while the story eventually reveals that Gaby's dreams are actual family histories, it remains unclear whether Gaby experienced these events firsthand or whether they became part of Gaby's consciousness through stories heard from others.

The archive, then, is the conflation of what might be considered two primary sources: the family histories of the participants and the understanding that La Comunidad Ixim is crafting future versions of their past experiences. One result of the primary source amalgamation is Gaby's historical consciousness of intermixed terror, joy, pleasure, and confusion. This particular archive does not seek to clarify or eliminate the ambiguity around Gaby but instead acknowledges it as part of the process of continuity. As Sarah Hunt poignantly asserts, "If we accept the alive and ongoing nature of colonial relations, and the lived aspects of Indigeneity as critical to Indigenous ontologies, any attempts to fix Indigenous knowledge can only be partial."[22] *Las aventuras de Gaby* practices this dynamic fluidity as a site not of loss but of multiplicity. It does so in three main ways: (1) It uses dreams as a way to embrace the ambiguity that results from inherited family histories that point to multiple displacements; (2) it visualizes intergenerational relationships in ways that account for the migrant labor of Maya parents; and (3) it uses family stories as a starting point to build relationships through and despite problematic institutions like schools.

3.1 Gaby dreaming of a familiar home. Line drawing by Gabriela Lopez-Morales for *Las aventuras de Gaby*.

In *Las aventuras de Gaby*, dreams serve to highlight the affective, physical, and temporal ruptures produced by intergenerational Indigenous dispossession. The dreams are a way to explore what it means for the children of the diaspora to challenge the linear nature of genealogy, storytelling, and even the distinction between lived memories and those that are inherited in more subtle and undisclosed ways. For instance, research often points to how Maya migrants experience either poverty or physical violence by the state and then migrate to the United States. The book challenges the linearity of this sequence by initially demonstrating Gaby's connection to Guatemala through a dream of "a familiar place ... somewhere far, far away" (see figure 3.1). Two pages later, Gaby has another dream in which

3.2 Gaby's nightmare of the familiar house on fire. Line drawing by Gabriela Lopez-Morales for *Las aventuras de Gaby*.

they, Alex the older brother, and Nan are crossing the border and hiding behind bushes. Nan reminds them that if the coyote—a young man wearing a baseball cap—tells them to run, then they need to run. Gaby, startled, awakes from the dream. The following night Gaby has a nightmare: the familiar home is on fire (see figure 3.2). The inclusion of these issues is critically important to ensuring that Maya children have a sense of personal history that includes state violence as visually represented by migration and the familiar yet geographically distant home burning. Just as critical is that these events are not chronologically sequenced as they would be in academic research; they all are presented as part and parcel of Gaby's existence.

The use of dreams and temporal rupture reflects the experience of many La Comunidad Ixim members who either migrated themselves or learned their families' migration stories. Even several of those who did not migrate recounted the multiple migrations of their families. Alongside these multiple migrations were also stories of siblings born on both sides of the border, women (mothers) who migrated alone, parents who had children with other partners, and even multiple migrations completed by the same parent. This breaking, remaking, and expansion of the familial structure again contests the gendered and nuclear family formation that transnational family literature has often challenged.[23] Araceli described the following:

> [My mom] was just scared that [my Dad] was not going to come back because she said that was common, for men to just go and never come back. And she was, like, no, this isn't happening. At that time they had three kids already, so then she came to the US, and she left my older brother and sister with my grandparents. My grandparents raised them over there, like, I think maybe two years, a year or two years? I don't know something around one to three years, and they brought my sister, who was the youngest at that time. So they lived here and then my older brother and sister lived over there, which is interesting because yesterday my grandparents were home and my grandma she just goes and hugs my sister. She's like, "Ah eres mi hija, I raised you for the first three years." It was just random, she just grabbed her and hugged her, and my sister was like, "Yeah, you were my mom." So she was her mom really. So, then my mom and my dad were here, what is it, maybe 1987 or so, and then my dad went back to go get my brother and my sister, and his younger brother, so then they came back that way.

The multiple, nonlinear migrations remain significant to Araceli's understanding of her family and the role her grandparents played in it, even though she was born and raised in South Central Los Angeles. I asked each of the Comunidad Ixim organizers, "See if you can tell me about your family's migration story." They all had stories that included multiple migrations across many generations. Gaby's dreams capture this sense of an expansive wealth of family history in relation to not only Guatemala but migration as well.

Gaby has no social network outside of her family to process these dreams and memories or sequence the events. This allows the book to act as a site of dialogue within the community and among family members rather than as a source of history for all Maya children. La Comunidad Ixim purposefully chose not to provide details about why the home was on fire or about the migration experience in part because of the book's aim to create space for multiple dialogues to occur within the Maya dias-

3.3 Gaby wakes to find Nan already boarding the bus for work. Line drawing by Gabriela Lopez-Morales for *Las aventuras de Gaby*.

pora. Rather than beginning from the place of intergenerational dialogue, however, the book moves toward this dialogue only after it references how challenging it can be to uphold intergenerational engagement across generations in the diaspora.

Gaby's interactions while awake remind the reader that this is also a story of what it means to be Maya in an urban Latina/o context. After having the nightmare about the homes burning, Gaby runs to tell Nan about the dream, only to find that her mom is already outside, boarding the bus to go to work (see figure 3.3). Making the maternal figure a working parent who was not necessarily available at the moment when Gaby needed her was an expression of what Mateo, Araceli, and Lisa all shared as a formative experience of their childhoods: having parents who worked all day to support the household, at times cleaning homes and caring for other people's children. When I asked Mateo about his migration as a young child, he tied his experience to the loss of two families: first, the loss of his family in Guatemala, and second, his parents' absence due to working long hours:

I think at that time I did not know my dad. I knew of him; I knew that he existed and so there was a lot of stories my family would tell me. And I was like, "Oh, wow, he exists, he's there." But seeing how he was in reality, as a human being, he was working two jobs, having to deal with a child that has leukemia, and having two other boys now, I think, and not understanding who I was as a little boy, I was flamboyant. At the beginning it felt really good, "It's my dad he's really here," but then later on I realized it's not going to be what I thought it was going to be. It wasn't the promised land, I feel cheated out of—I had a family [in Guatemala] and I no longer had them. My cousins, I lost connection. And my grandmother, that's when I realized I really miss my grandmother because she was there. I think living in Cudahy, my parents had to work so we were left alone pretty much all day. I had to learn how to cook. I turned seven in Cudahy and by eight years old, I remember my mom taught us how to cook; she taught my older brother and I that we need to take care of our younger brother and don't answer the door. I understood this is the reality and that's OK, I need to learn how to cook.

Mateo's experience shows us the overlap of what it means to be queer, Maya, and an undocumented child whose family suffers the health consequences of environmental racism and poverty. However, it is critical to understand that for Mateo and other participants, their organizing in multiple spaces provides them with the structural critique that allows Mateo to recognize the pressure his father was under. While he doesn't excuse his parents' absence or his father's homophobia, he has also learned that this is all part of the reality that he and his family lived. This demonstrates how critical intersectional organizing is for the Maya diaspora, and how participation in multiple spaces can benefit them beyond the skills and experience they acquire.

Araceli, whose father is K'anjob'al and whose mother is Ladina, stated that her parents also worked very long hours because they had an herbal and natural supplement store at a swap meet. Her parents rarely took time off and often required all of the children to help out at the store. In addition, this created a family structure that required older siblings to take on many caretaker responsibilities. Thus, the family structure within *Las aventuras de Gaby*, in both its visual and literary representations, exemplifies stories that are common among the group. In the scene where Nan is boarding the bus to work, Gaby is obviously disappointed that she is not home, but the storyline makes it clear that Nan has to go to work. The gap left by Gaby's mother is filled by a sibling named Alex. The story takes a neutral tone toward Gaby and Alex's relationship, but it is Alex who tells Gaby that the dreams are memories.

While Nan is not always available to provide emotional labor because she must provide economic sustenance as a single migrant mother, she nonetheless does appear in a pivotal moment toward the end of the story when Gaby is trying to decide what to share with her school classmates for show and tell. After experiencing the dreams and rejection from peers at school (discussed in more detail below), Gaby is conflicted. Nan's discussion with Gaby serves as a moment of resolution within the story. As they make tamales, Gaby finally tells Nan about the dreams, and Nan responds, "I see. Well, Gaby, I have a story to tell you . . ." While the text does not actually describe what Nan shares, the following morning we see Nan at Gaby's bedside holding a morral. The text reads, "The next morning, Nan gives Gaby a *morral* to wear to class for Show and Tell. She says, 'Wear this so you can always remember that we are a strong family and should not be ashamed of who we are.'" Both the shared story and the gifting of the morral as a material cultural and spiritual object have deep implications for Gaby as a Maya child in diaspora. The image on the morral is of the Kab'awil, a two-headed bird that visually represents duality within Maya cosmology; it is a common image on morrales and textiles sold all over Guatemala.

The visual and textual absence of Nan's actual story represents a conscious decision by La Comunidad Ixim organizers not to privilege any particular narrative of what it means to be Maya. That is, while Nan clearly states her reasons for sharing the morral, the absence of a backstory provides an opening for readers to discuss what Nan may tell Gaby and why listening and sharing between generations is important. The potential for these stories to ground the knowledge of elders is also premised on the notion that much shame still results from anti-Indigenous rhetoric, policy, and state violence in both Guatemala and the United States.[24] Finally, the collective clearly articulated that the absence of Nan's story invokes a Maya audience. Organizers knowingly chose to operate from the assumption that readers would be able to fill in the context of the war and the ways it has shaped the Maya experience in diaspora.

Although much of the story takes place in Gaby's home or subconscious, the storyline also showcases Gaby's interactions with peers and a teacher at school. Rather than position school as a site of learning, the collective uses it to confront US racial and ethnic categories that make Maya

3.4 At school, the teacher announces a Cinco de Mayo celebration to recognize Gaby's culture. Line drawing by Gabriela Lopez-Morales for *Las aventuras de Gaby*.

people invisible. In one instance, a teacher named Ms. Smith states that the class will soon be celebrating Cinco de Mayo with a Mexican hat dance, a show and tell, and the sale of nachos during lunch. Ms. Smith adds, "Don't forget that we are doing this to celebrate your culture!" A thought bubble above Gaby's head reads, "My culture?" (see figure 3.4). The creation of this page stemmed from conversations about how collective members remembered being forced to participate in events that centered Mexican history and culture: School personnel often presumed that all brown children were Mexican, and that these events would therefore be culturally relevant to all children with that skin tone. The organizers agreed that schools and educators impose superficial forms of multiculturalism that take Mexican and Mexican American culture as definitive of Latinidad, and as a result schools act as sites of assimilation even into Latinidad. This is an important note to make in conversations around the experiences of children and youth in the Maya diaspora. James Loucky writes, "For children and youth, some born in Guatemala and others in California, life in Los Angeles revolves around normative standards and institutions such as public schools that appear to have little or no connection to the homeland and experiences of their parents."[25] The collective's need to confront this experience directly speaks to the ongoing salience of premising Latina/o identity on Mexicanness.

The story does not solely blame the educator and school for this issue but also recognizes that non-Maya peers often perpetuate the same stereotypes. Gaby's first choice of what to present for show and tell is a photograph of Gaby, Nan, and Gaby's grandmother. When Gaby takes the photo to school and shows it to a group of friends, another child asks what the woman in the picture is wearing. Gaby responds simply "la ropa" (the clothes). In discussions around this scene, the collective specifically discussed how to mark the difference members felt growing up, especially in school, where they were often assumed to be Mexican yet lacked the terminology to explain to others that they were Maya or Indigenous. While such marginalization is not necessarily directly antagonistic or violent, being made to feel invisible through a mestizo Mexican/Latina/o identity is a common occurrence within Latinidad.

The scene in which Gaby shows her friends the photograph represents key shared experiences among the members of La Comunidad Ixim. The scene illustrates that children's ability to name Maya practices is often shrouded in euphemisms their parents learned. Therefore, rather than have Gaby explain that Nan is wearing Maya clothing or the p'ot, the group decided to label the clothes with the name they heard growing up, which was simply la ropa. The text on the page narrates this experience, while the image depicts Gaby's hand holding the photo in which all three people are smiling. The juxtaposition of Gaby's marginalization against the visual image of the photograph, which exudes happiness, represents another key moment. This symbolizes the diasporic contradiction of the joy one has in belonging to family and community while simultaneously being marginalized for not fitting a Latina/o paradigm, especially as it is (mis)understood by teachers and peers.

The story closes with a classmate introducing herself to Gaby and stating that her family is also "from Guatemala and they want to share their family story with Gaby." In the image, Gaby holds the morral and sits at a table talking with the classmate (see figure 3.5). This ending reflects the collective's project: defining Maya community by extending knowledge drawn from family stories to engage with others in the formation of non-biologically determined relationships.

3.5 Gaby meets a classmate who also is a Maya from Guatemala. Line drawing by Gabriela Lopez-Morales for *Las aventuras de Gaby*.

In addition to the coloring book, the other half of the collective's project is a set of activities for older children. These include a K'iche' word search, a maze with glyphs, a review of the Maya number system, and a set of questions and tips that young people can use to ask their elders about their family's genealogy and migration stories. It is critical to understand how *Las aventuras de Gaby* builds on the work of Irma Otzoy, who argues that Maya textiles can be considered as texts that are written by weavers, carried by wearers, and can be read by Maya people and those familiar with Maya systems of meaning.[26] In a similar fashion, the coloring book and activity set are directed at readers who have a diasporic Maya gaze that can draw meaning and connection from the activities and the moments of Gaby's life. As such, it gives primacy to the migrant Maya gaze while also allowing for that gaze to be defined through a series of open-ended experiences. The book does not simply allow for open-ended experiences; rather, it directly invites the reader to engage with memories of their families, to ask questions about Gaby's memories, and to realize that something as ubiquitous as a word search can incite a much larger effort to maintain and redefine Maya community outside of *and* in relation to our places of origin.

Conclusion: Kinship Beyond Family

The mobile archive of Indigeneity positions the Maya diasporic identity as a purposefully and consciously constructed identity which does not take for granted that a Maya diaspora already exists as a defined community. Through the mobile archive of a coloring book, its creators lay out and struggle over the parameters around Maya identity, both among themselves and in their cultural productions. While positioning any identity (whether queer, youth, diasporic, or Indigenous) as inherently radical is problematic, both La Comunidad Ixim and its archive center working-class, queer, Indigenous experiences in diaspora. This allows the collective to build connections with each other outside of nuclear families and see each other as sources of information, support, and care that anchor their own formation of Indigenous kinship. Often relying on group members' personal experiences of what it means to build a notion of justice that does not reproduce erasures, the organization expands what it means to be Maya in diaspora through its practice of kinship and community, as well as its facilitation of ongoing and open-ended conversations through *Las aventuras de Gaby*.

I do not position the book as solely a cultural production because the text and images are a historical account of violence as an integral part of what migrants and the diaspora confront. A central tension to this positioning is the interplay of the story's written text and its use of words and images to invoke oral storytelling. What is certain is that the intergenerational effects of multiple migrations and displacements require an engagement with Indigeneity as it is formed out of relationships with specific places and yet extends beyond those spaces.

As I have argued previously, the ability to challenge a settler imaginary must also be nestled within a recognition that Mayas are not indigenous to the places they migrate to. To some degree one must have a sense of nonbelonging to be able to challenge settler colonial politics. As a result, archives that continue to center migration experiences of the second generation are key to engaging in ongoing conversations about why thousands of Mayas have left Guatemala for the United States every year since the 1970s. However, what led the collective to be able to create La Comunidad Ixim has been their prior participation in spaces that may be easily read as Latina/o; that is, immigrants' rights movements, environmental justice organizations, and the like. Rather than completely dismiss Latinidad as always closed to Indigenous migrants, I would argue that Mayas draw attention to the ways in which even this category is neither seamless nor a finished product.

Within the diaspora, the positionalities embodied and constructed by La Comunidad Ixim function in a context that is informed by multiple generations confronting historical and contemporary settler colonialism. Participants in La Comunidad Ixim make sense of settler colonial realities through the stories passed down, or at times silenced, by generations of family in Guatemala and the United States, as well as their own experiences of brushing up against Latinidad in the settler colonial and white supremacist country of the United States. Maya positionalities in the diaspora create complex linkages between historical family legacies and the political economies of their places of origin, as well as the colonial structures of the Guatemalan and US nation-states—not to mention how these relationships are configured within Los Angeles. This complexity is also the richness that allows La Comunidad Ixim—and encourages other Maya collectives—to enact an archival practice that searches for and creates materials that can embrace multiplicity and a diverse understanding of Maya cultural practices.

4

Returning the Gaze, Reclaiming the Image

Contemporary Photography as Archive Making

In 2017 *Look* magazine published a layout of Francesca Kennedy's effort to "change Guatemala through artisanal high fashion."[1] Poised in the foreground center of the image is Francesca herself—thin, tall, and blonde. To the right and left behind her, as part of the backdrop, stand several smiling Maya women vendors. This widely criticized visual image reproduced the white Western gaze that has dominated how Guatemalan tourist industries and Ladino elites have visualized Maya women.[2] The photograph struck a chord of indignation because, while images of Indigenous women as backdrop producers of artisanal goods are common, this image was published at the exact time that Maya women across Guatemala were organizing protests and workshops to protect their weavings from being appropriated by high fashion houses and fast fashion. Movimiento Nacional de Tejedoras—Ruchajixik ri qana'ojb'äl, one of the leading organizations in the struggle to protect the communal right to weavings, has organized public protests and workshops and produced social media content that has been instrumental in positioning Maya women as leaders in the protection of Maya collective heritage. Through their social movement, Maya women are also forcing Guatemalan national law to grapple with Indigenous people as collectives. Rather than having individual weavers copyright their personal designs, the movement has determined that what is at stake is a collective process of social reproduction where the clothing upholds the social values, knowledge, and expert labor of Maya people themselves.[3] During the public protests led by weavers, another image emerged of a Maya woman holding a protest sign reading, "Somos las hijas de las abuelas que no morirán. Ellas viven en el universo de nuestros tejidos." (We are the daughters of the grandmothers who did not die. They live in the universe of our weavings.) The contradiction between the images of Maya women as background vendors versus as leading organizers in defense of their rights is a central tension in the politics of visual representation.

Beyond the visual aspects, these images speak to stark differences in how sectors of Guatemalan society articulate and organize for change. Francesca Kennedy's vision of change aligns with current inequalities that seek to provide small-scale support through capitalist businesses. However, this process necessarily forces Maya women to change what the textiles look like and how they are used because it relies on the purchasing power of non-Maya people. In contrast, the Maya women's movement seeks legal protections from the state for their ancestral weaving practices. These women also clearly articulate that if legal precedent does not exist, it can be created, and in using this strategy they are engaging the law as creators of the law, not solely as citizens under its established jurisdiction. This engagement, while it may limit what the movement is able to accomplish, is a strategy developed and led by the weavers themselves and inclusive of lawyers like Angelina Aspuac, who is Kaqchikel and reminds the world that ultimately, "Se trata de dignidad" (It is about dignity). The leaders' use of these legal mechanisms is ultimately about forcibly challenging the material conditions of poverty that Maya women face despite being used as tourist attractions. Leonarda Dionicio, one of the leaders of the weavers' movement, states, "El folklor nos convierte en curiosas, exóticas, en un objeto de comercialización mundial para fotografías de atracción." (Folklore converts us into curiosities, exotic, objects of global commercialization for photographs to attract tourism.)[4] Visual images of Maya women become politicized sites of history and serve as artifacts that document the lived realities of Maya communities. As a result, photography can both challenge erasure and redistribute the power to archive Maya histories of everyday experience.

In 2017, as these images circulated on social media, the contradiction between the visual representations of commodification versus social movement organizing motivated me to collaborate with Las Fotos Project to develop a project around youth, photography, and creating images of Maya women in the diaspora. The goals of Las Fotos Project is "to elevate the voices of teenage girls from communities of color through photography and mentoring, empowering them to channel their creativity for the benefit of themselves, their community, and future careers."[5] It does this by recruiting young girls of color and supporting them as they take on issues in their community or explore their creativity through photography. I first saw their work through an "Esta Soy Yo" self-portrait exhibit hosted at the community art organization Self Help Graphics and Arts in 2016. One image was a self-portrait of Paola Bautista, age fourteen, where she is wearing a school uniform and crouching in an alley. Her caption discussed the lack of infrastructure in her community of South Los Angeles that allowed alleys to become trash dump sites. The crouched figure of a young Latina—who used her body to signal and question the neglect of her community—intervened in the notion that these girls do not see the structural abandonment and that they cannot say anything about it. I was drawn to this image and remember it because there was something about the alley and architecture of the houses that instantly transported me back to where I grew up, South Central Los Angeles. This image was displayed alongside photographs of girls of color in their bedrooms, their backyards, and different parts of Los Angeles. Cumulatively, the images offered a wide representation of Latina girlhood that struck me as unique and powerful.

While most of the work of Las Fotos Project has not focused on specific ethnic communities, I approached Board of Directors President Emily Grijalva and Executive Director Eric Ibarra about recruiting Guatemalan girls to take on this unique endeavor. Both were excited at the prospect, and through our collaboration, we were able to build a program that included eleven weeks of political education, technical photography training, photo shoots, and exhibit planning, culminating in a photo exhibition. Via personal contacts, we publicly recruited Guatemalan participants, preferably ones of a Maya background, to be the photographers. Through the art project and exhibit, Maya Womxn in L.A. (MWLA), we were able to photograph more than forty women from ages four to ninety-six who self-identified as Maya. The final exhibition portrayed Maya women from different parts of Guatemala who lived in different neighborhoods of Los Angeles. In the process of creating the images, the majority were able to choose the date, location, and parameters of their photographs.[6] MWLA included images of Maya women wearing traditional clothing, but in both overt and subtle ways it shattered the temporal and geographic limitations so often imposed on Maya women. This is in part a result of how the youth photographers were trained and how the photo shoots were conducted. What emerged from the flexible process of MWLA was an expansive representation of Mayaness that also reflected the racialized geographies of Los Angeles.

This chapter considers how the MWLA youth photography project took up themes of transnational racism, intergenerational dialogue, and the flexible nature of new and old forms of cultural practice in the production of a photography exhibit that served as a form of documenting Maya experiences. Photographs have often been a complicated terrain for Maya people, who are positioned as ancient and exotic vestiges of a once-great civilization yet are simultaneously excluded from most parts of Guatemalan society that make decisions over their bodies, labor, and territory. On the other hand, for Maya migrants, photographs are also artifacts that tie us to our ancestral homelands, ancestors, and family members that are separated by settler borders.

MWLA emerged from the contradictions around the ways in which visual images are typically produced *about* Maya women, yet not necessarily with the explicit intention of challenging or even recognizing the underlying systems of power. Like the photography project, this chapter intentionally highlights the voices of the cultural producers themselves because mobile archives of Indigeneity are not just about the final archive that may be seen by a public audience. Much more attention can be paid to the complexities when the archivists who produce both the primary materials and the ways they are presented to the public are part of the analysis. From these interviews and photographs, we see that archives of Indigeneity can take up historically problematic tools like photography and redirect its use. Instead of simply taking images of random Maya women in corte, this project sought to highlight care and consent in its process; by doing so, MWLA was able to reflect complex stories of race and Indigeneity in the geographies of Los Angeles.

(Hyper)Visibility, Representation, and Erasure

Photography has historically been used as a technology of settler colonialism because of the ways that visual images have exoticized and fixed Indigenous people as static vestiges of the past rather than contemporary political subjects.[7] Most famously, the images captured by Edward Curtis have been widely critiqued for their investment in reinforcing the notion of a vanishing Indian archetype. Nonetheless, photographs of Native people in historical archives create additional routes of claiming and knowing that enrich family narratives, oral histories, and other forms of research or documentation.[8] In writing on contemporary art in Central America, Kency Cornejo reminds us, "The visual thingification of Indigenous and enslaved African peoples was accelerated with the invention of photography in the nineteenth century and projects that aimed to prove racial inferiority through the visual."[9] Historical photos of Indigenous people are a distinct visual archive from those presented in this chapter, but even contemporary images should be understood in relation to a troubled history of settler colonial dispossession that included images of unnamed Indigenous people, often without their consent. As Indigenous scholars contend with the evolving access to and meaning of these historical images, contemporary practices perpetuate the same logics and tropes as earlier confrontations with the production of photos.

In Guatemala, the photographing of Maya women dressed in Maya clothing has been a strategy for developing a tourism industry that is heavily reliant on tropes of Maya people as exotic but passive adornments. In popular tourist destinations, it is very common to see people taking photographs of Maya women in traditional dress, and now some women request payment for capturing their image. Yet Mayas still experience high levels of extreme poverty even though tourism is a billion-dollar industry in Guatemala. As Gloria Chacón writes, "The Indigenous past... has been systematically appropriated and packaged as a commodity by nation-states through official institutions. This distancing forecloses projects of autonomy."[10] Tourism in Guatemala is so deeply intertwined with the commodification of Maya people that at the Aurora International Airport in Guatemala City, travelers are greeted by large images of Maya women in their clothing, cacao on a grinding stone, and other markers of Maya life. In the highly visual economy of tourism, it is the bodies and labor of Maya people, and Maya women especially, that are offered as a defining feature of Guatemala as a country. As a result, an entire national economy is built around visually marketing Maya culture, which is not actually controlled by or benefiting many Maya people. In this sense, the hypervisibility of Maya women and the widespread ties to strict notions of traditional culture produced by the tourist industry function to erase the settler colonial reality of Guatemala.

However, photographs are also a mobile archive of Indigeneity that migrants typically carry with them or have access to, unlike their limited access to physical territory or goods. Migrants use photographs to document their own moments of life and grief, as well as to connect to older generations and homelands. Migrants and their children may or may not have official birth, death, or marriage certificates from government institutions, but they may have photographs of elders who have passed away or of communal cultural practices. These become key epistemological sites, and when reproduced via social media or physical duplication, their impact and relevance are further extended. Paul Joseph López Oro argues, "Therefore, ancestral memory offers us the theoretical space to reimagine alternative multi-sited archivings that do not adhere to colonial governance of documentation, namely ancestral memory as an archive of resistance and survival in the afterlife of the Middle Passage and slavery."[11] While López Oro is discussing the legacies that the Black Indigenous Garifuna communities call upon, his analysis can be extended to how the Maya diaspora extends kinship circles through the digital sharing or physical reproduction of images. Even in the context of creating new images for the exhibit, many individuals and families chose to incorporate images of their own elders and relatives, and we were able to develop their use of older images within contemporary photographs as a thread throughout the exhibit (figure 4.1). This draws distinct temporalities into the photograph to center an ancestor-based genealogy that informs and shapes the contemporary photograph. By virtue of the images of grandparents and great-grandparents typically being older, the contemporary subjects are able to visually signal the ongoing relevance of their ancestral relative to their own contemporary Indigeneity. This emerged as a theme across various subjects who did not know each other and were not advised to showcase these images, demonstrating the ongoing relevance of ancestors and elders even in the context of migration to a radically distinct environment like urban Los Angeles. Digital sharing of images like these — on or off social media — opens conversations as generations figure out who is pictured and their relationships to ancestors and to each other.

These differences in how and to what ends images are produced are important within the context of intergenerational and multilingual communities and families. While Maya women elders are key knowledge holders and many are survivors of the genocide, they may have limited literacy in speaking or reading Spanish. Two of the elders documented for this project were unable to, or preferred not to, speak Spanish. They happened to come from nearby towns in Huehuetenango; when they met each other at the exhibit opening, they happily began to communicate in K'anjob'al and Acateco, which are distinct but related languages. A daughter of the Acateca elder later commented that she especially appreciated that the elders were able to engage with the event and that her mother could navigate the material without necessarily having to read all the captions. Nonetheless, issues around capturing images of Maya women without their consent were present even at the opening, as attendees around the two elders began to take photographs of them without their express permission. I was alerted to this after the fact, and it was an important reminder of how normalized

4.1 A portrait of a woman wearing ceremonial dress and holding a photograph of her great-grandmother. Image produced by Isabel for Maya Womxn in L.A. Courtesy of Las Fotos Project.

this lack of consent is and how even those who understood the general aim of this project could still perpetuate the very issue around consent we were attempting to address.

These tensions point to larger questions of how visual images reproduce or intervene in ideologies that are intertwined with transnational racial geographies. The same desires that fuel the settler gaze of Maya people as exotic vestiges of an ancient but vanished civilization in Guatemala can also be present when we imagine Maya communities in the diaspora. By analyzing interviews with youth participants, I unpack how mobile archives of Indigeneity can use traditionally problematic media, like photography, in ways that anchor and expand how we think about consent, reciprocity, and relationality, as well as engage youth and young adults as part of the formation of mobile archives. These multiple frictions informed and became apparent in the Maya Womxn in L.A. project, which placed Guatemalan or Maya girls as photographers of self-identified Maya women in diaspora.

Youth Photography and Transnational Racial Geographies in Los Angeles

Two years after MWLA concluded, I interviewed the youth photographers and mentors to understand the overall impact of the program as well as the choices they made as youth leaders within the project. Interviewing the cultural producers expands the process of archive building by considering how their experiences inform their decisions to participate and also become part of the archive-as-documentation process. The time between the exhibit and the interviews helped me understand that the youths' experience with this project was as much about being Maya or Guatemalan as it was about making space in a city that is heavily Mexican, where Latina/o is read as "Mexican," and "Mexican" is often read as non-Indigenous. Their responses revealed that intra-Latinx difference is spatialized even within a local geography like Los Angeles.

While it has been documented that redlining has historically played a pivotal role in shaping the city and suburbs of Los Angeles, it is also true that Indigeneity has played a role in how Latinidad takes up space. The Pico Union–Westlake neighborhood is a specific space where Indigenous and Central American migrants have built networks of support that have become embedded in place through their storefronts, their use of sidewalks for outdoor markets, and the location of community organizations that serve these communities. Since the 1970s and 1980s, the Pico Union–Westlake area has been a site of organizing for Maya refugees and organizations, but in the contemporary moment Maya migrants live in every part of Los Angeles County, and they are not necessarily visible as a collective in spaces that remain predominately "Mexican."

For example, Julia was recruited as a photographer for MWLA because she happened to be enrolled in Emily Grijalva's Latin American literature class when Emily announced that Las Fotos Project was looking for Guatemalan girls. Julia was hesitant and didn't fully understand the level of commitment that was required, but she did fill out the recruitment form and remained a consistent participant in the project. She described having moved from Westlake to Boyle Heights at the beginning of her high school journey. These two neighborhoods are less than five miles away from each other but are spatially divided by downtown Los Angeles, with Pico Union–Westlake to the west of downtown and Boyle Heights to the east. Both neighborhoods are majority Latina/o, but most Latinas/os in Boyle Heights are of Mexican birth or ancestry. Though the majority of Latinas/os in the Pico Union–Westlake area are of Mexican birth or ancestry, Guatemalans and Salvadorans represent a more substantial part of the population. None of these national categories (Mexican, Guatemalan, or Salvadoran) is a perfect stand-in for the complex racial and historical context of these neighborhoods. But importantly, even at the very basic level of national origin, the two neighborhoods are different, and consequently, so are their restaurants, businesses, school populations, and other characteristics.

The transition from one neighborhood to another would be difficult for any young person, but Julia's experience also demonstrates the ways in which these geographies of Latinidad are not seamless. She noted the difference in moving from a neighborhood of people who were like her to a neighborhood that was predominately Mexican: "Once I came to Boyle Heights, I would constantly get asked, 'Oh, where are you from?' When before that I wouldn't as much, I wouldn't get asked that. I just feel mostly shy and not ashamed. Just feel left out from everyone else." This is especially meaningful because Julia actively participated with her family in Maya spaces and celebrations: More than once she was crowned the *reina* (representative) of the community group her family participated in.[12] She stated, "I would participate, and the events would happen over there in Westlake and not over here in Boyle Heights. And I would notice that I wouldn't even mention it to my friends or invite people because I just, I thought it was just me and my family and people we know, if that makes sense really. I wouldn't speak about it at all. I wouldn't share about it." Julia was very clear that she resolved neighborhood racial and ethnic differences by not telling her friends in Boyle Heights about the Maya spaces she participated in. This protective silence is a response to the erasure that happens within the Latinx community. Lourdes Alberto penned a powerful essay on the consequences of this tension between her own Indigenous community and the Latinx community. She writes, "Despite our deep commitments to our *pueblos*, that quotidian reality was never reflected in the world outside of my community. I did not see it in our curriculum, on Spanish-language television, or even among my fellow Latina/o peers' experiences as racialized subjects in the US."[13] We can read Julia's response as one of silence, but it is a silence compelled by social structures and social relations within the Latinx community, where Indigenous bodies and cultures are already cast as inferior in Guatemala and as unrecognizable in the Latinx population.

Julia articulates her response to these differences in spatial geography as tied to "being shy." Certainly, Julia does have that affect, but she also understands that this personality trait is intertwined with how people in different parts of Los Angeles read and interrogate her difference. Interestingly, for Julia and the other participants, this difference can be tied to national (Guatemalan versus Mexican) and racial (Indigenous versus non-Indigenous) differences. Just as salient is that her peers continuously ask her where she was from, indicating they also are keenly aware of these distinctions. The micro-scales of intra-Latinx racial difference permeate a multitude of spaces, including small businesses, churches, and schools.

These differences that become occluded through a larger discourse of Latinidad are intergenerational realities that we grapple with even as adults. Emily Grijalva, the president of Las Fotos Project's board of directors and a coleader of MWLA, discussed some of her own experiences in Boyle Heights. Emily spent her early years in Pico Union being raised by her single mother, who is Guatemalan. She was sent to Quetzaltenango for her middle school and high school education then returned to Los Angeles to attend college and eventually become an educator. As an educator who is committed to an ethnic studies approach to pedagogy, she decided that she would live in the local community where she was hired to teach. She stated that she wanted to be aware of local community dynamics as part of her dedication to teaching and advocating for her students. As a result, when she was hired at a school in Boyle Heights, she moved to the neighborhood. However, she shared having thought back on instances where she perhaps acclimated so quickly to the local Mexican and Chicana/o community that she missed opportunities to create space for Central Americans at her own campus:

> When I first started teaching... there was a time where I was coaching Students Run L.A., and I had a lot of Guatemalan girls running the marathon. I remember we were having conversations; their moms had brought us some *paches* [rice, corn, or potato-based tamales wrapped in banana or *maxán* leaves]. It was so awesome. I was like, "Oh, could I

create a Central American space?" Then I remember I turned to some of our Mexican students, and I was like, "Would you feel, I don't know, kind of pushed aside if I started a Central American club?" They were kind of like, "Yeah!" But then why, you have MEChA, but why did I feel the need to ask that question and check in with them? If there's a need for a Central American support group, that's fine. I should be able to make that.

It is especially telling that Emily, an adult educator and advocate, found it challenging to walk the line between honoring the local Mexican, Mexican American, and Chicanx community and making space for Central American students. As a result, this project became a space where every participant acknowledged that MWLA was the only time we were in a collective of Maya and Guatemalan women outside of our biological relatives. The act of being in a space that centered critical and historically informed conversations about state violence and race was a rare reprieve in a city with more than a quarter million Guatemalans precisely because the youth and mentors were all primarily located on the eastside.

Even though most of us do not operate in primarily Guatemalan spaces unless we live in particular neighborhoods, many of us still see ongoing issues through a Central American, Guatemalan, or Maya lens. These various lenses are difficult to disentangle from how race is socially constructed and how Indigeneity is embodied as a lived experience. For example, despite Julia's affinity for organized Maya community events and the fact that all her Los Angeles elders spoke fluent K'iche', she didn't necessarily identify herself as Maya. Given the context laid out in the introduction to this book, we can tie her hesitation to the way that the Guatemalan government often positions Indigenous people as inferior and the fact that movements that cohere a Maya political subjectivity often miss many community members. I argued in the introduction that this blurring between national, Indigenous, and localized geographies often works in the service of Indigenous elimination. Like the children's book produced by La Comunidad Ixim, MWLA is a reminder that the process of archive making can actually open a space for conversations between young people and within families, and ultimately even for each young person to learn about Maya history and respect for Maya people.

The young Ladina women who participated also articulated that the project was unique in their experience and that, as a result, they were better able to understand the complex issues around Indigeneity and power. Nicole, for example, grew up and completed most of her schooling in Guatemala. However, she mentioned several times that this project was the first time she had learned about the civil war and had a concrete conversation around racism in Guatemala. She noted that this history is not taught in Guatemalan schools, so she learned a lot alongside her peers. When we discussed challenges, Nicole noted, "After the project happened, I start analyzing how we tend to take up spaces because overall we feel connected to it. We feel like we fit that description. But the more I think about the program, the more I analyze like I was taking a space that it wasn't completely made for me. But it still felt like I was part of something that needed to be done." To provide a space for Ladinas in diaspora to be clear that they are not Indigenous is also important. Within the Guatemalan context, Ladinidad correlates to a racial/social category of people who lack or disavow Indigeneity and who wield their power and privilege against Indigenous people whom they deem inherently inferior. However, I often wonder what it means for Guatemalan Ladina/o youth to experience marginalization in the United States and lose access to the privilege they would have in Guatemala. As research on Indigenous migrant communities has shown, compatriots can weaponize racism from their country of origin in the US context, and many need to unlearn the mindset they inherited from their families, who perpetuate this racism in material and ideological ways. Consequently, within the diaspora it also becomes necessary to do political education that analyzes these (Indigenous, Ladina) categories and experiences so that Ladina youth can affirm that they are not Indigenous but still consider it their responsibility to learn about Indigenous issues and create spaces for Indigenous people.

Geographies of Indigenous Diasporas

The geographies of race across borders that play out for Maya women in schools are also lived in other spatial arrangements and layers. For instance, Julia chose an image of her aunt for the exhibit (figure 4.2). What stands out is the aunt's smile, partially covered by her hand but unmistakably joyful. Her beautiful blue-toned huipil and corte stand out against the orange backdrop, which interestingly enough, was well known as Wyvernwood, a sprawling housing complex in the Eastside–Boyle Heights neighborhood that has since been repainted in tones of blue and gray. In chapter 1, I discussed the ways in which a spatial awareness that is locally specific to par-

4.2 Julia's portrait of her aunt for the Maya Womxn in L.A. project. Courtesy of Las Fotos Project.

ticular Guatemala regions is embedded into the design of Maya clothing. One of the elements that emerged in the MWLA photographs is that Maya geography can be read in relation to a Los Angeles geography which has histories of race and class embedded into its architecture or urban planning. In the case of Wyvernwood, there has been a protracted struggle to confront the threat of gentrification in Boyle Heights as a whole, but the struggle has also been waged against the "redevelopment" of this low-income housing complex in particular. In a way, Wyvernwood represents both a lucrative opportunity and a heated site because it houses more than six thousand of the lowest-income residents in Los Angeles. Among them is Julia's family, including her aunt.

We can read this photograph for its relationship to the struggle over space in Los Angeles and as a representation of Maya continuity and survival, and other stories emerge when we see the photograph and the subject beyond this single visual image. When I interviewed Julia, she recounted the experience of photographing her aunt:

> **Julia** [My aunt] was happy. I clearly remember asking her if she can be a model for the photo shoot. Because she is my tía, it was more emo-

tional, more connected. She got to wear corte, my corte because she didn't have one. So when she put it on, she got emotional and started talking about family.... Her hardship, her hard experiences coming over here at a young age and leaving her mom mostly.

Author What do you think it is about the clothes and putting them on that made her say or feel those things or share those things?

Julia I know it's because Guatemalans, that's their clothing, that's what they use every day. And over here, it isn't. Jeans, the shirt, and shoes. I think it's the feeling of missing your country, your culture, your customs.

How does insight into Julia's aunt's life and the relationship between Julia and her aunt change or add to how we see the image itself? The photograph takes on a distinct, layered sense of the struggle against loss and displacement. Rather than simply being about documenting Indigenous existence, this intimate moment allowed for a transmission of stories that can inform how Julia understands migration and Indigeneity. This mobile archive of Indigeneity also supported Maya social reproduction because Julia was able to offer her own Indigenous clothing for her aunt to use in the portrait. The sharing of clothing, then creates a larger space that affirms Indigenous life. A practice that Julia engages in takes on new significance when it allows her aunt to articulate her own reality as a displaced Indigenous migrant. This exchange speaks to the embodied and everyday engagement in the struggle to survive as Indigenous people at the margins who have already lost so much (a country, cultural practices, customs, and family) and yet confront in Los Angeles similar racial struggles under distinct rubrics (poverty and gentrification). As we have seen, in Los Angeles gentrification is another form of dispossessing those who are already marginalized.

Interestingly, gentrification also came up as a theme in relation to the photo of Mina (see figure 4.3). This was one of the first student-produced images and eventually became the lead image for MWLA outreach materials. Part of the young women's training was to practice taking pictures of their relatives to start understanding composition, lighting, and other elements of photography. The photographer of this image was Marisol, Mina's older sister. They are Jewish on their father's side, and their mother is a Guatemalan born and raised in Los Angeles. Their mother is a social worker whose mother had migrated at a young age. While Marisol's mother openly

4.3 A portrait of Mina Alvarado Goldberg by her sister, Marisol, produced for the Maya Womxn in L.A. project. Courtesy of Las Fotos Project.

identifies as Indigenous, Marisol has poignant questions around what Indigeneity means without ties to a specific land, language, or people. Like many young people, Marisol is working through notions of Indigeneity that open tensions between self-identification versus collective belonging. At the time I interviewed her, she was still working through these questions and thoughts, but she was also in the process of articulating what growing up in the eastside neighborhood of Echo Park has meant as the neighborhood has been redeveloped from a working-class community to a gentrified, upper-middle-class neighborhood.

Marisol took another photo, of the Macario family, that also contains layered geographies of dispossession and survivance. This, however, was not the impetus for the photo: the Macario family participated in the project because they had a previous relationship with Marisol's mother. Part of their relationship was grounded in being Guatemalan, but perhaps more importantly, the families were drawn together decades ago because they have deaf relatives and therefore know American sign language. The Macario family, while not fluent K'iche' speakers, nonetheless remember some words and are quatrilingual (English, Spanish, K'iche', and American sign language). Their participation in the project demonstrates the many important spaces and ties among the Guatemalan and Maya community, including involvement in the deaf community.

Set against an architecturally stunning home in South Los Angeles, the Macario mother and daughter pose in their Maya clothing. In addition to the beautiful clothes that speak to the Maya geography of their ancestral territory, the image communicates the gendered intimacy that is the bedrock of what it means to pass down this practice. Vivian, the mother, sits a step above her daughter, and rests her hand firmly on her daughter's shoulder. Vivian's chin is slightly lifted, conveying a deep sense of pride and guidance. She is the elder in the image, a knowledge holder in her own right. Jackelyn, wearing a joyful smile, rests one step below her mother, her hands in her lap. Jackelyn may not yet have been to Guatemala, but her connection to her ancestral homeland is embodied through her relationship with the women elders in her family.

The architecture of the home is also reflective of the architecture of South Los Angeles. Since the era of the Great Migration and racial covenants in Los Angeles, South Los Angeles has been a predominantly Black neighborhood. The neighborhood architecture is much more spacious than surrounding neighborhoods given the relatively high rate of homeownership since the early twentieth century.[14] While residential architectural styles vary across Los Angeles, it is not uncommon to find tall front steps, pillars, and other details that make South Los Angeles homes distinct. While South Los Angeles became an affordable place where some migrant families, including Maya families, could buy a home, this affordability was driven by the dispossession of African Americans due to deindustrialization, loss of union jobs, ongoing governmental neglect, criminalization, and the so-called War on Drugs. One of the consequences is that parts of South Los Angeles also constitute the geography of Indigenous diaspora. Perhaps most notable are spaces like the Garden of Roses, where beautifully curated roses become a financially and geographically accessible backdrop for wedding and birthday photos for families in the neighborhood, including Indigenous diasporic families. For viewers who are from Los Angeles, these photographs can be read for a layered geography that includes both Maya regional dress and the Los Angeles built environment.

Understanding the Spectrum of Maya Women's Experiences

While we have seen in earlier chapters that families and collectives play critical roles in either continuing old practices or creating new ones to disseminate Maya cultural production and denounce current regimes while envisioning future possibilities, the MWLA exhibit opened a new and necessary space for a multitude of visual representations of the diasporic experience. But unpacking diasporas is especially critical because we often—and rightfully so—think about them as being unified in some shape or form. Paying attention to the ways diasporic Indigenous people use their bodies and the geography of their multiple communities to call attention to various politics at play creates an opportunity for us to explore the multitude of experiences that make up a deeply dynamic people. While we put out a public call for self-identified Maya women in Los Angeles to participate in MWLA, we did not call on them to wear Maya clothing. Our reasons for not doing so included the politics highlighted in chapter 1, where for some Mayas, connection comes later in life due to multiple systems of oppression, and the barriers to the ongoing use of Maya clothing discussed in chapter 2. As a result, the photographed women ranged from Maya women who continued to wear Maya clothing as an everyday practice to young women who changed its use.

For instance, one young woman decided to wear a shirt fashioned from the Guatemalan flag. Initially, this raised questions within the project of what exactly was Maya about the image. However, this too is part of the diasporic experience. The reality that terms like *Chapin* or symbols like the national flag take on distinct significance in the diaspora is critical. There are people within the diaspora who would never raise the Guatemalan national flag precisely because it symbolizes the nation that has committed atrocities against our collective people. Yet there are also others for whom the flag remains a symbol of connection and claiming because the Guatemala they know is in fact Maya. This claiming of a national symbol is distinct from how the US government imposes the nationality of "Guatemalan" to erase Indigenous rights and specific needs of Indigenous Guatemalans. Both claims are not only valid but deserving of careful consideration to understand why people or institutions make the claims they do. In this young woman's case, her relationship to Maya heritage is through her father, and while she understands herself as Maya, wearing a shirt with the Guatemalan national flag is her choice for how to represent herself. This self-representation breaks away from notions of a singular, rigid form of Maya visual representation.

Part of the work achieved by mobile archives of Indigeneity is to center these shifts in meaning to highlight how dynamic the Maya diaspora is. For Maya people, Maya dress is linked to embodied politics and Indigenous geographies, but that does not preclude it from also being used by Ladinos to sell Guatemala as a site of cultural commodification. Similarly, many Mayas in Guatemala and the diaspora have no affinity for the national flag, and yet for some the flag represents a marker of reconnection with their origin. In the same way that Julia attributes her Maya dress to the clothes people wear in Guatemala, this conflation points to part of the complexity arising because Guatemalan has at times become a stand-in for Indigenous, especially in the diaspora. That is, even though the flag symbolizes a settler colonial country, it is also a terrain of struggle against being forced into a pan-Latinidad identity defined through mestizo Mexican or Chicana/o cultural nationalism. Within that context, the flag can serve as a way to tie oneself to a geography that is peripheral within the United States.

The reclaiming of self-representation is an intervention against the ways in which Maya migrants are made invisible or denied robust subjectivities. Therefore, giving the subjects of the photographs the opportunity to self-select and choose how, where, when, and with whom they wanted to be photographed is an important interruption of these politics. One image in the exhibit portrays a group of high school girls who were recent immigrants from Guatemala. Interestingly, when I interviewed the youth photographer, Marisol, she told me that even though these girls were Guatemalan, they would often say they were Mexican. Attempting to pass as Mexican as a strategy to avoid deportation to Guatemala has been well documented in the literature on Central American migrants. In addition, the attempt to pass as Mexican in environments with large Mexican populations can be an attempt to lessen social stigma in places like schools, even when this stigma is not directly a result of legal status.[15] But with the encouragement of educators and staff at the school who understood these girls' actual backgrounds—alongside the encouragement of Marisol herself, who comes from a radically different socioeconomic background but is also Guatemalan—the students agreed to the photo shoot. The resulting image is joyous, with the young women smiling, engaging with each other, and using Maya textiles to make themselves visible. Given the context of passing as Mexican and the politics of hiding due to the ways Indigenous Guatemalan women are vulnerable to interpersonal and systemic violence during migration, the perseverance and joy of these young women breathes life into how we think about the contours of the diaspora. We cannot deny or minimize that the diaspora is forged by vulnerable families and communities, yet this project provided options and opportunities that the girls took up with joy.

The moment of laughter captured in the image reminds us to think of Maya women as more than victims, remembering that they are always more than the challenges and silence and that in the right moment and with the right support, they will claim their collective belonging and refuse both the settler politics of deportation and Mexicanization as a survival strategy. These young women bear the brunt of what Shannon Speed labels as a process of being made structurally vulnerable.[16] For Speed, the emphasis on how Indigenous women are made vulnerable results from scholars' tendency to mark Indigenous women as inherently vulnerable rather than thinking about the ways in which these women are made vulnerable by the intersection of interpersonal violence, narcoviolence against women, and violence from government entities like the police or military. Through powerful and heartbreaking testimonios from migrant Indigenous women being held in detention, Speed argues that this assumption of vulnerability is gendered violence that pushes Indigenous women to migrate, confronts them along the journey, and characterizes much of their experience in detention. This framing also emerges out of how Native and Indigenous women and femmes have long understood the false binary between interpersonal and state violence, which both ultimately are rooted in settler colonialism regardless of the actual hands that commit the violent act. Therefore, the decision of the young women to try to publicly pass as Mexican is one response to heightened levels of neglect and marginalization.

In the image, the girls sit in front of a beautiful purple textile that functions as a backdrop. However, although the adults who hold up the textile attempt to stand behind it, we can see their hands at the top edges. The group of girls also extends beyond the textile's frame. A professionally trained photographer may have made different choices about composition. However, this image is about more than the final product. It is about the context and the process of everyone involved: the young photographer, the girls in the image, and even the adults who came to the photo shoot to support these students. Although we do not know their individual stories, we know that these young girls are marginalized subjects and members of a community that most often makes the news because of the state violence it experiences. For these reasons, images like this interrogate the ways in which Maya girls and women can feel and embody joy and connection outside of the confines of state violence. In addition, the fact that the photo was taken at a public high school, which is a public institution, also points to the gaps that hinder or create possibilities. These girls were honest about the ways in which they confront stigma in those hallways and protect themselves with the relational privilege Mexicans have compared to Guatemalans or Mayas. This demonstrates that work, time, and resources are all necessary to create a different, albeit momentary, space that does not reproduce the social hierarchies these young women are confronting and navigating.

In these often systematically silenced gaps—in places like schools or under the notions of immigration politics—we can document silence and survivance as part of a Maya diasporic experience. While Las Fotos Project typically asks the young women photographers to write captions for the images they produce, for this exhibit the voices of women in the photographs were given priority. The photographic subjects were able to write, or in some cases have their loved ones write, part of their story to accompany their images. This gave rise to a multivocal process that further interrupted the objectification of Maya women. By interpreting not just the images of Maya women, but also their statements about themselves, the viewer is reminded that Maya women already have a critical perspective on many of their life experiences. Part of what it means to return the gaze is that while Mayas may not fully control who is the audience of these archives of Indigeneity, they can still ensure that images and their accompanying texts proclaim a politics of life on their own terms. What Maya women have to say about themselves is as significant as what we see in the visual image.

In one family, four sisters and their mother were all part of the photo shoot, so the sisters wrote individual captions then one of them transcribed her mother's words to include. One of the images portrays the five of them, all wearing Maya dress, sitting around their dining table, chatting and laughing. The mother sits at the head of the table surrounded by her daughters, which conveys an intergenerational, vibrant, and joyful family. In the context of genocide, upholding these bonds across generations is a direct testament to survival. One line from the mother's caption stated: "That is how we migrated, with my baby on my back, your dad carrying your brother, and your poor siblings walking for a very long time. We left everything behind. You think we wanted to leave? We wanted to live. We had to escape." The caption spells out a coerced displacement that occurred as a matter of life and death. In turn, the daughters similarly described their own memories as children. One of the daughters wrote:

> By the age of 7 years old, I had crossed 2 borders. As a child, I never quite understood the Civil War in Guatemala. All I knew was that we needed to survive. The constant disruption and moves that I went through as a child is what makes me a strong and resilient person today. Through my migration from country to country, I felt both sadness and hope. Now, I can never thank my parents enough for their sacrifice. I will never know how strong they are, not only physically, mentally, or emotionally, but spiritually. They have endured many obstacles and yet remain strong in all aspects of life.

These narratives that accompany the portraits are a critical intervention that interrupts the settler gaze that uses images of Maya women for the sake of a depoliticized cultural voyeurism and marks them as exotic. Instead, the narratives and images, as well as the process, lay out a distinct possibility to create space for joy and survival that is politicized precisely because of the state violence Maya women themselves articulate.

For Maya women, embodying multiple geographies is also about claiming an ancestral survival and resilience that defies erasure and elimination. Julia photographed one of the subjects, Maricela, on the steps in front of her apartment building. In the image, a smiling Maricela is wearing their corte and huipil. Maricela wrote the following caption for the photograph:

> More than representation, wearing my corte in Los Angeles is a responsibility. Knowing that I wear the stories, the life, the love of my ancestors is beyond powerful; it is tenacious, it is resilient. My ancestors, my grandparents, my parents have lived through colonization, wars, and genocide, yet here I stand wearing the one corte that I own, the one corte that my grandmother and I share; that is resilience. By wearing my corte in Los Angeles, I am telling white supremacy, "Look at me. You tried to erase my existence, but here I am." My resilient ancestors prevailed.

Maricela links the various forms of structural racism that displaced their family in Guatemala with the forms of exclusion they have faced in the United States, drawing on the much longer historical trajectory that public discourses often miss in relation to violence against Mayas today. Maricela names this system white supremacy, a term that usually refers to racial hierarchies in the United States, but is also applicable to Guatemala, whose racial hierarchy is primarily based on Indigenous and Ladino groups. Social media more recently has coined the term "whitemalans," essentially a merger of white as a racial category and Guatemalan as a national category. Narratives produced by diasporic subjects like Maricela are critical in demonstrating that it is imperative to "not just take Indigenous peoples' experience seriously but also take *their understanding* of it seriously."[17] This type of self-representation is much more than an individual reclaiming by the photographer or the subject. The building of an archival artifact by a Mam subject like Maricela and a K'iche' photographer like Julia is the ongoing engagement between two very old Indigenous nations with entire histories together. In Guatemala, the Mam and K'iche' are located next to each other and as a result have long histories of exchange. This shared moment within the larger Maya diaspora, then, is also an echo of these ancient Indigenous nation-to-nation engagements, which also upsets the settler colonial logic of solely thinking about the photographer and subject as children of Guatemalan immigrants.

The strength of the MWLA exhibit is not solely that it expanded the spectrum of how we visualize or understand Maya women, but also that it allowed us to see multiple manifestations of an Indigenous diaspora's claim to life and futurity. When the elder woman says, "We wanted to live"; when young girls, even for a brief moment, engage with each other as Maya girls, and when Maricela reminds us that there is joy and power in the act of surviving, they are all demonstrating that this diaspora wants to survive as Maya people. Despite all the powerful genocidal logics that materially incentivize forgetting and assimilating, they instead lean on each other and on elders to persist.

Communal Archive Making

The opening of our exhibit saw one of the largest crowds Las Fotos Project had ever drawn to one of its shows. More than three hundred people waited in line with friends and family to take turns crowding into a small gallery space in Lincoln Heights to witness the power and beauty of the photographers and the exhibit. What began as a humble possibility became a multimedia project that included images, textiles, interactive community mapping, and audio interviews. The success of the exhibit largely relied on people who contributed their time, talent, and labor simply because this project was important: it created a space to hold our collective refusals of assimilation and erasure. Moreover, exhibiting the ongoing persistence of Maya women also opened opportunities for the community to participate in and engage with an archive. That is, I would argue that the documentation of the opening night in videos and photos was also a process of archive making that transcended the youth photographers and the Maya women they photographed.

As I noted earlier in this chapter, isolated visual images of Maya women can be decontextualized from lived experiences of surviving genocide and displacement. The text that appeared alongside these images was a critical intervention against the erasure of this larger sociopolitical context. In addition, the exhibit facilitated the creation of other artifacts that helped attendees think about these textiles alongside a longer history of Maya cultural practice. This was in part accomplished using a historical timeline designed in the form of a ceiba tree. Because the ceiba has its own significance within Maya cosmologies, its use aligns with the claim that Maya people have their own epistemologies. The ceiba is part of the ontological world making found in the Pop Wuj creation story, and it continues to represent a relationship with the flora and fauna beyond their utilitarian value. Placing a historical timeline alongside the ceiba establishes a continuity from the precolonial era to the present and future. This continuity is in itself a political claim against the historical erasure perpetuated by Guatemalan elites who would have us believe that the great thinkers, artists, astronomers, and scientists of the Maya civilization disappeared.

One of the artifacts memorialized in photographs of the opening event was an interactive map. This mapping activity invited attendees to chart their own or their family's migration to the United States. We drew a map with instructions for attendees to use pushpins and lengths of yarn to locate where in Guatemala their family came from and where in the United States they migrated to. The map became a communal instance of archive making that took an Indigenous ontological practice—weaving threads together to create a narrative—and simplified it for audience participation. The converging strings of thread were reminders that, in addition to the women shown in the photographs, many other people from Guatemala were present at the event. This interactive activity became an embodied, geographic, and intergenerational documentation of Guatemalan and Maya existence (see figures 4.4 and 4.5). Simultaneously, it reframed migration as a site of connection rather than one necessarily of dispossession or alienation.

4.4 An attendee at the opening of the *Maya Womxn in L.A.* exhibit adds a thread to the communal mapping interactive activity. Courtesy of Las Fotos Project.

The opening reception also created a multisensory experience for the audience that historically contextualized the images and text that were the central focus. Audio interviews that were prerecorded with some of the photo subjects and live marimba music on the sidewalk outside the gallery created a space where multiple social issues were addressed while joy and resistance remained central. In one of the audio interviews, Sinnai Avila states that she buys directly from weavers to resist the appropriation of Maya textiles by major brands like H&M and Forever 21. Audio excerpts of interviews conducted by the young photographers with two of the subjects featured in the photographs also reflected an effort to include an aural aspect to this archive. These aural registers provided glimpses into how Indigenous culture accompanies a politicized interruption of settler logics that are premised on the elimination of Indigenous subjecthood. As Daina Sanchez writes, "Through soundscapes that include music, language, and sounds associated with their hometowns, Serranos can engage in and show belonging through millennial and ever-evolving forms of Indigenous communal life."[18] The oral/aural component of our exhibit was especially important given the multilingual nature of the Maya community, but it also provided additional means of experiencing Maya history, politics, and resilience beyond a written text. Photographs and videos of the

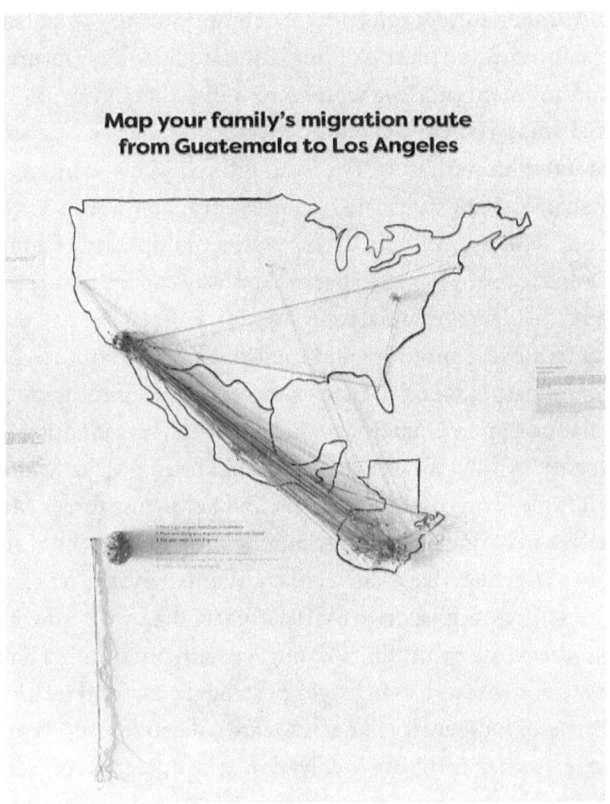

4.5 The communal migration map created at the *Maya Womxn in L.A.* exhibit. Courtesy of Las Fotos Project.

event add significance to the actual images, and as a result are included in the archive that now exists online—a record of not just the gallery exhibit but the community that came together to celebrate the MWLA project and share their stories of migration.

Conclusion: Archiving Collective Refusals

In the context of transnational racial geographies, MWLA intervened in how we think about Los Angeles as Guatemalan girls documented the experiences of Maya women. MWLA elucidated that Los Angeles is not just a city of immigrants; it is a city of Indigenous survivance that has defied settler erasure across borders. Part of what allowed MWLA to complicate the notion of a city of immigrants is that the collaborative and historically informed photographs became an opportunity to document and unpack the interrelated nature of migration, Indigenous erasure, and the ongoing commitment of Maya women to refuse their absorption into settler colonialism in the United States. MWLA was able to do this because it documented more than forty self-identified Maya women and expanded the visual, textual, and aural narratives available about Maya women in diaspora. The project held up for view a multiplicity of generations, forms of violence, borders, and spaces. For Maya space to be embodied and lived outside of settler social reproduction will require discourses on Indigeneity to include mobility and multiplicity. Each of the young women photographers and each of the women and girls photographed has a different relationship to Guatemalan history and Maya identity. Beyond simply diversifying how we visualize and understand Maya women, engaging with multiple forms of displacement and belonging forces Maya women themselves to define how they share themselves with the world.

As a collective archive, Maya Womxn in L.A. was less concerned with the settler impulse to preserve objects than with how it created space for the diasporic community to engage with one another and address difficult histories without losing sight of struggle, joy, and relationality. Mobile archives of Indigeneity like MWLA are collective refusals to forget, to deny, to hide. Rather, for those involved in this project as subjects, photographers, mentors, educators, or organizers, it was an opportunity to highlight Maya histories, experiences, and knowledge on Maya terms despite the erasure or outright elimination that occurs in many settings. Ultimately, this project was not about defining the Maya diaspora as a binary experience where you either do or do not speak a Maya language, or where you either wear or do not wear Maya clothing, and so on. On the contrary, we made space for Maya women to come forward *as they are* to tell their stories through both images and text. In the process, we collectively shaped and built a project that is millennia in the making.

Conclusion

Much of this book has focused on the moments of joy, life, continuity, and historical memory within the diaspora. Our communities, like many others, are fractured by colonial violence, and we experience that violence in a multitude of embodied ways. This includes conflicts between communities and within communities. However, when I considered what themes resonated across multiple interviews, one that stood out was the way that connection acted as a balm to sites of conflict and sorrow. These relationships are expansive and diverse, and I intentionally emphasized how cultural production weaves a Guatemalan Maya diaspora across various families and communities. These stories of connection across our internal differences are all part of shaping how we are understood and what stories get told about us within academic institutions. However, this is not to say that we have moved beyond the original terror that began more than five hundred years ago. Both in our territories and in our diasporas, we continue to face challenges as we also continue to migrate back and forth in ways that reflect a multitude of positions, endeavors, and hopes. These challenges are a byproduct of multiple countries that have sought to dispossess Maya people of their labor, culture, history, and epistemology, even their very lives. In response, and alongside other dispossessed communities, Maya people have fought for centuries to create a life where their children can eat and learn without having to give up their relationship to the land and culture of their ancestors. As Indigenous diaspora scholar Luis Urrieta reminds us, "Decolonization is painful, but it's a necessary and enduring process toward healing that we must continue to fight for, not only for ourselves, but for future generations."[1] This struggle remains salient even for those of us who are now legal US citizens but continue to watch the violence wrought upon our community members.

In the spring of 2018, as the images of Maya Womxn in L.A. hung on the walls of the Las Fotos Project gallery, Claudia Patricia Gómez González, a young Maya Mam migrant woman, was murdered by a Border Patrol agent in Laredo, Texas, as she was crossing into the United States. Her death was a stark reminder that transnational politics of displacement continue to shape the experiences of Maya women. The earliest news coverage called Claudia Patricia an unnamed immigrant woman, an assailant, and an illegal border crosser. For those of us in the Maya diaspora, she was a relative who took the same journey that so many of our families had taken and that was deemed not only "illegal" but also punishable by death. In 2018 we then saw the deaths of at least five Maya children in detention centers over eighteen months. These losses were devastating in part because we knew their names and we knew that each one stood for so many others whose names we will not know and whose bodies will not be found. As the relatives of these children and youth denounced the loss of their loved ones, those of us in the diaspora saw their grief, and it felt painfully familiar. We felt again and again the grief that we often set aside to continue our work, our search for place, our demands for lives with dignity. We organized altars and commemorations in multiple spaces, attended spaces organized by others, shared our grief in poetry and art, and we continue to remember all these young ones as part of our diaspora. Images and stories about Claudia Patricia, her parents, and her relatives remain embedded in my own diasporic consciousness as I write about the many ways that our survival is a joyous political act against the necropolitical imperative of settler governments. Documenting these losses and our persistent continuity in the face of loss remains part of a multigenerational endeavor to archive ourselves on our own terms and with our own materials.

Throughout this book, I primarily discussed mobile archives of Indigeneity as a process of drawing on Maya epistemological practices to articulate and challenge transnational forms of violence using critical materials. The material objects that make up the archives, along with the stories of Maya people themselves, generate opportunities for those in the diaspora, especially youth, to continue building their own visions of Maya collectivity. As a result, even as we consider how to cope with such painful structures as displacement or dehumanization wrought by Immigration and Customs Enforcement (ICE) we turn to candles, seeds, incense, water, textiles, writing, and photos to help us process pain and loss. Despite physical displacement from our territories, the ability of future generations to return or even continue land-based practices in Tovangaar will remain critical to anchoring our responses to settler violence in our cosmologies.

As the arc of this book contends, the ongoing struggle to build community on occupied Indigenous territory is occurring within a settler colonial structure that has deployed Latinidad in its project of dispossession. Latinidad limits the space available for representing the Maya diaspora. Indigenous and Afro-Latinx people are often used as examples of why Latinidad is not an inclusive term; however, the nuances and complexities within our large and diverse Maya diaspora rarely become part of the conversation. Rather than use the Maya diaspora as a symbol to point out why either Latinidad is diverse or does not work as a unifying term, I sought to engage with some of the multiplicities within our community. This book is only a glimpse into a community that contains millions of people and dozens of distinct communities across multiple countries. Even so, Maya diasporic existence in the United States should force us to remember that Latinidad is a category born out of imperialism and settler colonialism. Part of the work that our cultural materials do is to position us as outsiders to the US nation-state and its definitions of Latinidad. What I hope this book offers to other similarly positioned communities is the knowledge that this position of not belonging does not have to be solely about painful exclusion; instead, it can also inform powerful critiques of ICE, schools, media, government policies, legal citizenship procedures, and other institutions.

The coerced inclusion into a Latinidad that is premised on Mexican mestizaje also creates a critical tension with the original caretakers of Los Angeles, who continuously point out that settler colonial structures have led to the exploitation and erasure of the water and land their communities continue to fight for. Charles Sepulveda notes that the Indigenous theory and practice of Kuuyam can be a guide for living in good relationships with Native people and land, but "the status of *Kuuyam* is neither demanded nor ordered. It is instead a relationship offered and chosen."[2] This means that we must be intentional in how we work to build our Maya diasporic community so that we can understand Native people in an Indigenous-to-Indigenous relationship. As a result, I anchored much of this work in the idea that rather than make the claim that Maya migrants are Indigenous and therefore are not Latinx, we should disentangle the way in which Indigeneity is a field of power, as Aída Hernández Castillo points out.[3] The reality of being good Indigenous relatives may be a long time coming, and some readers may perceive the idea as impossibly utopian, but for many who center a Maya cultural production that is intersectional and invested in justice, it is part of a life-asserting project that is built in hypervisible and everyday moments.

My hope is that this book will add to the conversations that continue to be central to many Indigenous scholars and communities who live outside of our ancestral territories. Among those are how we can acknowledge the stories told about us in academia and complicate them to include our own views, priorities, and strategies for survivance. Many of us in academia continue to explore how we juxtapose the importance of land with the reality of mobility and diaspora, even as we move beyond the notion that to be Indigenous is to stay (physically, spiritually, and culturally) in one place. Despite what settler colonialism would have us imagine, these communal dialogues do not occur over emptied land or in a vacuum. As noted in the introduction, the relationship between Indigeneity and land is both deeply spiritual and critically important, while simultaneously being fraught sites though which settler colonial and imperial violence is often enacted by constricting how these relationships are created. Mobile archives of Indigeneity exemplify that when Indigenous communities take meaning making into their own hands, they create the materials that communicate historical memory and a life-centered politics that are cognizant of the power dynamics of what it means to be Indigenous in the twenty-first century. In particular, my discussion of Maya dress emphasized that the relationships Maya peoples have built to particular places over thousands of years remains foundational. However, those relationships shift as we consider migration and the ongoing power of distinct nation-states to form regimes of anti-Indigenous violence. Migration forces specific communities to rearticulate what aspects of their experiences are dynamic and which remain collectively rooted in a millennial history and practice. In that expansive space of building relationships across time, geography, and the physical world of the living we can see the critical work that people commit to. Instead of making their struggle legible to white Western audiences through a sense of "in-between-ness," we can read their organizing as exceeding the bounds of settler borders and time. Maya migrants themselves begin to lay out the threads that will bind them—and their children—back to Maya communities that are still seeking justice and dignity.

Part of the process of creating mobile archives requires a consideration of the aspects of Indigenous life that cannot be captured by material artifacts. The mobile archive of Indigeneity, as I have conceptualized it throughout the book, is about the *process* of working through layered temporal and spatial understandings of what it means to be Indigenous and collectively thinking about the power of archival materiality beyond an individual or even a nuclear family. In the case of Maya clothing, the appropriation by fashion designers of weavings as mere fabric emptied of its meaning repurposes a historied practice into a mode of production in the service of profit. Maya clothing used and shared among chosen kin and family members forms an archival practice that contains and transmits the history of violence and the experience of migration as an extension of that violence. The clothing is critical not just because it is a cultural practice but because within the context of genocide in Guatemala and erasure in the United States, it remains political to claim places of origin through Maya aesthetics. It is these practices that continue to be upheld as sites of belonging and collective meaning in spite of state violence.

Just as Maya clothing is a transnational practice that acts as a container for collective histories across generations, so are new forms of memory making like alternative forms of literature. Among those are grassroots projects like the coloring book produced by La Comunidad Ixim. Through their collective efforts, La Comunidad Ixim is shifting how we understand second-generation Mayas as not only engaging with their cultural practices, but also as a group that can draw resources from their organizing to develop critical interventions within Maya communities. In particular, they make visible that femmes and queer people have Maya identities and lead Maya collectives. The Maya Womxn in L.A. project takes up similar themes of creating an archive that uses the historically problematic medium of photography in ways that anchor and expand how we think about consent, reciprocity, and relationality and how we engage youth and young adults as part of the formation of mobile archives of Indigeneity. Both of these cultural productions seek to denaturalize Maya inclusion into a generic Latinx category by pointing out the ways that the oversimplified notions of Latinidad need to be questioned. In addition, mobile archives of Indigeneity create an opportunity to destabilize what is understood as an archive. Institutional archives are indeed incredibly important to the ongoing efforts by Maya people across borders and to other Indigenous people as well. However, I would argue that historically we have not been included as part of the public that can access these archives, so we have simultaneously created our own.

Ultimately, this book has been about celebrating moments of history and continuity to highlight the work that community members commit to. By continuing to tell their stories, they refuse to forget who they are and where they belong. The memories are never quite nostalgic, since many fled under dire circumstances that they continue to discuss, but they recognize that displacement is not the natural order of things. Instead, members of the diaspora often remember a time when, even briefly, their homelands felt like home, a time before war, or perhaps more accurately, moments that were not defined solely by war. In these contexts, elders who migrated have passed down histories and practices diasporic youth can use to build connections to each other. These efforts are valuable in so many ways that one book can never do justice to all of the complexity, nuance, and power they hold. Instead, I want to end this book by inviting more members of the Maya community to continue telling their stories in whatever mediums make sense to them, to their families, and to the other Mayas they want to build relationships with. Even if we are the only ones listening, the continued practice of telling and listening is an important and enduring rebellion against erasure and forgetting.

Notes

Introduction

1. For a detailed account of the initial complaint, the trials and prosecutions, and the appeals that followed, see Dill, "International Human Rights and Local Justice." In addition, note that it was members of the civilian patrol who were prosecuted. While established and overseen by the military, the patrol was not considered an official part of the military. As a result, the successful prosecution of these officials still safeguarded military personnel.
2. I use the term *testimony* because the play uses Tecú Osorio's court testimony. However, Tecú Osorio's book and public appearances rely on his *testimonio*. A testimonio differs from testimony in that it does not rely on normative understandings of truth and instead centers the stories of marginalized people as legitimate counterstories to disciplining discourses. See Beverly, "Margin at the Center"; Montejo, *Testimony*.
3. In the context of Central American state violence, war, and massive displacement, cultural production takes on a sharp political edge that, according to Karina Alvarado (now Karina Alma), "is not the passing down of a historical artifact or past but the process through which people dialogue, engage, and transform these from their current and present locations." Alvarado, "Cultural Memory and Making," 490.
4. For more on survivance in Native Studies, see Vizenor, *Manifest Manners*.
5. Ester Hernández states, "Within Los Angeles public space, Central American identity symbols provide mnemonic cues to individual, collective, and intergenerational pasts of Angeleno/Salvadoran/Central American social justice struggles." In the context of ongoing silence and erasure, we cannot assume that there is a consensus regarding what stories should be told and how. Instead, Hernández draws our attention to specific sites that Central Americans have created and the multitude of perspectives that emerge as they create venues to engage history, including the histories of state repression. Hernández, "Remembering Through Cultural Interventions," 144.

6   De León, *Land of Open Graves*; Vogt, *Lives in Transit*.
7   Estrada, "Reclaiming Public Space."
8   Featherstone, "Archive."
9   Cotera, "Unpacking Our Mothers' Libraries," 305.
10 Hartman, *Lose Your Mother*.
11 Adams-Campbell et al., "Introduction," 110.
12 Adams-Campbell et al., "Introduction," 111.
13 Taylor, *Archive and the Repertoire*; Alma, *Counterpoetics*.
14 Hall, "Cultural Identity," 394.
15 Schweizer's "Counter-Archive" discusses how we can think about counter-archives, migrant archives, postcolonial archival theory, and dissemination alongside the new possibilities of open archives. Among important interventions against traditional and normative archives are Kelly Lytle Hernández's *City of Inmates*; Genevieve Carpio's "Tales from the Rebel Archive," and Alana de Hinojosa's "El Rio Grande as Unruly Archive."
16 Appadurai, "Archive and Aspiration," 16.
17 Lazo, "Migrant Archives"; Magaña, "Multimodal Archives of Transborder Belonging," 707; Appadurai, "Archive and Aspiration," 20.
18 Bradley, "Seductions of the Archive," 108.
19 Derrida, *Archive Fever*, 10.
20 Menjívar and Rodríguez, *When States Kill*.
21 Indigenous geography is complex, and I use the term *Native* primarily in relation to nations that exist within the territories of Turtle Island currently occupied by the United States. I use *Indigenous* as a pantribal term, especially in reference to nations located in territories occupied by the countries of Latin America.
22 Shannon Speed points to Daiva Stasiulis and Nira Yuval-Davis's earlier articulation of settler societies, which was then popularized by Patrick Wolfe. Since these earlier writings, settler colonialism has also been utilized in conceptualizing sexuality, gender and feminism, environmental studies, migration, and the occupation of Palestine. See Speed, "Structures of Settler Capitalism in Abya Yala"; Stasiulis and Davis, *Unsettling Settler Societies*; Wolfe, *Settler Colonialism*.
23 Commission for Historical Clarification, *Guatemala*.
24 Menjívar and Rodríguez's *When States Kill* is an excellent anthology that demonstrates the interrelated projects of state violence that continually link the United States with economic and political elites in Latin American countries.
25 Speed, "Structures of Settler Capitalism in Abya Yala," 786.
26 Batz, "Ixil University." Mega projects are typically funded by entities like the International Monetary Fund or foreign corporations (such as mining companies). These have been the site of social conflicts related to land disputes because they dispossess Indigenous people, and when Indigenous communities resist, they are deemed terrorists, criminals, and

enemies. For more information on key sites of contemporary struggle in Guatemala, see Rasch, "Transformations in Citizenship"; Grandia, "Road Mapping."

27 Castro and Picq, "Stateness as Landgrab."
28 Jennifer Cárcamo's documentary *Eternos Indocumentados* features Irma Alicia Velásquez Nimatuj giving a presentation in which she utilizes a map that overlays the sites of massacres and sites of social conflict. See also Batz, "Ixil University."
29 Global Witness, "Enemies of the State Report."
30 For more information on these issues, I strongly recommend the news outlet of Prensa Comunitaria, as well as North American Congress in Latin America reports written by Giovanni Batz.
31 Hunt, "Violence, Law and the Everyday Politics of Recognition"; Speed, *Incarcerated Stories*.
32 Hale, "Rethinking Indigenous Politics."
33 Jason de León has noted that human smugglers have increased their charges in parallel with the increased danger of crossing the border since the United States implemented Operation Gatekeeper and prevention through deterrence. In addition, Lauren Heidbrink looks at the impact of debt on migrants and their families in their homelands, as well as the ways debt is (un)regulated in Guatemala. See de León, *Land of Open Graves*; Heidbrink, "Coercive Power of Debt."
34 There has been ongoing discussion on the relationship between social death and genocide. In this book, I use social death to mark the consequences of state violence beyond the destruction of bodies or villages. The genocide Mayas experienced in the 1980s fits the criteria set by the United Nations to be classified as genocide. What I lay out in this chapter, however, is also a concern for the enduring consequences that make Maya social reproduction difficult. This includes the murder of large swaths of elders, children, organizers, and healers. It also includes children who are orphaned or are born outside of their ancestral territory as a result of the violence of the genocide. The concept of social death was developed by Orlando Patterson in relation to the experience of Black enslavement; however, this framework can also help us analyze the situation of bodies that survive but have to remake themselves into communities while living in dehumanizing conditions. For more, see Patterson, *Slavery and Social Death*; Card, "Genocide and Social Death."
35 Montejo, *Maya Intellectual Renaissance*. It is important to distinguish between the terms *Ladina/o* and *Latina/o*. *Ladina/o* is a term used for Guatemalans who do not identify as Indigenous and instead highlight their European ancestry. For an excellent analysis of contemporary Ladina/o identity, I recommend Charles Hale's *Más Que Un Indio*.
36 Hernández Castillo, "Indigeneity as a Field of Power," 379.
37 Little, *Mayas in the Marketplace*.

38   The work of Gladys Tzul Tzul is also an in-depth examination of how Indigeneity functions through communal organization in the community of Chuimeq'ena' (Totonicapán). These critiques about the limitations of a larger umbrella term *Maya*, alongside the importance of specific Indigenous governance models, are critical in the context of Guatemala, and my hope is that they will also shape diasporic conversations and formations. See Xón Riquiac, *Entre*; Tzul Tzul, *Sistemas de Gobierno*.
39   Esquit, "Nationalist Contradictions"; Cojtí Cuxil, "Politics of Mayan Revindication"; Raxche', "Maya Culture."
40   Herrera, "Racialized Illegality."
41   Estrada has estimated that half of Guatemalan migrants are Maya based on personal communications with both the Guatemalan embassy and grassroots organizations. See Estrada, "Ka Tzij" and "Ixoq tzi'j." In *Migranthood*, Heidbrink also notes that according to the Guatemalan government, 95 percent of minors ages birth to seventeen who are deported are Indigenous.
42   On language, see Peñalosa, "Trilingualism in the Barrio." On migration after state violence, see Foxen, *In Search of Providence*; Hagan, *Deciding to Be Legal*; Wellmeier, "Rituals of Resettlement." On economic and cultural practices in Los Angeles, see Popkin, "Guatemalan Mayan Migration to Los Angeles" and "Emergence of Pan-Mayan Ethnicity." Finally, on undocumented migrants, see Camayd-Freixas, "Interpreting After the Largest ICE Raid in US History"; Reynolds, "(Be)laboring Childhoods."
43   Loucky and Moors, *Mayan Diaspora*.
44   For critical reflections on these contradictions, see Batz, "Maya Cultural Resistance in Los Angeles"; López and Irrizary, "Somos pero no somos iguales"; Lopez, "CRT and Immigration." Other works have described the experiences of Mayas through a sociological lens; see, for example, O'Connor and Canizales, "Thresholds of Liminality"; Canizales, "American Individualism."
45   Barillas Chón, "K'iche', Mam, and Nahua Migrant Youth."
46   Estrada, "Ka Tzij," 213; Batz, "Maya Cultural Resistance in Los Angeles," 195.
47   LeBaron, "When Latinos Are Not Latinos"; Hiller et al., "I Am Maya."
48   Alberto, "Nations, Nationalisms, and Indígenas"; Chacón, "Metamestizaje."
49   Lytle Hernández, *City of Inmates*; Carpio, *Collisions at the Crossroads*.
50   Sepulveda, "Our Sacred Waters"; Lytle Hernández, *City of Inmates*.
51   Calderon, "Speaking Back to Manifest Destinies"; Rifkin, "Settler Common Sense."
52   International Mayan League, "Indigenous Peoples' Rights to Exist."
53   On Indigenous survivance, see Vizenor, *Manifest Manners*.
54   Turner, *This Is Not a Peace Pipe*.
55   Velásquez Nimatuj, "Memory/Memoir."
56   Wilson, *Research Is Ceremony*, 14.

57 Cadena, *Indigenous Mestizos*.
58 See Stoll, *Rigoberta Menchú*; Menchú, *I, Rigoberta Menchú*; Arias, "Rigoberta Menchú's History"; Nance, *Can Literature Promote Justice?*
59 Scholar-activist literature in anthropology has broadly challenged notions of objectivity, especially with respect to research about marginalized communities that face a disproportionate degree of violence and discrimination. These interventions recognize that knowledge production is fundamentally political. Mariana Mora's work on Kuxlejal politics with Zapatista communities recognizes that, when these communities set boundaries and procedures for research, they are acknowledging that dialogue, autonomy, and knowledge production are intertwined in such a fashion that all three take place at once during interviews with elders. In addition, Aída Hernández Castillo has critically acknowledged that her own work on the violence Indigenous women have faced under the rubric of "traditional" law was used by Mexican conservatives to argue that Indigenous communities should not have autonomy because they would violate the rights of women within the community. Hernández Castillo documents this as part of her conversation about thinking through the consequences of our research. Scholars like Aída Hernández Castillo, Shannon Speed, Mariana Mora, and Charles Hale have all advanced a critical conversation around research with Indigenous people caught in complex and ultimately repressive relationships with settler nations. See Hernández Castillo, "Indigeneity as a Field of Power"; Hale, "Rethinking Indigenous Politics"; Heidbrink, *Migranthood*; Mora, *Kuxlejal Politics*; Speed, *Incarcerated Stories*.
60 Tuck and Yang, "Decolonization Is Not a Metaphor."
61 Simpson, "On Ethnographic Refusal," 78; emphasis in the original.
62 Simpson, *As We Have Always Done*.
63 Arista, "Navigating Uncharted Oceans of Meaning."
64 Chacón, *Indigenous Cosmolectics*, 12.
65 In "Familia and Comunidad-Based Saberes," Luis Urrieta lays out how forms of teaching and learning within Indigenous heritage communities in Mexico are part of everyday life, involve various generations including small children, and create a social world that anchors children and youth to extended kinship networks and community.
66 Mixed methodology is typically defined as a mixture of quantitative and qualitative methods. Multimethod is a more accurate description of the approach I use in the book because I mix qualitative sociological methods with those of cultural studies and humanities. Rather than focus on one strictly defined method, I approach each set of oral histories and cultural objects to glean what they can say that has not already been said about the Maya diaspora. I analyze the cultural objects, the interviews, and their relationships to each other through an inductive method, and in each chapter I include a method section to more directly state how I

developed the methodology for that study. For more on multimethodology, see Brewer and Hunter, *Foundations of Multimethod Research*.
67 Batz, *Fourth Invasion*.
68 Gray and Gómez-Barris, *Toward a Sociology of the Trace*, viii.

Chapter One. Contesting the Logics of Displacement in the Production of the Indigenous Migrant

1 The Hague Convention on Protection of Children and Co-operation in Respect of Intercountry Adoption sets out parameters regarding international adoption that seek to curb child trafficking by ensuring that biological parents give consent to the adoption. While the United States signed the convention in 1994, implementation did not occur until April 2008. Articles of the convention can be found at the HCCH (Hague Conference on Private International Law) website, "Convention of 29 May 1993 on Protection of Children and Co-Operation in Respect of Intercountry Adoption": https://www.hcch.net/en/instruments/conventions/full-text/?cid=69.
2 Posocco, "On the Queer Necropolitics."
3 Rotabi et al., "International Child Adoption."
4 Rotabi and Bromfield, *From Intercountry Adoption to Global Surrogacy*, 66.
5 From this point forward I will use "Denese/Dominga" to refer to the protagonist of the documentary. Rather than privilege either "the American Denese" or "the Guatemalan Dominga," as she states in the film, I will use both to emphasize the reality of multiplicity and give space to the possibility that the two can remain distinct and yet connected as part of her experience. In her critique of how Chicana/o nationalism attempts to create resistance narratives through the practice of naming, Nicole Marie Guidotti-Hernández uses this strategy of double naming the historical figure of Josefa/Juanita because "by calling attention to all of Josefa/Juanita's names, we defy the practice of making her nameless and problematize the question of truth in historical scholarship" (Guidotti-Hernández, *Unspeakable Violence*, 43). Use of the name Denese/Dominga challenges the assumption that either name is her "real" name, because both names are inextricably tied to the macro processes and personal experiences that are part of her story.
6 In *Beyond Terror*, Elizabeth Swanson Goldberg argues that human rights films emerge in a post–World War II context to document extreme forms of political violence in order to direct international pressure toward stopping these forms of brutality. However, human rights films also make use of the documentary form, which Trinh T. Minh-Ha critiques as uniquely producing "a whole aesthetic of objectivity" grounded in "the power of the film to capture reality 'out there' for us 'in here.' The moment of ap-

7   Alsultany, "Arabs and Muslims in the Media." Alsultany's notion of simplified complex representations names how visual production attempts to produce a more progressive perspective of a marginalized community by offsetting negative portrayals of Arab/Muslim characters with positive or redeeming Arab/Muslim victims of discrimination. Alsultany argues that these characterizations may seem humanizing but often reinforce discourses of terrorism and security while simultaneously acknowledging that there will unfortunately be individual casualties of these discourses. She argues that "these representations often challenge or complicate earlier stereotypes yet contribute to a multicultural or postrace illusion" (162). I extend this analysis because Alsultany exemplifies the need to read beyond the narrative and images before us to see their implications for justifying structural issues even as they highlight the potential pitfalls of these policies and politics.

propriation and of consumption is either simply ignored or carefully rendered invisible according to the rules of good and bad documentary." Minh-Ha, "Documentary Is/Not a Name," 80.

8   Laplante, "Memory Battles," 621. Laplante meticulously charts the general strategy of denying genocide by reinforcing either that it was a time of war against communists (now labeled terrorists) or that, while crimes were committed, the charge of genocide is excessive — or worse, unfounded. Her case study for outlining what she terms "memory battles" is the court trial of Efraín Ríos Montt. Laplante privileges the courtroom, but other scholars on Guatemala and memory have emphasized the struggle over memory in terms of visual art (Hoelscher, "Angels of Memory"), linguistic practice among Ixil communities (García, "Long Count of Historical Memory"), and the existence of police archives (Lovell, "Archive That Never Was").

9   Estrada, "A'Co Nuq'."

10 For the Meskwaki's own account of their tribal history, which has been privileged here, please see Meskwaki Nation, "The Meskwaki Nation's History," https://www.meskwaki.org/history. Also see Zimmer, "Settlement Sovereignty" and "Building the Red Earth Nation." For other understandings of the Black Hawk War of 1832, see Hall, *Uncommon Defense*; Jung, "Black Hawk War (1832)" and *Black Hawk War of 1832*.

11 Rifkin, *Settler Common Sense*, xvi. Rifkin also goes on to argue that looking at the assumed absence of Native people allows us to conceptualize "indigeneity as a reservoir for signifiers of aberrance instead of as a potential challenge to the legitimacy of U.S. law and jurisdiction." This is especially critical to how we conceptualize transnational adoption as existing outside of the original genocide that gave way to the formation of the United States and that continues to wreak havoc on Native nations and communities today.

12 Estrada, "A'Co Nuq.'"
13 Rifkin, "Settler Common Sense," 331.
14 Briggs, *Somebody's Children*.
15 Briggs, "Mother, Child, Race, Nation."
16 Philips, "Indian Child Welfare Act in the Face of Extinction," 352.
17 Chinchilla et al., "Sanctuary Movement," 105.
18 It is important to note the ways that the growing literature around CASM has built on itself. Rossana Pérez and Henry A. J. Ramos's *Flight to Freedom* is critical here because their book contains primarily firsthand accounts of Central Americans involved in multiple aspects of these movements. In addition, recent research has begun to take up an especially useful framework focused on settler colonialism. The literature around this movement is still in formation and continuously sharpens its critiques and theoretical framing. See Nepstad, *Convictions of the Soul*; Stuelke, "Reparative Politics."
19 To learn more about the various entities that were involved in the Central American solidarity movement, their strategies, goals, and achievements, refer to Nepstad, *Convictions of the Soul*; Rodríguez, *Dividing the Isthmus*.
20 Nepstad, "Oppositional Consciousness," 666; Stuelke, "Reparative Politics," 768.
21 Here it is useful to turn to Sophia Villenas's "Latina Mothers and Small Town Racisms," in which she writes about the notion of "benevolent racisms" that are supposed to be distinct from hostile racism, yet do not challenge the structural racism that informs these seemingly inoffensive, yet deficit perspectives. She writes, "[Benevolent racism] was also more difficult to confront precisely because it was posed as a rational, humane, welcoming, and thus 'nonracist' response in comparison to the irrational, unwelcoming, and thus racist response of Hope City residents often referred to as 'small-town rednecks'" (9).
22 Tuck and Yang, "Decolonization Is Not a Metaphor."
23 Stuelke's "Reparative Politics," in particular, builds on Indigenous studies and examines a novel in which Maya refugees are asked (perhaps obligated) to play the role of Native American parents in order for the protagonist, a white lesbian US citizen, to be able to keep a Cherokee child as her adoptee. This novel exemplifies transborder anti-Indigenous politics in that it positions one Indigenous person as participating in the dispossession of Native people through the orchestrated stealing of a Native child.

Ana Patricia Rodríguez's work, "The Fiction of Solidarity," points to the appropriation of Central American diasporic narratives in the service of Chicana feminist agendas. While her work does not focus on Indigenous or Maya narratives, she highlights the tensions and failures that occur when a Chicana feminist lens is used to read Central American

24 experiences in the absence of a committed dialogue with Central American people themselves.
24 For more on Indigenous dispossession through adoption by white families, see Briggs, *Somebody's Children*, and Jacobs, *White Mother to a Dark Race*, which examine closely the adoption of Native children into white families as a strategy of colonization and dispossession.
25 Briggs, *Somebody's Children*, xx.
26 Stephen, *Transborder Lives*, 6.
27 Aguirre, "Chixoy Dam," 2; on the massacre, see Dill, "International Human Rights and Local Justice"; Pacenza, "A People Damned."
28 Way, *Mayan in the Mall*, 125.
29 Recent scholarship has applied settler colonial theory to Latin America generally and Guatemala in particular. The December 2017 special issue of *American Quarterly* on settler colonialism in Latin America featured an article by Shannon Speed in which she writes that to ignore the condition of Latin America as settler colonialism is to accept "the basic premise that the settler has settled, and is now from here, rather than acknowledging that there is a state of ongoing occupation, in Latin America as elsewhere in the hemisphere," Speed, "Structures of Settler Capitalism in Abya Yala" (786). In the same issue, Castro and Picq trace a clear historiography which demonstrates that on all sides of the political spectrum there has been a consistent project of territorial dispossession that marks a fundamental feature of settler colonialism. Part of the challenge here is to understand settler colonialism as a framework with specific characteristics that can be useful to analyzing issues across borders rather than to take it as coincidence that something like mass detention would take place just as there is an influx in Indigenous migrants being displaced from their ancestral territories. Castro and Picq, "Stateness as Landgrab."
30 Lytle Hernandez, *City of Inmates*, 4.
31 I would especially like to highlight the anthology coedited by Herman Gray and Macarena Gómez-Barris, *Toward a Sociology of the Trace*, because they "propose a sociology of the trace as a way to attenuate the distance between observable social worlds and those things that are not easily found through methodologies that attempt to empirically account for social reality" (5). A singular emphasis on the white gaze would also elide the ways in which these problematic representations are not fully determinant and how the glimpses into the connection to Maya activism can be important sites of analysis. My attempt to read these fleeting moments is an attempt to engage with the reality that, while this film circulates as human rights film, it also offers an opportunity for Mayas in the United States to reflect on the challenges they face in the diaspora.

Chapter Two. Weaving Maya Geographies, Textiles, and Relationality in Diaspora

1 I distinguish my research from most literature that focuses on issues of second-generation migrants by thinking about migration in relation to Indigeneity. Because immigration literature often thinks about generational issues in relation to socioeconomic mobility and integration, it often overlooks how Indigeneity plays a critical role in the way people conceptualize their transnational practices. While I occasionally use generational terminology like "second-generation" or "1.5 generation," these types of categories often diminish the possibilities of understanding the critical continuities that have enabled communities to survive colonialism for centuries. See Fernandez-Kelly and Curran, "Nicaraguans"; Portes and Rumbaut, *Legacies*; Portes and Zhou, "New Second Generation"; Rumbaut, "Crucible Within."

The term traje is popularly used in Guatemala and the diaspora, among Mayas and non-Mayas alike, to refer to traditional Indigenous clothing. The shift to "regional clothing" or "Maya clothing" marks an ongoing conversation among scholars and activists who challenge the folklorization of Maya culture. The concern revolves around how English translations of traje as traditional clothing do not clearly articulate the diversity of textiles that exists, the textiles' relationship to particular geographic and regional areas, and their specificity to the Maya experience. In this chapter, I use the term traje when my interview participants specifically used that term but use *regional clothing* or *Maya clothing* when using my own words. My desire not to change interviewees' wording is grounded in my respect for their words, because political consciousness is a lifelong process that not everyone begins at the same time or in the same way. I preserve their words to honor that our elders and youth are incredible sites of strength and knowledge who live Indigeneity in the everyday, and their words are part of how they share their knowledge with the world.

2 Tejada, "Transplanting the Organizing Seed"; Levitt and Schiller, "Conceptualizing Simultaneity"; Espiritu, *Home Bound*.

3 These sites of terror from the war saturate what look like normal sites, so this is not an uncommon occurrence. Given the discussion in the introduction, similar sites of terror from the colonial invasion to now could be considered the same way.

4 Ramírez, "Mercedes Coroy."

5 See O'Brien, *Firsting and Lasting*; Rifkin, *Settler Common Sense*.

6 In "We Are Not Dreamers," Leisy J. Abrego and Genevieve Negrón-Gonzales note that even undocumented youth (part of the 1.5 generation) experience different social and political realities from their parents. According to these authors, this experience often changes once youth turn eighteen and find that both legal labor and financial support for college

are foreclosed because of their status. In addition, in "Speaking Back to Manifest Destinies," Dolores Calderon argues that because public education reinforces settler colonial history and politics, these youth are exposed to settler colonial logics in ways that differ from adults' experiences.

7   Grandin, *Blood of Guatemala*, 6; Otzoy, "Maya Clothing and Identity."
8   Arroyo Calderón, "Racismo y desvalrización."
9   See Carey and Torres, "Precursors to Femicide"; Musalo and Bookey, "Crimes Without Punishment"; Velasco, "Guatemalan Femicide"; Fregoso and Bejarano, *Terrorizing Women*. For more on femicide in the Guatemalan context, see Godoy-Paiz, "Not Just 'Another Woman'"; Hartviksen, "Towards a Historical Materialist Analysis." For a regional analysis on femicides in Central America, see Prieto-Carrón et al., "No More Killings!" These studies point to femicide as a growing crisis grounded in a continuing mindset of disposability that works disproportionately to eliminate poor and Indigenous people.
10 Velásquez Nimatuj, "Transnationalism and Maya Dress," 526.
11 Barrios Escobar and Cap Sir, "Formas de discriminación."
12 Velásquez Nimatuj, "Transnationalism and Maya Dress," 527–28.
13 Chacón, "Material Culture," 54.
14 World Bank, "Guatemala."
15 Bobb, "Proenza Schouler Alum." Backstrap loom weaving is a precolonial method of producing textiles where the weaver kneels on the ground and uses the tension created between a tree and their back to produce the weaving.
16 Chacón, "Material Culture," 66.
17 Guzmán Bockler and Herbert, *Guatemala*, 117. Christopher Loperena's *Ends of Paradise* highlights the Indigenous territorial dispossession that occurs when nations rely on tourism through the case study of contemporary land struggles on Garifuna territory in Honduras.
18 Varagur, "Mexico Prevents." Since the writing of this chapter, Maya women have formed the Movimiento Nacional de Tejedoras—Ruchajixik ri qana'ojb'äl (National Movement of Weavers). On February 23, 2017, they presented Initiative 5247, which would create a series of reforms and procedures that guarantee a collective patrimony for Maya women in relation to their textiles. Check their Facebook page for the most up-to-date information on this initiative and their public demonstrations.
19 Equipo de Estudios, *Tejidos que lleva el alma*.
20 Barillas Chón, "Indigenous Immigrant Youth's Understandings of Power."
21 This resembles the process that Lisa Cacho argues is part of producing the immigrant as contradictory to lawfulness in *Social Death*.
22 Castañeda et al., "Mexicanization."
23 Batz, "Maya Cultural Resistance in Los Angeles," 199.
24 In relation to Hmong story cloths, Viet Nguyen comments, "For refugees, the imagination of past, present, and future countries can occur si-

multaneously, in refusal of the progressive notion of time that belongs to the nation, marching relentlessly from past to future," Nguyen, "Refugee Memories," 934.

25 Nicolas, "Pertenencia Mutua"; Urrieta, "Diasporic Community Smartness."
26 Boj Lopez, "Maya Youth and Cultural Sustainability."
27 Harman, *Aging and Intergenerational Relations*.
28 Boj Lopez, "Weavings That Rupture."
29 Macleod, "Mayan Dress as Text," 682–83.
30 Estrada, "Reclaiming Public Space."
31 Macleod, "Mayan Dress as Text."
32 Otzoy, "Maya Clothing and Identity," 144.
33 Vizenor, *Manifest Manners*.
34 Byrd, *Transit of Empire*.
35 Saranillio, "Colliding Histories," 304.
36 Goeman, *Mark My Words*, 12.
37 Lourdes Alberto and María Eugenia Cotera and María Josefina Saldaña-Portillo, among others, have pointed out that making claims premised on generic understandings of Indigeneity can perpetuate erasures. See Alberto, "Topographies of Indigenism"; Cotera and Saldaña-Portillo, "Indigenous But Not Indian?"
38 Tuck and Yang, "Decolonization Is Not a Metaphor," 21.

Chapter Three. La Comunidad Ixim and Organizing in the Maya Diaspora

1 For examples of the former scholarship, see Williams et al., *A Place to Be*; Wellmeier, "Santa Eulalia's People in Exile."
2 For example, Shannon Speed argued that the Mexican state project of erasure through assimilation in the early twentieth century worked through shrinking the Indigenous community by only identifying those that speak a Maya language and wear Maya clothing as Indigenous. She writes, "From the perspective of those in power, a homogenous, modern Mexican population was required. The disappearance of Indigenous peoples though the manipulation of census data was but one means to achieve that end" (Speed, *Incarcerated Stories*, 96).
3 In *City of Inmates*, Kelly Lytle Hernández effectively argues that the criminalization of so-called vagrants is tied to their inability to form nuclear families that would support the project of private property.
4 Guzmán Bockler and Herbert, *Guatemala*.
5 Hale, *Más Que Un Indio*. Note that other works about Guatemala's history also point to *Ladino* as being a term anchored in Jewish identity (see Martínez Salzar, *Global Coloniality*) and as being used to include nonwhite racial others such as mixed-race and Black people (see Gudmunson and Wolfe, *Blacks and Blackness in Central America*).

6   On localized understandings of Indigeneity, see Grandin, *Blood of Guatemala*; on the Maya movement, see Montejo, *Maya Intellectual Renaissance*.
7   Scholars like Audra Simpson remind us that political sovereignty reflects a system of governance that Native and First Nations people ardently protect because it is the bedrock on which they understand and defend themselves. She poignantly argues against cultural recognition and multicultural inclusion and uplifts how Mohawks of Kahnawà:ke refuse US and Canadian citizenship. On the other hand, scholars like Jennifer Nez Denetdale note that nationhood was a foreign form of political organization for Navajo people, producing a new set of challenges when the nation coheres around a masculine, heteronormative, patriarchal figure or organizational structure like the nuclear family. Indigenous collectives have engaged such a wide array of responses in diverse historical contexts that it becomes necessary to be specific rather than make broad statements about Indigenous belonging. At the same time, given the propensity of some white people to falsely claim Indigeneity when they have neither living relationships to the people nor any documented lineage, it can also be irresponsible to uphold ideas of self-identification or self-Indigenization. In this discourse, Kim TallBear's work is central. For scholars in Native and Indigenous studies, especially for those who write about diasporas and want to be responsive to both systems of belonging from our homelands and the places we arrive to, it is important to be aware of this complex landscape. See Simpson, *Mohawk Interruptus*; Denetdale, "Return"; TallBear, "Indigenous Genocide."
8   One clear example of this is the Q'eqchi' struggle over Agua Caliente near Lake Izabal that the Goldman Environmental Prize campaign documented when they awarded Rodrigo Tot the prize in 2017. The video shows that the documents recording Indigenous land titles had been torn out of the official land registry so that the land could be permitted to a nickel-mining company. See https://www.goldmanprize.org/recipient/rodrigo-tot/.
9   Recovery of Historical Memory Project, *Guatemala: Never Again!*, 37.
10 Pidduck, "Queer Kinship and Ambivalence," 444.
11 Vera-Rosa, "Breaking and Remaking of Everyday Life," 3.
12 Burns, *Maya in Exile*.
13 Lutz and Lovell, "Survivors on the Move"; Batz, "Ixil Maya Resistance."
14 Mattiace and Loret de Mola, "Yucatec Maya Organizations," 210.
15 "Xinachtli Profile," accessed August 1, 2015, formerly at https://callink.berkeley.edu/organization/xinaxtli/about.
16 See Nicholls, *DREAMers*, and for an important intervention into this discourse from the standpoint of undocumented people themselves, see Abrego and Negrón-Gonzales, *We Are Not Dreamers*.
17 Ramirez, *Native Hubs*.
18 Alvarado Cifuentes, "Our Skins," 18.

19 Finley, "Decolonizing the Queer Native Body," 34.
20 Byrd, "What's Normative Got to Do with It?," 105.
21 Nguyen, "Minor Threats," 15.
22 Hunt, "Ontologies of Indigeneity," 31.
23 Vera-Rosas, "Regarding 'the Mother of Anchor-Children'"; Parreñas, *Children of Global Migration*; Abrego, *Sacrificing Families*.
24 Giovanni Batz correlates the self-identification of some Maya youth as Latina/o or Hispanic with "parents [who] may themselves feel ashamed of being Maya and see no value in teaching their children an Indigenous culture. Discrimination within the Guatemalan community contributes to this attitude, and so does daily life in Los Angeles neighborhoods." Batz, "Maya Cultural Resistance in Los Angeles," 203.
25 Loucky, *Maya in a Modern Metropolis*, 214.
26 Otzoy, "Maya Clothing and Identity."

Chapter Four. Returning the Gaze, Reclaiming the Image

1 While the June 2017 *Look Magazine* cover was concerning because of its composition, the business model for Francesca Kennedy's company, IX Style, is a social enterprise that attempts to value textiles, and by extension, the labor of Maya women differently. In exchange for textiles, Kennedy both pays the weavers and supplies them with water filters because local sources of water that families rely on have been contaminated. We have to look at companies and business models like these as a symptom of the historical and utter neglect faced by Maya families: Their participation in such enterprises is never equitable, yet it is preferable to not having clean drinking water. One of the primary polluters of local water sources near Atitlán are the hotels, one of which is owned by Francesca Kennedy's parents. In addition, her mother is Guatemalan, and Kennedy has dual citizenship.
2 Kency Cornejo's *Visual Disobedience* argues that one of the moves that produce visual coloniality is "visual thingification," which includes "the colonialist practice of fabricating visual evidence for the dehumanization of the colonized through a series of negations for the purpose of justifying elimination" (22–23).
3 The Asociación Femenina para el Desarrollo de Sacatepequez (AFEDES) has self-published a book that discusses the roots of these issues, the development of their movement, the political strategy they have utilized, and the barriers and challenges they have faced. In this text is a section on the limits of current Guatemalan constitutional law and their approach to overcome them. AFEDES, *Nuestro Tejidos*.
4 López, "Mujeres tejedoras."
5 Las Fotos Project, "About Us," accessed December 12, 2021, https://www.lasfotosproject.org/about.

6   Las Fotos Project, Exhibition Archives, Maya Womxn in L.A., 2018, https://www.lasfotosproject.org/exhibition-archives/project-four-mdxm3.
7   In "Photography and Critical Heritage," Jane Lydon insightfully draws our attention to the way photography can create an opportunity for reconnection if it revisits the conditions of separation, stolen generations, and forcible assimilation.
8   Amy Lonetree's "Heritage of Resilience" is an excellent example of the power of visual archives that become "archives of resilience." Critical to her understanding is that this archive was not intended to be an ethnographic accounting of a vanishing race, like Edward Curtis's photographs, but instead were paid studio portraits that showed the range and intergenerational strength of Ho-Chunk people who made the choice to have their photos taken.
9   Cornejo, *Visual Disobedience*, 23.
10 Chacón, *Indigenous Cosmolectics*, 17.
11 López Oro, "Digitizing Ancestral Memory," 173–74.
12 Various communities annually elect a young woman or girl as the representative for their community. Each community has its own name and process for doing so, and many diasporic communities continue this practice.
13 Alberto, "Coming Out as Indian" 248.
14 Stephens and Pastor, "What's Going On?"
15 Boj Lopez, "Contesting Exclusion and Erasure."
16 Speed, *Incarcerated Stories*.
17 Speed, *Incarcerated Stories*, 8; emphasis in the original.
18 Sanchez, *Children of Solaga*, 175.

Conclusion

1   Urrieta, "Indigenous Reflections," 10.
2   Sepulveda, "Our Sacred Waters," 54.
3   Hernández Castillo, "Indigeneity as a Field of Power."

Bibliography

Abrego, Leisy J. *Sacrificing Families: Navigating Laws, Labor, and Love Across Borders*. Stanford, CA: Stanford University Press, 2014.

Abrego, Leisy J., and Genevieve Negrón-Gonzales, eds. *We Are Not Dreamers: Undocumented Scholars Theorize Undocumented Life in the United States*. Durham, NC: Duke University Press, 2020.

Acosta, Oscar Zeta. *The Revolt of the Cockroach People*. New York: Vintage Books, 1973.

Adams-Campbell, Melissa, Ashley Glassburn Falzetti, and Courtney Rivard. "Introduction: Indigeneity and the Work of Settler Archives." *Settler Colonial Studies* 5, no. 2 (2015): 109–16. https://doi.org/10.1080/2201473X.2014.957256.

AFEDES (Asociación Femenina para el Desarrollo de Sacatepequez). *Nuestro tejidos son los libros que la colonia no pudo quemar: El camino del Movimiento Nacional de Tejedoras Mayas de Guatemala*. Guatemala: Tujaal Ediciones, 2020.

Aguirre, Monti. "Chixoy Dam." Carnegie Council for Ethics in International Affairs. *Human Rights Dialogue* ser. 2, no. 11 (2004). https://www.carnegiecouncil.org/media/series/dialogue/human-rights-dialogue-1994-2005-series-2-no-11-spring-2004-environmental-rights-online-exclusives-interview-with-cristobal-osorio-sanchez.

Alberto, Lourdes. "Coming Out as Indian: On Being an Indigenous Latina in the US." *Latino Studies* 15 (2017): 247–53.

Alberto, Lourdes. "Nations, Nationalisms, and Indígenas: The 'Indian' in the Chicano Revolutionary Imaginary." *Critical Ethnic Studies* 2, no. 1 (2016): 107–27.

Alberto, Lourdes. "Topographies of Indigenism: Mexico, Decolonial Indigenism, and the Chicana Transnational Subject in Ana Castillo's Mixquiahuala Letters." In *Comparative Indigeneities of the Américas: Toward a Hemispheric Approach*, edited by M. Bianet Castellanos, Lourdes Gutiérrez Nájera, and Arturo J. Aldama. Tucson: University of Arizona Press, 2012.

Alma, Karina. *Central American Counterpoetics: Diaspora and Rememory*. Tucson: University of Arizona Press, 2024.

Alsultany, Evelyn. "Arabs and Muslims in the Media after 9/11: Representational Strategies for a 'Postrace' Era." *American Quarterly* 65, no. 1 (2013): 161–69.

Alvarado, Karina. "Cultural Memory and Making by US Central Americans." *Latino Studies* 15, no. 4 (2017): 476–97. https://doi.org/10.1057/s41276-017-0093-8.

Alvarado Cifuentes, Mario [Mac]. "Our Skins: Critical Maya Aesthetics as Resistance to the Cisgender Heteronormative Binary." PhD diss., University of California, Los Angeles. https://escholarship.org/uc/item/48s8778f.

Appadurai, Arjun. "Archive and Aspiration." In *Information Is Alive*, edited by Joke Brouwer and Arjen Mulder, 14–25. Rotterdam: N2_Publishing/NAI Publishers.

Arias, Arturo. "Rigoberta Menchú's History Within the Guatemalan Context." In *The Rigoberta Menchú Controversy*, edited by Arturo Arias and David Stoll. Minneapolis: University of Minnesota Press, 2001.

Arista, Noelani. 2010. "Navigating Uncharted Oceans of Meaning: *Kaona* as Historical and Interpretive Method." *PMLA: Publications of the Modern Language Association of America* 125, no. 3: 663–69. https://doi.org/10.1632/pmla.2010.125.3.663.

Arroyo Calderón, Patricia. Racismo y desvalorización del trabajo de las mujeres indígenas en Guatemala: Desde la economía doméstica hasta el Caso Sepur Zarco. *EntreDiversidades: Revista de Ciencias Sociales y Humanidades* 7, no. 2 (2020): 94–126.

Barillas Chón, David W. "Indigenous Immigrant Youth's Understandings of Power: Race, Labor, and Language." *Critical Latinx Indigeneities and Education* 13, no. 2 (2019): 15–41. https:doi.org/10.24974/amae.13.2.427.

Barillas Chón, David W. "K'iche', Mam, and Nahua Migrant Youth Navigating Colonial Codes of Power." *Urban Education* 59, no. 4 (2024): 1224–51. https://doi.org/10.1177/00420859211073902.

Barrios Escobar, Lina Eugenia, and Lilia Irene Cap Sir. "Formas de discriminación por el uso del traje maya en campus central y centros universitarios de Quetzaltenango y Chimaltenango de la Universidad de San Carlos de Guatemala USAC." Final report. Universidad de San Carlos de Guatemala, Instituto de Estudios Interétnicos, November 2015. http://www.repositorio.usac.edu.gt/4793/1/INF-2015-12.pdf.

Batz, Giovanni. *The Fourth Invasion: Decolonizing Histories, Extractivism, and Maya Resistance in Guatemala*. Oakland: University of California Press, 2024.

Batz, Giovanni. "Guatemala's Democracy in Tatters." *NACLA Report on the Americas* 55, no. 2 (2023): 110–13. https://doi.org/10.1080/10714839.2023.2213048.

Batz, Giovanni, "Ixil Maya Resistance Against Megaprojects in Cotzal, Guatemala." *Theory and Event* 23, no. 4 (2020): 1016–36.

Batz, Giovanni. "The Ixil University and the Decolonization of Knowledge." In *Indigenous and Decolonizing Studies in Education: Mapping the Long View*, edited by Linda Tuhiwai Smith, Eve Tuck, and K. Wayne Yang. New York: Routledge, 2019.

Batz, Giovanni. "Maya Cultural Resistance in Los Angeles: The Recovery of

Identity and Culture Among Maya Youth." *Latin American Perspectives* 14, no. 3 (2014): 194–207. https://doi.org/10.1177/0094582X14531727.

Beverly, John. "The Margin at the Center: On Testimonio." In *The Real Thing: Testimonial Discourse and Latin America*, edited by George M. Gugelberger. Durham, NC: Duke University Press, 1996.

Bobb, Brooke. "A Proenza Schouler Alum Launches a Line Made from Traditional Guatemalan Textiles." *New York Times*, August 27, 2014. https://archive.nytimes.com/tmagazine.blogs.nytimes.com/2014/08/27/caroline-fuss-harare-proenza-schouler-alum-fashion-line-made-from-traditional-guatemalan-textiles/.

Boj Lopez, Floridalma. "Contesting Exclusion and Erasure: The Educational Experiences of Guatemalans in Los Angeles." *Latin American Research Review* 61, no. 2 (2026).

Boj Lopez, Floridalma. "Maya Youth and Cultural Sustainability in the United States." In *Latinos and Latinas at Risk: Issues in Education, Health, Community, and Justice*, edited by Gabriel Gutiérrez. Santa Barbara, CA: Greenwood, 2015.

Boj Lopez, Floridalma. "Weavings That Rupture: The Possibility of Contesting Settler Colonialism Through Cultural Retention Among the Maya Diaspora." In *U.S. Central Americans: Reconstructing Memories, Struggles, and Communities of Resistance*, edited by Alicia Ivonne Estrada, Ester Hernández, and K. Oliva-Alvarado. Tucson: University of Arizona Press, 2017.

Bradley, Harriet. "The Seductions of the Archive: Voices Lost and Found." *History of the Human Sciences* 12, no. 2 (1999): 107–22. https://doi.org/10.1177/09526959922120270.

Brewer, John, and Albert Hunter. *Foundations of Multimethod Research*. Thousand Oaks, CA: Sage, 2005.

Briggs, Laura. "Mother, Child, Race, Nation: The Visual Iconography of Rescue and the Politics of Transnational and Transracial Adoption." *Gender and History* 15, no. 2 (2003): 179–200. https://doi.org/10.1111/1468-0424.00298.

Briggs, Laura. *Somebody's Children: The Politics of Transracial and Transnational Adoption*. Durham, NC: Duke University Press, 2012.

Burns, Allan F. *Maya in Exile: Guatemalans in Florida*. Philadelphia: Temple University Press, 1993.

Byrd, Jodi. A. *Transit of Empire: Indigenous Critiques of Colonialism*. Minneapolis: University of Minnesota Press, 2011.

Byrd, Jodi A. "What's Normative Got to Do with It? Towards Indigenous Queer Relationality." *Social Text* 38, no. 4 (2020): 105–23.

Cacho, Lisa Marie. *Social Death: Racialized Rightlessness and the Criminalization of the Unprotected*. New York: New York University Press, 2012.

Cadena, Marisol de la. *Indigenous Mestizos: The Politics of Race and Culture in Cuzco, Peru, 1919–1991*. Durham, NC: Duke University Press, 2000.

Calderon, Dolores. "Speaking Back to Manifest Destinies: A Land Education-

Based Approach to Critical Curriculum Inquiry." *Environmental Education Research* 20, no. 1 (2014): 24–36. https://doi.org/10.1080/13504622.2013.865114.

Camayd-Freixas, Erik. "Interpreting After the Largest ICE Raid in US History." In *Behind Bars: Latino/as and Prison in the United States*, edited by Suzanne Oboler. New York: Palgrave Macmillan, 2009. https://doi.org/10.1057/9780230101470_10.

Canizales, Stephanie L. "American Individualism and the Social Incorporation of Unaccompanied Guatemalan Maya Young Adults in Los Angeles." *Ethnic and Racial Studies* 38, no. 10 (2015): 1831–47.

Cárcamo, Jennifer, dir. *Los Eternos Indocumentados*, 2018. Film. Accessed March 15, 2025. https://eternosindocumentados.com.

Card, Claudia. "Genocide and Social Death." *Hypatia* 18, no. 1 (2003): 63–79. https://doi.org/10.1111/j.1527-2001.2003.tb00779.x.

Carey, David, Jr., and M. Lisa Torres. "Precursors to Femicide: Guatemalan Women in a Vortex of Violence." *Latin American Research Review* 45, no. 3 (2010): 142–64.

Carpio, Genevieve. *Collisions at the Crossroads: How Place and Mobility Make Race*. Berkeley: University of California Press, 2019.

Carpio, Genevieve. "Tales from the Rebel Archive: History as Subversive Practice at California's Margins." *Southern California Quarterly* 102, no. 1 (2020): 57–79.

Carrie Ellison, Treva. 2019. "Black Femme Praxis and the Promise of Black Gender." *Black Scholar* 49, no. 1: 6–16.

Castañeda, Xóchitl, Beatriz Manz, and Allison Davenport. "Mexicanization: A Survival Strategy for Guatemalan Mayans in the San Francisco Bay Area." *Migraciones Internacionales* 1, no. 3 (2002): 103–23.

Castro, Juan, and Manuela Lavinas Picq. "Stateness as Landgrab: A Political History of Maya Dispossession in Guatemala." *American Quarterly* 69, no. 4 (2017): 791–99. https://doi.org/10.1353/aq.2017.0065.

Chacón, Gloria E. *Indigenous Cosmolectics: Kab'awil and the Making of Maya and Zapotec Literatures*. Chapel Hill: University of North Carolina Press, 2018.

Chacón, Gloria E. "Material Culture, Indigeneity, and Temporality: The Textile as Legal Subject." *Textual Cultures: Text, Contexts, Interpretation* 13, no. 2 (2020): 49–69.

Chacón, Gloria E. "Metamestizaje and the Narration of Political Movements from the South." *Latino Studies* 15, no. 2 (2017): 182–200. https://doi.org/10.1057/s41276-017-0062-2.

Chinchilla, Norma Stoltz, Nora HaMateo, and James Louky. "The Sanctuary Movement and Central American Activism in Los Angeles." *Latin American Perspectives* 36, no. 6 (2009): 101–26.

Cojtí Cuxil, Demetrio. "The Politics of Mayan Revindication." In *Maya Cultural Activism in Guatemala*, edited by Edward F. Fischer and R. McKenna Brown. Austin: University of Texas Press, 1996. https://www.jstor.org/stable/10.7560/708501.

Comisión para el Esclarecimiento Histórico. *Guatemala, Memory of Silence: Tz'inil Na'tab'al*. Report of the Commission for Historical Clarification, Conclusions and Recommendations. Guatemala: CEH, 1998.

Cornejo, Kency. *Visual Disobedience: Art and Decoloniality in Central America*. Duke University Press, 2024.

Cotera, María Eugenia. "Unpacking Our Mothers' Libraries: Practices of Chicana Memory Before and After the Digital Turn." In *Chicana Movidas: New Narratives of Activism and Feminism in the Movement Era*, edited by Dionne Espinoza, María Eugenia Cotera, and Maylei Blackwell. Austin: University of Texas Press, 2018.

Cotera, María Eugenia, and María Josefina Saldaña-Portillo. "Indigenous But Not Indian? Chicana/os and the Politics of Indigeneity." In *The World of Indigenous North America*, edited by Robert Warrior. New York: Routledge, 2015.

De León, Jason, with Michael Wells, photographer. *The Land of Open Graves: Living and Dying on the Migrant Trail*. Berkeley: University of California Press, 2015.

Denetdale, Jennifer Nez. "Return to 'The Uprising at Beautiful Mountain in 1913': Marriage and Sexuality in the Making of the Modern Navajo Nation." In *Critically Sovereign: Indigenous Gender, Sexuality, and Feminist Studies*, edited by Joanne Barker. Durham, NC: Duke University Press, 2017.

Derrida, Jacques. *Archive Fever: A Freudian Impression*. Translated by Eric Prenowitz. Chicago: University of Chicago Press, 1998.

Dill, Kathleen. "International Human Rights and Local Justice in Guatemala: The Rio Negro (Pak'oxom) and Agua Fria Trials." *Cultural Dynamics* 17, no. 3 (2005): 323–50. https://doi.org/10.1177/0921374005061993.

Equipo de Estudios Comunitarios y Acción Psicosocial. *Tejidos que lleva el alma: Memoria de las mujeres maya sobrevivientes de violación sexual durante el conflicto armado*. Guatemala: ECAP, 2009.

Espiritu, Yen Le. *Home Bound: Filipino American Lives Across Cultures, Communities, and Countries*. Berkeley: University of California Press, 2003.

Esquit, Edgar. "Nationalist Contradictions: Pan-Mayanism, Representations of the Past, and the Reproduction of Inequalities in Guatemala." In *Decolonizing Native Histories: Collaboration, Knowledge, and Language in the Americas*, edited by Florencia E. Mallon. Durham, NC: Duke University Press, 2012. https://doi.org/10.1515/9780822394853-009.

Estrada, Alicia Ivonne. "'A'Co Nuq': Maya Women in Post-1996 Guatemalan Cinematic Productions." *Istmo: Revista Virtual de Estudios Literarios y Culturales Centroamericanos* 13 (2006).

Estrada, Alicia Ivonne. "Ixoq tzi'j: palabra y cuerpo en La rueda de Maya Cú Choc." *Revista Canadiense de Estudios Hispánicos* 39, no. 1 (2014): 147–63. https://www.jstor.org/stable/24388800.

Estrada, Alicia Ivonne. "Ka Tzij: The Maya Diasporic Voices from Contacto Ancestral." *Latino Studies* 11, no. 2 (2013): 208–27. https://doi.org/10.1057/lst.2013.5.

Estrada, Alicia Ivonne. "Reclaiming Public Space and Place: Maya Community Formation in Westlake/MacArthur Park." In *U.S. Central Americans: Reconstructing Memories, Struggles, and Communities of Resistance*, edited by Karin Alvarado, Alicia Ivonne Estrada, and Ester Hernández. Tucson: University of Arizona Press, 2017.

Featherstone, Mike. "Archive." *Theory, Culture and Society* 23, no. 2–3 (2006): 591–96. https://doi.org/10.1177/0263276406023002106.

Fernandez-Kelly, Patricia, and Sara Curran. "Nicaraguans: Voices Lost, Voices Found." In *Ethnicities: Children of Immigrants in America*, edited by R. G. Rumbaut and A. Portes. Berkeley: University of California Press, 2001.

Finley, Chris. "Decolonizing the Queer Native Body (and Recovering the Native Bull-Dyke): Bringing 'Sexy Back' and Out of Native Studies' Closet." In *Queer Indigenous Studies: Critical Interventions in Theory, Politics, and Literature*, edited by Qwo-Li Driskill, Chris Finley, Brian Joseph Gilley, and Scott Lauria Morgensen. Tucson: University of Arizona Press, 2011.

Flynn, Patricia, dir. *Discovering Dominga: A Survivor's Story*. Film. Berkeley, CA: Berkeley Media, 2003.

Foxen, Patricia. *In Search of Providence: Transnational Mayan Identities*. Nashville, TN: Vanderbilt University Press, 2008.

Fregoso, Rosa-Linda, and Cynthia Bejarano. *Terrorizing Women: Feminicide in the Americas*. Durham, NC: Duke University Press, 2010.

García, María Luz. "The Long Count of Historical Memory: Ixihl Mayan Ceremonial Speech in Guatemala." *American Ethnologist* 41, no. 4 (2014): 664–80.

Global Witness. "Enemies of the State?" July 30, 2019. https://www.globalwitness.org/en/campaigns/environmental-activists/enemies-state/.

Godoy-Paiz, Paula. "Not Just 'Another Woman': Femicide and Representation in Guatemala." *Journal of Latin American and Caribbean Anthropology* 17, no. 1 (2012): 88–109. https://doi.org/10.1111/j.1935-4940.2012.01192.x.

Goeman, Mishuana. *Mark My Words: Native Women Mapping Our Nations*. Minneapolis: University of Minnesota Press, 2013.

Goldberg, Elizabeth Swanson. *Beyond Terror: Gender, Narrative, Human Rights*. New Brunswick, NJ: Rutgers University Press, 2007.

Goldman Environmental Prize. *Rodrigo Tot: 2017 Goldman Environmental Prize Winner*. https://www.goldmanprize.org/recipient/rodrigo-tot/.

Grandia, Liza. "Road Mapping: Megaprojects and Land Grabs in the Northern Guatemalan Lowlands." *Development and Change* 44, no. 2 (2013): 233–59. https://doi.org/10.1111/dech.12020.

Grandin, Greg. *The Blood of Guatemala: A History of Race and Nation*. Durham, NC: Duke University Press, 2000.

Gray, Herman, and Macarena Gómez-Barris, eds. *Toward a Sociology of the Trace*. Minneapolis: University of Minnesota Press, 2010.

Gudmundson, Lowell, and Justin Wolfe, eds. *Blacks and Blackness in Central America: Between Race and Place*. Durham, NC: Duke University Press, 2010.

Guidotti-Hernández, Nicole Marie. *Unspeakable Violence: Remapping U.S. and Mexican National Imaginaries.* Durham, NC: Duke University Press, 2011.

Guzmán Bockler, Carlos, and Jean-Loup Herbert. *Guatemala: Una interpretación histórico-social.* Guatemala: Cholsamaj, 1975.

Hagan, Jacqueline Maria. *Deciding to Be Legal: A Maya Community in Houston.* Philadelphia: Temple University Press, 1994.

Hale, Charles. *Más que un indio (More Than an Indian): Racial Ambivalence and the Paradox of Neoliberal Multiculturalism in Guatemala.* Santa Fe, NM: School of American Research Press, 2006.

Hale, Charles. "Rethinking Indigenous Politics in the Era of the 'Indio Permitido.'" NACLA *Report on the Americas* 38, no. 2 (2004): 16–21. https://doi.org/10.1080/10714839.2004.11724509.

Hall, John W. *Uncommon Defense: Indian Allies in the Black Hawk War.* Cambridge, MA: Harvard University Press, 2009.

Hall, Stuart. "Cultural Identity and Diaspora." In *Colonial Discourse and Post-Colonial Theory,* edited by Patrick Williams and Laura Chrisman. London: Routledge, 2015.

Harman, Robert. "Intergenerational Relations Among Maya in Los Angeles." In *Selected Papers on Refugee Issues,* vol. 4, edited by Anne M. Rynearson and James Phillips. Arlington, VA: American Anthropological Association, 1996.

Hartman, Saidiya. *Lose Your Mother: A Journey Along the Atlantic Slave Route.* New York: Farrar, Straus and Giroux, 2008.

Hartviksen, Julia. "Towards a Historical Materialist Analysis of Femicide in Post-Conflict Guatemala." Master's thesis, Queen's University, 2014.

Heidbrink, Lauren. "The Coercive Power of Debt: Migration and Deportation of Guatemalan Indigenous Youth." *Journal of Latin American and Caribbean Anthropology* 24, no. 1 (2019): 263–81. https://doi.org/10.1111/jlca.12385.

Heidbrink, Lauren. *Migranthood: Youth in a New Era of Deportation.* Stanford, CA: Stanford University Press, 2020.

Hernández, Ester. "Remembering Through Cultural Interventions: Mapping Central Americans in L.A. Public Spaces." In *U.S. Central Americans: Reconstructing Memories, Struggles, and Communities of Resistance,* edited by Karina O. Alvarado, Alicia Ivonne Estrada, and Ester E. Hernández. Tucson: University of Arizona Press, 2017.

Hernández Castillo, R. Aída. "Indigeneity as a Field of Power: Multiculturalism and Indigenous Identities in Political Struggles." In *The SAGE Handbook of Identities,* edited by Margaret Wetherell and Chandra Talpade Mohanty. Los Angeles: Sage, 2010. https://dx.doi.org/10.4135/9781446200889.n21.

Herrera, Juan. "Racialized Illegality: The Regulation of Informal Labor and Space." *Latino Studies* 14, no. 3 (2016): 320–43. https://doi.org/10.1057/s41276-016-0007-1.

Hiller, Patrick T., J. P. Linstroth, and Paloma Ayala Vela. "'I Am Maya, Not Guatemalan, Nor Hispanic'—The Belongingness of Mayas in Southern Florida." *Forum: Qualitative Social Research* 10, no. 3 (2009): Article 10. https://doi.org/10.17169/fqs-10.3.1361.

Hinojosa, Alana de. "El Rio Grande as Unruly Archive: Submerged Histories of the Chamizal Dispute." Thesis, University of California, Los Angeles, 2017.

Hoelscher, Steven. "Angels of Memory: Photography and Haunting in Guatemala City." *GeoJournal* 73, no. 3 (2008): 195–217. https://doi.org/10.1007/s10708-008-9203-3.

Hunt, Sarah. "Ontologies of Indigeneity: The Politics of Embodying a Concept." *Cultural Geographies* 21, no. 1 (2013): 27–32. https://doi.org/10.1177/1474474013500226.

Hunt, Sarah. "Violence, Law and the Everyday Politics of Recognition." Paper presented at the Native American and Indigenous Studies Association (NAISA), Washington, DC, June 4–6, 2015.

International Mayan League. "Indigenous Peoples' Rights to Exist, Self Determination, Language and Due Process in Migration," Accessed September 23, 2022. https://www.mayanleague.org/indigenous-peoples-rights-to-exist.

Jacobs, Margaret D. *White Mother to a Dark Race: Settler Colonialism, Maternalism, and the Removal of Indigenous Children in the American West and Australia, 1880–1940*. Lincoln: University of Nebraska Press, 2009.

Jung, Patrick J. "Black Hawk War (1832)." In *The Encyclopedia of War*, edited by Gordon Martel. Hoboken, NJ: Blackwell, 2011.

Jung, Patrick J. *The Black Hawk War of 1832*. Norman: University of Oklahoma Press, 2007.

Kauanui, J. Kēhaulani. *Hawaiian Blood: Colonialism and the Politics of Sovereignty and Indigeneity*. Durham, NC: Duke University Press, 2008.

Laplante, Lisa J. "Memory Battles: Guatemala's Public Debates and the Genocide Trial of José Efraín Ríos Montt." *Quinnipiac Law Review* 32, no. 3 (2014): 621.

Lazo, Rodrigo. "Migrant Archives: New Routes in and out of American Studies." In *States of Emergency*. Chapel Hill: University of North Carolina Press, 2009.

LeBaron, Alan Verne. "When Latinos Are Not Latinos: The Case of Guatemalan Maya in the United States, the Southeast, and Georgia." *Latino Studies* 10, no. 1 (2012): 179–95. https://doi.org/10.1057/lst.2012.8.

Levitt, Peggy, and Nina Glick Schiller. "Conceptualizing Simultaneity: A Transnational Social Field Perspective on Society." *Conceptual and Methodological Developments in the Study of International Migration* 38, no. 3 (2004): 1002–39. https://doi.org/10.1111/j.1747-7379.2004.tb00227.x.

Little, Walter E. *Mayas in the Marketplace: Tourism, Globalization, and Cultural Identity*. Austin: University of Texas Press, 2004.

Lonetree, Amy. "A Heritage of Resilience: Ho-Chunk Family Photographs in the Visual Archive." *Public Historian* 41, no. 1 (2019): 34–50. https://doi.org/10.1525/tph.2019.41.1.34.

Loperena, Christopher. *The Ends of Paradise: Race, Extraction, and the Struggle for Black Life in Honduras*. Stanford, CA: Stanford University Press, 2023.

López, Josué. "CRT and Immigration: Settler Colonialism, Foreign Indigeneity, and the Education of Racial Perception." *University of Maryland Law Journal of Race, Religion, Gender, and Class* 19, no. 1 (2019): 134–65.

López, Josué, and Jason G. Irizarry. "Somos pero no somos iguales/We Are But We Are Not the Same: Unpacking Latinx Indigeneity and the Implications for Urban Schools." *Urban Education* 57, no. 9 (2022): 1539–64.

López, Kimberly Rocio. "Mujeres tejedoras: Afuera somos exóticas, acá las "'Marías.'" Plaza Pública. Updated January 16, 2021. https://www.plazapublica .com.gt/content/mujeres-tejedoras-afuera-somos-exoticas-aca-las-marias.

López Oro, Paul Joseph. "Digitizing Ancestral Memory: Garifuna Settlement Day in the Americas and in Cyberspace." In *Indigenous Interfaces, Spaces, Technology, and Social Networks in Mexico and Central America*, edited by Jennifer Gómez Menjívar and Gloria Elizabeth Chacón. Tucson: University of Arizona Press, 2019.

Loucky, James. *Maya in a Modern Metropolis: Establishing New Lives and Livelihoods in Los Angeles*. Philadelphia: Temple University Press, 2000.

Loucky, James, and Marilyn M. Moors. *The Mayan Diaspora: Guatemalan Roots, New American Lives*. Philadelphia: Temple University Press, 2000.

Lovell, W. George. "The Archive That Never Was: State Terror and Historical Memory in Guatemala." *Geographical Review* 103, no. 2 (2013): 199–209. https://doi.org/10.1111/gere.12009.

Lutz, Christopher Hayden, and W. George Lovell. "Survivors on the Move: Maya Migration in Time and Space." Paper presented to the Latin American Studies Association, Washington, DC, April 5, 1991.

Lydon, Jane. "Photography and Critical Heritage: Australian Aboriginal Photographic Archives and Stolen Generations." *Public Historian* 41, no. 1 (2019): 18–33.

Lytle Hernández, Kelly. *City of Inmates: Conquest, Rebellion, and the Rise of Human Caging in Los Angeles, 1771–1965*. Chapel Hill: University of North Carolina Press, 2017.

Macleod, Morna. "Mayan Dress as Text: Contested Meanings." *Development in Practice* 14, no. 5 (2004): 680–89. https://www.jstor.org/stable/4029896.

Magaña, Maurice Rafael. "Multimodal Archives of Transborder Belonging: Murals, Social Media, and Racialized Geographies in Los Angeles." *American Anthropologist* 124, no. 4 (2022): 703–20. https://doi.org/10.1111/aman.13772.

Martínez Salazar, Egla. *Global Coloniality of Power in Guatemala: Racism, Genocide, Citizenship*. Lanham, MD: Lexington Books, 2012.

Mattiace, Shannan L., and Patricia Fortuny Loret de Mola. "Yucatec Maya Organizations in San Francisco, California: Ethnic Identity Formation Across Migrant Generations." *Latin American Research Review* 50, no. 2 (2015): 201–15. https://www.jstor.org/stable/43670296.

Menchú, Rigoberta. *I, Rigoberta Menchú: An Indian Woman in Guatemala*. Edited by Elisabeth Burgos-Debray. New York: Verso, 1983.

Menjívar, Cecilia, and Leisy J. Abrego. "Legal Violence: Immigration Law and the Lives of Central American Immigrants." *American Journal of Sociology* 117, no. 5 (2012): 1380–1421. https://doi.org/10.1086/663575.

Menjívar, Cecilia, and Leisy Abrego. "Legal Violence in the Lives of Immigrants: How Immigration Enforcement Affects Families, Schools, and Workplaces." *American Progress*, 11 December 2012. https://www.americanprogress.org/article/legal-violence-in-the-lives-of-immigrants/.

Menjívar, Cecilia, and Néstor Rodríguez. *When States Kill: Latin America, the U.S., and Technologies of Terror*. Austin: University of Texas Press, 2005.

Minh-Ha, Trinh T. "Documentary Is/Not a Name." *October* 52 (Spring 1990): 76–98. https://www.jstor.org/stable/778886.

Montejo, Victor D. *Maya Intellectual Renaissance*. Austin: University of Texas Press, 2005. https://www.jstor.org/stable/10.7560/706842.

Montejo, Victor D. *Testimony: Death of a Guatemalan Village*. Evanston, IL: Curbstone Press, 1987.

Mora, Mariana. *Kuxlejal Politics: Indigenous Autonomy, Race, and Decolonizing Research in Zapatista Communities*. Austin: University of Texas Press, 2017.

Musalo, Karen, and Blaine Bookey. "Crimes Without Punishment: An Update on Violence Against Women and Impunity in Guatemala." *Hastings Race and Poverty Law Journal* 10 (2013): 265–92.

Nance, Kimberly A. *Can Literature Promote Justice?: Trauma Narrative and Social Action in Latin American Testimonio*. Nashville, TN: Vanderbilt University Press, 2006.

Nepstad, Sharon Erickson. *Convictions of the Soul: Religion, Culture, and Agency in the Central America Solidarity Movement*. New York: Oxford University Press, 2004.

Nepstad, Sharon Erickson. "Oppositional Consciousness among the Privileged: Remaking Religion in the Central American Solidarity Movement." *Critical Sociology* 33, no. 4 (2007): 661–88.

Nguyen, Mimi Thi. "Minor Threats." *Radical History Review*, no. 122 (2015): 11–24.

Nguyen, Viet Thanh. "Refugee Memories and Asian American Critique." *Positions: East Asia Cultures Critique* 20, no. 3 (2012): 911–42.

Nicholls, Walter J. *The DREAMers: How the Undocumented Youth Movement Transformed the Immigrant Rights Debate*. Stanford, CA: Stanford University Press, 2013.

Nicolas, Brenda. "Pertenencia mutua: Indigenous Oaxacans Contesting Settler Colonial Grammars." *American Quarterly* 76, no. 2 (2024): 241–71.

O'Brien, Jean M. *Firsting and Lasting: Writing Indians Out of Existence in New England*. Minneapolis: University of Minnesota Press, 2010.

O'Connor, Brendan H., and Stephanie L. Canizales. "Thresholds of Liminality: Discourse and Embodiment from Separation to Consummation Among Guatemalan Maya Youth Workers in Los Angeles." *International Journal of the Sociology of Language* 2023, no. 279 (2023): 155–79.

Otzoy, Irma. "Maya Clothing and Identity." In *Maya Cultural Activism in Guatemala*, edited by Edward F. Fischer and R. McKenna Brown. Austin: University of Texas Press, 1996.

Pacenza, Matt. "A People Damned: The Chixoy Dam, Guatemalan Massacres and the World Bank." *Multinational Monitor* 17, no. 7–8 (1996).

Parreñas, Rhacel Salazar. *Children of Global Migration: Transnational Families and Gendered Woes*. Stanford, CA: Stanford University Press, 2005.

Patterson, Orlando. *Slavery and Social Death: A Comparative Study*. Cambridge, MA: Harvard University Press, 1982.

Peñalosa, Fernando. "Trilingualism in the Barrio: Mayan Indians in Los Angeles." *Language Problems and Language Planning* 10, no. 3 (1986): 229–52. https://doi.org/10.1075/lplp.10.3.01pea.

Pérez, Rossana, and Henry A. J. Ramos. *Flight to Freedom: The Story of Central American Refugees in California*. Houston: Arte Público Press, 2008.

Philips, Sloan. "The Indian Child Welfare Act in the Face of Extinction." *American Indian Law Review* 21, no. 2 (1997): 352.

Pidduck, Julianne. "Queer Kinship and Ambivalence: Video Autoethnographies by Jean Carlomusto and Richard Fung." *GLQ* 15, no. 3 (2009): 441–68. https://doi.org/10.1215/10642684-2008-031.

Popkin, Eric. "The Emergence of Pan-Mayan Ethnicity in the Guatemalan Transnational Community Linking Santa Eulalia and Los Angeles." *Current Sociology* 53, no. 4 (2005). https://doi.org/10.1177/0011392105052721.

Popkin, Eric. "Guatemalan Mayan Migration to Los Angeles: Constructing Transnational Linkages in the Context of the Settlement Process." *Ethnic and Racial Studies* 22, no. 2 (1999): 267–89. https://doi.org/10.1080/014198799329486.

Portes, Alejandro, and Rubén G. Rumbaut. *Legacies: The Story of the Immigrant Second Generation*. Berkeley: University of California Press, 2001.

Portes, Alejandro, and Min Zhou. "The New Second Generation: Segmented Assimilation and Its Variants." *The ANNALS of the American Academy of Political and Social Science* 530, no. 1 (1993): 74–96. https://doi.org/10.1177/0002716293530001006.

Posocco, Silvia. "On the Queer Necropolitics of Transnational Adoption in Guatemala." In *Queer Necropolitics*, edited by Jin Haritaworn, Adi Kuntsman, and Silvia Posocco. New York: Routledge.

Prieto-Carrón, Marina, Marilyn Thomson, and Mandy Macdonald. "No More Killings! Women Respond to Femicides in Central America." *Gender and Development* 15, no. 1 (2007): 25–40. https://www.jstor.org/stable/20461179.

Ramírez, Claudia. "Mercedes Coroy se pronuncia por comentario racista sobre la indumentaria maya." *El Periódico*, August 20, 2021.

Ramirez, Renya K. *Native Hubs: Culture, Community, and Belonging in Silicon Valley and Beyond*. Durham, NC: Duke University Press, 2007.

Rasch, Elisabet Dueholm. "Transformations in Citizenship: Local Resistance against Mining Projects in Huehuetenango (Guatemala)." *Journal of Developing Societies* 28, no. 2 (June 2012): 159–84. https://doi.org/10.1177/0169796X12448756.

Raxche'. "Maya Culture and the Politics of Development." In *Maya Cultural Activ-*

ism in Guatemala, edited by Edward F. Fischer and R. McKenna Brown. Austin: University of Texas Press, 1996. https://www.jstor.org/stable/10.7560/708501.

Recovery of Historical Memory Project. *Guatemala, Never Again!* Guatemala City: Human Rights Office, Archdiocese of Guatemala, 1999.

Reynolds, Jennifer F. "(Be)Laboring Childhoods in Postville, Iowa." *Anthropological Quarterly* 86, no. 3 (2013): 851–89. https://www.jstor.org/stable/43652639.

Rifkin, Mark. "Settler Common Sense." *Settler Colonial Studies* 3, no. 3–4 (2013): 322–40. https://doi.org/10.1080/2201473X.2013.810702.

Rifkin, Mark. *Settler Common Sense: Queerness and Everyday Colonialism in the American Renaissance.* Minneapolis: University of Minnesota Press, 2014.

Rodríguez, Ana Patricia. *Dividing the Isthmus: Central American Transnational Histories, Literatures, and Cultures.* Austin: University of Texas Press, 2009.

Rodríguez, Ana Patricia. "The Fiction of Solidarity: Transfronterista Feminisms and Anti-Imperialist Struggles in Central American Transnational Narratives." *Feminist Studies* 34, no. 1–2 (2008): 199–228. https://www.jstor.org/stable/20459190.

Rotabi, Karen Smith, and Nicole F. Bromfield. *From Intercountry Adoption to Global Surrogacy: A Human Rights History and New Fertility Frontiers.* New York: Routledge, 2017.

Rotabi, Karen Smith, A. W. Morris, and M. O. Weil. "International Child Adoption in a Post-Conflict Society: A Multi-Systemic Assessment of Guatemala." *Journal of Intergroup Relations* 34, no. 2 (2008): 9–41.

Rumbaut, Rubén G. "The Crucible Within: Ethnic Identity, Self-Esteem, and Segmented Assimilation Among Children of Immigrants." *International Migration Review* 28, no. 4 (1994): 748–94. https://doi.org/10.1177/019791839402800407.

Sanchez, Daina. *Children of Solaga: Indigenous Belonging Across the US-Mexico Border.* Stanford, CA: Stanford University Press. 2024.

Saranillio, Dean Itsuji. "Colliding Histories: Hawaiʻi Statehood at the Intersection of Asians 'Ineligible to Citizenship' and Hawaiians 'Unfit for Self-Government.'" *Journal of Asian American Studies* 13, no. 3 (2010): 283–309.

Schweizer, Yvonne. "Counter-Archive." *Terms: CIHA Journal of Art History* 1 (2023): 27–38.

Sepulveda, Charles. "Our Sacred Waters: Theorizing Kuuyam as a Decolonial Possibility." *Decolonization: Indigeneity, Education and Society* 7, no. 1 (2018): 40–58.

Simpson, Audra. *Mohawk Interruptus: Political Life Across the Borders of Settler States.* Durham, NC: Duke University Press, 2014.

Simpson, Audra. "On Ethnographic Refusal: Indigeneity, 'Voice,' and Colonial Citizenship." *Junctures* 9 (2007): 67–80.

Simpson, Leanne Betasamosake. *As We Have Always Done: Indigenous Freedom Through Radical Resistance.* Minneapolis: University of Minnesota Press, 2017.

Speed, Shannon. *Incarcerated Stories: Indigenous Women Migrants and Violence in the Settler-Capitalist State*. Chapel Hill: University of North Carolina Press, 2019.
Speed, Shannon. "Structures of Settler Capitalism in Abya Yala." *American Quarterly* 69, no. 4 (2017): 783–90. https://doi.org/10.1353/aq.2017.0064.
Stasiulis, Daiva, and Nira Yuval-Davis, eds. *Unsettling Settler Societies: Articulations of Gender, Race, Ethnicity and Class*. Los Angeles: Sage, 1995.
Stephen, Lynn. *Transborder Lives: Indigenous Oaxacans in Mexico, California, and Oregon*. Durham, NC: Duke University Press, 2007.
Stephens, Pamela, and Manuel Pastor. "What's Going On?: Black Experiences of Latinization and Loss in South Los Angeles." *Du Bois Review: Social Science Research on Race* 17, no. 1 (2020): 1–32. https://doi.org/10.1017/S1742058X20000053.
Stoll, David. *Rigoberta Menchú and the Story of All Poor Guatemalans*. Boulder, CO: Westview Press, 1999.
Stuelke, Patricia. "The Reparative Politics of Central America Solidarity Movement Culture." *American Quarterly* 66, no. 3 (2014): 767–90.
TallBear, Kim. "Indigenous Genocide and Reanimation, Settler Apocalypse and Hope." *Aboriginal Policy Studies* 10, no. 2 (2023): 93–111. https://doi.org/10.5663/aps.v10i2.29425.
Taylor, Diana. *The Archive and the Repertoire: Performing Cultural Memory in the Americas*. Durham, NC: Duke University Press, 2003.
Tejada, Karen. "Transplanting the Organizing Seed: Understanding the Political Habitus of Salvadorans in the Metro D.C. Area." *APSA 2010 Annual Meeting Papers*. https://papers.ssrn.com/sol3/papers.cfm?abstract_id=1643987.
Tuck, Eve, and K. Wayne Yang. "Decolonization Is Not a Metaphor." *Decolonization: Indigeneity* 1, no. 1 (2012): 1–40.
Turner, Dale. *This Is Not a Peace Pipe: Towards a Critical Indigenous Philosophy*. Toronto, ON: University of Toronto Press, 2006.
Tzul Tzul, Gladys. *Sistemas de gobierno comunal indígena: Mujeres y tramas de parentesco en chuimeq'ena'*. Mexico City: Instituto Amaq', 2018.
Urrieta, Luis, Jr. "Diasporic Community Smartness: Saberes (Knowings) Beyond Schooling and Borders." *Race, Ethnicity and Education* 19, no. 6 (2016): 1186–99.
Urrieta, Luis, Jr. "Familia and Comunidad-Based Saberes: Learning in an Indigenous Heritage Community." *Anthropology and Education Quarterly* 44, no. 3 (2013): 320–35. https://doi.org/10.1111/aeq.12028.
Urrieta, Luis, Jr. "Indigenous Reflections on Identity, Trauma, and Healing: Navigating Belonging and Power." *Genealogy* 3, no. 2 (2019): 26. https://doi.org/10.3390/genealogy3020026.
Varagur, Krithika. "Mexico Prevents Indigenous Designs from Being Culturally Appropriated—Again." Huffpost.com, March 17, 2016. https://www.huffpost.com/entry/mexico-prevents-indigenous-designs-from-being-culturally-appropriated-again_n_56e87879e4b0b25c9183afc4.

Vargas, Deborah R., Lawrence La Fountain-Stokes, and Nancy Raquel Mirabal, eds. *Keywords for Latina/o Studies*. New York: New York University Press, 2017.

Velasco, Natalie Jo. "The Guatemalan Femicide: An Epidemic of Impunity." *Law and Business Review of the Americas* 14, no. 2 (2008): Article 8.

Velásquez Nimatuj, Irma Alicia. "Memory/Memoir, Challenges, and Anthropology." Translated by Isabel Dulfano. In *Indigenous Feminist Narratives: I/We: Wo(men) of an(Other) Way*, edited by Isabel Dulfano. New York: Palgrave Macmillan, 2015.

Velásquez Nimatuj, Irma Alicia. "Transnationalism and Maya Dress." In *The Guatemala Reader: History, Culture, Politics*, edited by Greg Grandin, Deborah T. Levenson, and Elizabeth Oglesby, 523–31. Durham, NC: Duke University Press, 2011. https://doi.org/10.1215/9780822394679-101.

Vera-Rosas, Gretel H. "The Breaking and Remaking of Everyday Life: Illegality, Maternity and Displacement in the Americas." PhD diss., University of Southern California, 2013.

Vera-Rosas, Gretel H. "Regarding 'the Mother of Anchor-Children': Towards an Ethical Practice of the Flesh." Special issue, *Decolonial Gesture* 11, no. 1 (2014). https://hemisphericinstitute.org/en/emisferica-11-1-decolonial-gesture.html.

Villenas, Sophia. "Latina Mothers and Small-Town Racisms: Creating Narratives of Dignity and Moral Education in North Carolina." *Anthropology and Education Quarterly* 32 (2001): 3–28.

Vizenor, Gerald. *Manifest Manners: Narratives on Postindian Survivance*. Lincoln: University of Nebraska Press, 1999.

Vogt, Wendy A. *Lives in Transit: Violence and Intimacy on the Migrant Journey*. Berkeley: University of California Press, 2018.

Way, John T. *The Mayan in the Mall: Globalization, Development and the Making of Modern Guatemala*. Durham, NC: Duke University Press, 2012.

Wellmeier, Nancy. "Rituals of Resettlement: Identity and Resistance Among Maya Refugees." *Popular Culture* 29, no. 1 (1995): 43–60. https://doi.org/10.1111/j.0022-3840.1995.2901_43.x.

Wellmeier, Nancy J. "Santa Eulalia's People in Exile: Maya Religion, Culture, and Identity in Los Angeles." In *Gatherings in Diaspora: Religious Communities and the New Immigration*, edited by R. Stephen Warner and Judith G. Wittner. Philadelphia: Temple University Press, 1998.

Williams, Philip J., Timothy J. Steigenga, and Manuel A. Vásquez, eds. *A Place to Be: Brazilian, Guatemalan, and Mexican Immigrants in Florida's New Destinations*. New Brunswick, NJ: Rutgers University Press, 2009.

Wilson, Shawn. *Research Is Ceremony: Indigenous Research Methods*. Black Point, NS: Fernwood, 2008.

Wolfe, Patrick. *Settler Colonialism: The Politics and Poetics of an Ethnographic Event*. London: Bloomsbury, 1998.

World Bank. "Guatemala." Poverty and Equity Brief: Latin America and the Caribbean. April 2020. https://databank.worldbank.org/data/download

/poverty/33EF03BB-9722-4AE2-ABC7-AA2972D68AFE/Global_POVEQ_GTM.pdf.

Xón Riquiac, María Jacinta. *Entre la exotización y el mayámetro: Dinámicas contemporáneas del colonialismo.* Guatemala: Catafixia Editorial, 2022.

Zimmer, Eric Steven. "Building the Red Earth Nation: The Civilian Conservation Corps–Indian Division on the Meskwaki Settlement." NAIS: *Journal of the Native American and Indigenous Studies Association* 2, no. 2 (2015): 106–33. https://doi.org/10.1353/nai.2015.a635788.

Zimmer, Eric S. "Settlement Sovereignty: The Meskwaki Fight for Self-Governance, 1856–1937." *Annals of Iowa* 73 (2014): 311–47. https://doi.org/10.17077/0003-4827.12145.

Index

Page numbers in italics refer to figures.

Abrego, Leisy J., 152n6
Acateca, 66–67, 116
Acosta, Oscar Zeta, 94
adoption: Laura Briggs, 39; child trafficking, 148n1; and colonial processes of adoption and missionization, 41; Denese/Dominga, 38–39, 41; displacement, 34; erasure, 33, 38; framed in a discourse of difference, 45; genocide as a cause of, 149n11; Indigenous dispossession, 37, 151n24; Maya migrants categorized as Guatemalans and Latinos, 38; multiracial, 39; Native American children, 39, 42; settler common sense, 37; settler logics, 33, 36; transnational, 34, 37, 45, 149n11; transnational Indigenous, 33; as a transnational strategy of genocide, 45. *See also* Hague Convention on Protection of Children
adoptive family: assimilation, 42; as a corrective for Guatemalan genocide, 37, 39; father, 44; as kind and loving, 37; mother, 38, 42–43; notions of sanctuary, 35, 41; remaining passive in the face of violence, 42
African Americans, 126
Afro-Latinx, 139
Alberto, Lourdes, 17, 119, 154n37
aldeas, 87
Algona, Iowa: constructed as a white town, 43; Denese/Dominga's adoption, 34, 37, 42, 44; discourse of "not knowing," 41, 45; erasing Native existence, 38, 41; history of Indigenous dispossession, 29, 36, 41, 45; racism and exclusion, 46; white adult citizens of, 38, 41–42
Alsultany, Evelyn, 149n7
Alvarado, Karina (Karina Alma), 143n3
Alvarado Goldberg, Marisol, 124–25, 128
Alvarado Goldberg, Mina, 124, 125
American Quarterly, 151n29
American sign language, 125–26
anti-Indigenous politics: borders, 38, 75; clothing, 78; cultural production, 1; deconstructed, 46; *Discovering Dominga*, 42, 46, 52, 150n23; in Guatemala, 44
Araceli: family and tradition, 92; family migration, 102; interviews with, 75; learning K'anjob'al, 91; parents' work, 103–4; skin-color privilege, 76–77; wearing Maya clothing in the diaspora, 68, 70; joining Xinachtli, 94–95
archival: artifacts, 132; materials, 7; materiality, 141; methods, 27, 31; practice, 8, 17, 110, 141; process, 31; records, 86; research, 27; theory, 144n15
Arista, Noelani, 24
Appadurai, Arjun, 7
Árbenz, Jacobo, 9
archives: autonomous, 6; counter-archives, 6, 144n15; digital, 6; institutional, 4–6, 141; migrant, 6, 8, 144n15; multimodal, 6–7; police, 149n8; rebel, 6, 46; unruly, 6
Arévalo, Bernardo, 12
Asociación Femenina para el Desarrollo de Sacatepequez (AFEDES), 156n3
Aspuac, Angelina, 112
asylum, 33

Index 175

Atitlán, Sololá, 59, 156n1
Aztec, 17–18

backstrap loom weaving, 59, 153n15
Baja Verapaz, 1, 29
Barrios Escobar, Lina Eugenia, 58
Batz, Giovanni, 11, 26, 66, 144n26, 156n24
Becker, Denese Joy, 29, 34
Bejarano, Cynthia, 57
Black archives, 5
Black enslavement, 145n34
Black Hawk War of 1832, 36, 149n10
Black Indigenous Garifuna, 116
Black people, 84, 126, 154n5; survival, 19
Black radical movement, 17
Black studies, 4, 22
Boj Chojolan, Oscar Ubaldo, 20
Briggs, Laura, 39, 151n24
Bromfield, Nicole, 34

Cabrera, Thelma, 12
Cacho, Lisa, 153n21
Calderon, Dolores, 18, 152n6
Calderón, Patricia Arroyo, 57
Camila, 66–67, 69, 89, 95
camisa, 70
Cap Sir, Lilia Irene, 58
Carlos, 87, 96
Castañeda, Xóchitl, 66
Castro, Juan, 11, 151n29
Central American Sanctuary Movement (CASM; also known as one part of the Solidarity Movement or the Central American Peace and Solidarity Movement), 39–40, 42
ceremonies, 4, 48, 92
Chacón, Gloria, 17, 24, 58–59, 115
Chapina/Chapin, 87
Chinchilla, Norma, 40
Chixoy Dam, 44
Chuimeq'ena' (Totonicapán), 146n38
Cifuentes, Mario Alvarado, 96
Cinco de Mayo, 106
clothing. See also *corte*; *huipiles*; textiles
Cojtí Cuxil, Demetrio, 15
colonization: history of, 38; Indigenous dispossession, 47, 151n24; Spanish, 11; survival, 131
The Colors of Guatemala: Las aventuras de Gaby, 82, 97–105, 121, 141
Comité de Desarrollo Campesino (Committee on Peasant Development, CODECA), 12

La Comunidad Ixim: *The Colors of Guatemala: Las aventuras de Gaby*, 97–105, 121, 141; background, 30, 81; community belonging, 89; confronting settler colonialism, 110; family genealogies, 82; kinship, 83, 89; Maya identity formation, 90–91, 109; mobile archive, 2, 97–99; not privileging any particular narrative of what it means to be Maya, 105; queerness and contesting heteronormativity, 97; relationships with matriarchal elders, 92; shared collective responsibilities, 93–94, 97; as a social justice space, 95, 109; use of dreams and temporal rupture, 101; youth in diaspora, 85, 87–88, 91, 107
conservatives, 147n59
constitutional law, 156n3
Co-operation in Respect of Intercountry Adoption, 148n1
Corbett, Jim, 40
Cornejo, Kency, 114
corte: as an act of refusal, 56; as the act of wearing a history of place, defiance, and dispossession, 20; as an archive shaped by ancestors, 6; assistance from elders, 20, 70; as a blanket, 70; as celebration, 20, 92; and class, 90; connection to hometown, 65; maintaining relationships to land and kin based on Indigenous ontologies, 64; MWLA, 114; received as a gift, 65; reflections on colorism among Maya in the diaspora, 76; resulting in discrimination and racial slurs, 63; as a tube-top dress, 71; worn with pride and happiness, 64, 76, 122, 124, 131; worn in public, 73; zippers, 69
Cotera, María Eugenia, 4, 154n37
cultural artifacts, 3
cultural genocide, 64
cultural productions, 1–2, 27, 51–52, 109, 141
culture bearers, 4
Curtis, Edward, 114

Davenport, Allison, 66
deaf, 125–26
decolonization, 79, 137
de Landa, Diego, 10
de León, Jason, 145n33
Denetdale, Jennifer Nez, 155n7
diaspora: Black Indigenous Garifuna community, 116; children in, 106; colorism,

76; *The Colors of Guatemala: Las aventuras de Gaby*, 97, 99–100, 103, 105; La Comunidad Ixim, 81, 83, 90, 95, 109–10; contemporary racial structure of Guatemala, 84–85; Garden of Roses, 126; Claudia Patricia Gómez González, 138; Guatemalan national flag, 127–28; identity formation, 90, 109; intergenerational imaginaries, 92; intersectional organizing, 104; joy, 137; kinship ties, 82, 116; Ladinas, 122; Las Fotos Project, 112, 138; mobile archives of Indigeneity, 84; MWLA, 118, 127, 132, 138; not as a binary, 136; notions of "the family," 88; second-generation Maya, 65, 80–81, 92, 98; settler colonialism, 132; settler gaze, 117; state violence, 88; wearing Maya clothing in, 68, 70

diasporic: accountability in scholarship, 23, 27; archival practices, 8, 96–97; belonging, 96; building communities through Indigenous geographies, 55, 67; Chicana feminist lens, 150n23; community knowledge, 68, 71; consciousness, 138; contradiction, 107; cultural artifacts, 3, 67, 72; erasure of Indigenous people, 17, 71; geography of Indigenous families, 126; Indigenous scholars, 23, 26; Las Fotos Project, 130; linguistic or cultural practices, 83; Maya community, 14, 21, 27, 136, 139; Maya gaze, 108; Maya identity, 109, 146n38; Maya relationality, 21; multiple generations, 56, 87, 142; MWLA, 127; scholarship in Black studies and Indigenous studies, 4; self-representation in narratives, 132, 136; transnational ties, 21; understanding Latinidad in the context of imperialism and settler colonialism, 139; using Maya epistemologies to make sense of life in Los Angeles, 2; youth intersectional politics, 96

Dill, Kathleen, 143n1

Dionicio, Leonarda, 112

Discovering Dominga, 34–36, 41–42, 47; background, 29

discrimination: against Maya women, 57–58, 63; Arab/Muslim victims, 149n7; as cause of Maya immigration, 15; clothing as an archive, 64, 68, 80; in *Discovering Dominga*, 43; and Indigeneity, 87; Maya clothing as resistance to, 60, 75, 80; notions of objectivity, 147n59; racist, 16, 63; within the Guatemalan community, 74–75, 77, 86, 156n24

displacement: adoption, 34; anti-Indigenous, 84, 109; *The Colors of Guatemala: Las aventuras de Gaby*, 99; *Discovering Dominga*, 35, 43, 46; discrimination, 80; and dispossession, 62, 90; experience of conducting research, 26; family separation, 88; ICE, 138; Indigenous elimination, 9; intergenerational archive making, 68; intergenerational imaginaries, 46, 50; intergenerational memory, 47, 90–91; material objects, 34; mobile archives of Indigeneity, 4, 53, 61, 64; multiple generations of, 7, 90; in photography, 124, 130, 133, 136; poverty, 63; process of racialization for youth, 88–89; settler colonialism, 79; state violence, 143n3; textiles, 61, 63; undocumented status, 66; use of Maya clothing in the diaspora, 2, 66, 68, 71; youth leadership, 92–93

dispossession: across borders, 36, 38–39; of African Americans, 126; Algona, Iowa, 29, 36, 41, 45; colonization, 47, 151n24; considered foreign in the United States, 44–45; cultural productions, 51; defiance, 20, 62; Denese/Dominga's story, 37–38; and displacement, 62, 90; drought and violent extractive projects, 12; erasure, 18, 37; framing migration as a site of connection, 133; Indigenous adoption, 34, 45, 151n24; Indigenous resistance to, 13, 25, 27; intergenerational, 85, 100; labor exploitation, 57; Latinidad, 139; layered geographies of, 125; Los Angeles history, 18; maintain community ties and practices, 4; material artifacts, 3; Maya as an umbrella term, 13; memory, 49; mobile archives of Indigeneity, 4, 80; "moves to innocence," 40–41; Native American, 36–37, 78, 150n23; relationship to economic development and modernization, 44; research methodology, 25–27; settler colonial logic, 115; settler colonialism, 14, 36, 79, 95, 115; state violence, 9; territorial, 11–13; wearing *corte*, 20; wearing Maya clothing as an act of history of place, defiance, 20, 62

drought, 11–12

Echo Park, 125
elder knowledge, 75
erasure: and assimilation, 154n2; claiming an ancestral survival and resilience, 131, 133; clothing, 60, 71, 80, 141; cultural production, 8; dispossession, 18, 37; and DIY, 98; and forgetting, 142; of Indigenous people, 17–19; Las Fotos Project, 132–33; photography, 112; political critique of, 80; protective silence, 119; refusal of, 60; settler logics, 33, 36; and silence, 6, 143n5; and state-driven identifications, 82; state violence, 9; survivance, 135–36; systematic, 71; transnational adoption, 45; of water and land, 139. *See also* genocide
Esquit, Edgar, 14
Estrada, Alicia Ivonne, 37, 146n41

femicide, 13, 57–58; research, 153n9
Fernandino, 94
fiestas, 69
Fife, John, 40
Finley, Chris, 97
Flynn, Patricia, 34, 48
forgetting: assimilation, 132; discourses of, 1; and erasure, 142
fostering, 33
Fregoso, Rosa-Linda, 57
Fuss, Caroline, 59

Gabrielino, 56, 71, 94
García, Raquel, 55
gender nonconforming, 95
genocide: adoption as a result of, 39, 45; Algona, Iowa, 29, 36; context of colonial waves in Guatemala, 11–12; context of impunity, 57; cultural, 64; Denese/Dominga learning about, 34–35; denying, 1, 35, 149n8; *Discovering Dominga*, 35, 37; dispossession, 25; emigration from Guatemala, 11, 15, 89; erasure, 18, 29, 36, 133; genealogical ties, 88; historical memory, 52; history writing, 6; Indigeneity and queerness, 97; intergenerational imaginaries, 46; intergenerational memory, 47–48; legacy of, 26; living through, 131; longer project of, 21; Maya clothing worn in response to, 56; Maya women elders, 116; mission projects in schools, 18; Native Americans, 9, 149n11; official state narratives, 1; politics of claiming places of origin, 141; portrayal of United States as land of sanctuary, 35–36, 41; relationship to economic development and modernization, 44; relationship to social death, 13, 65, 145n34; sexual violence, 60; surviving, 6, 19, 116, 130, 133; systematic, 42; transnational adoption wave, 34, 45
gentrification, 123–24
Giammattei, Alejandro, 12
Gilroy, Paul, 5
Goldberg, Elizabeth Swanson, 148n6
Gómez-Barris, Macarena, 151n31
Gómez González, Claudia Patricia, 138
Grandin, Greg, 57, 155n6
Gray, Herman, 151n31
Grijalva, 113, 120
Guatemala, Never Again!, 88
Guatemala: anti-Indigenous politics, 44; causes of emigration, 15; civil war, 3, 11, 26, 36, 84, 122, 131; emigration from, 11, 15, 89; erasure of settler colonialism, 36; genocide and international adoption, 37, 39; national flag, 127–28; population and violence, 10; racism, 76, 82, 122; second generation learning about, 76; state violence, 9, 16
Guidotti-Hernández, Nicole Marie, 148n5

Hague Convention on Protection of Children, 33, 148n1
Hale, Charles, 147n59, 154n5
Hall, Stuart, 6
Hartman, Saidiya, 4
Heidbrink, Lauren, 145n33, 146n41
Herbert, Jean-Loup, 153n17
Hernández, Ester, 143n5
Hernández, Kelly Lytle, 46, 155n3
Hernández Castillo, R. Aída, 14, 139, 147n59
Herrera, Juan, 15
historical erasure, 133
Ho-Chunk, 157n8
hometown associations (HTAS), 81, 89
homophobia, 95, 104
Huehuetenango, 30, 81, 116
huipiles, 20, 55, 67
Hunt, Sarah, 12, 99

Ibarra, Eric, 113
Immigration and Customs Enforcement (ICE), 138–39
Indian Removal Act of 1830, 37
intergenerational imaginaries, 46–48, 50, 92; transborder, 46

178   Index

International Monetary Fund, 144n26
intersectional politics, 82–83
Ixil communities, 11, 149n8

Jewish, 124, 154n5
Joj, Walter Amilcar Paz, xvii
Julia: Indigeneity and identity, 121; navigating race topics, 119–20, 128; photographer for MWLA, 118, 131–32; photographing her aunt, 122–23; sharing clothing with her aunt, 124

Kab'awil, 105
K'anjob'al: communication, 116; ethnic identity, 73, 81, 90–91, 104; prayers, 92
Kennedy, Francesca, 111–12, 156n1
K'iche': communication, 22, 29, 48, 108, 121, 125–26; ethnic identity, 57, 62, 81, 90, 92, 96, 132; Rigoberta Menchú, 92; story, 93
Kizh, 56, 71, 94
Koana, 24
Kuxlejal, 27, 147n59
Kwe, 24

Ladina/o, 75–76, 104, 122, 145n35
land tenure, 7
Laplante, Lisa, 149n8
Las Fotos Project: background, 112; collaboration with, 113; gallery exhibit, 132, 138; participation with, 118; photos, 117, 123, 125, 134, 135; written statements from participants, 130
Latina/o: Boyle Heights, 119; identity, 16–17, 66, 77, 107, 113; and Native American experiences, 78; organizations, 94; paradigm, 107; Pico Union–Westlake, 119; as racialized subjects in the US, 120; read as non-Indigenous, 118, 156n24; space, 109; studies, 16; urban context, 103
Latinidad, 3–4; as a category of power, 31; assimilation into Mexicanness, 7; being made to feel invisible, 107; erasure of Indigenous roots, 17; erasure through absorption, 18; read as non-Indigenous, 107, 109–10, 118, 156n24
Lazo, Rodrigo, 7
lengua, 87
Lisa, 86–87, 94, 98, 103
logics: decolonial spatial, 78; genocidal, 132; Indigenous, 21; of power, 97; settler, 33, 84, 134; settler colonial, 29, 34–36, 38, 78, 97, 152n6; settler colonial dispossession, 115
Lonetree, Amy, 157n8
Look magazine, 111, 156n1
López Oro, Paul Joseph, 115–16
Loret de Mola, Patricia, 89
Lydon, Jane, 157n7

Macario family, 125: Jackelyn, 126; Vivian, 126
Magaña, Maurice, 7
Manz, Beatriz, 66
Maricela, 131–32
massacre: against Achí community, 34–35; Algona, Iowa, 46; Denese/Dominga's story, 12, 41, 43, 45, 50; *Discovering Dominga*, 49; during the 1980s, 11; intergenerational memories, 47, 49; maps, 145n28; by military, 1; Jesús Tecú Osorio's testimony, 2, 51; Río Negro, 1, 29, 34, 41, 44, 50
Mateo, 90, 92, 94–95, 103–4
Mattiace, Shannan, 89
Maya Achí: Denese/Dominga's story, 35, 51; survivors of massacres, 29, 34, 47, 51
Maya cosmovision, 54, 70, 72, 81
Maya epistemologies: ceremonies, 49; collectivity in diaspora, 97; connections with Maya identity through grandparents, 91; cultural productions, 2; historical memory, 3; mobile archive of Indigeneity, 53, 75, 82; survival strategies, 46
Maya Womxn in L.A. (MWLA): background, 113–14; as a collective of Maya and Guatemalan women, 121; exhibit with community support, 127, 132, 135–36; gentrification, 124; Emily Grijalva, 120; Maya geography, 123; as process of archive making, 121, 136; research interviews, 118
McConahay, Mary Jo, 34
memory: archives of Indigeneity, 8; cosmolectics for Mesoamerica, 24; in diaspora, 3, 49; genocide, 52; intergenerational, 47–48; historical, 3, 29, 35, 52; and historical materiality, 5; and land, 51; Maya epistemologies, 3; mobile archives of Indigeneity, 35; multidirectional intergenerational, 3; as part of an ongoing struggle, 149n8; power of, 1; rejecting Indigenous dispossession, 27; spirituality, 49; state violence, 35, 49, 53

Menchú, Rigoberta, 22, 92
Menjívar, Cecilia: role of US, 9; state violence, 144n24
Meskwaki, 36–38
mestizaje, 4, 7, 17, 139
migration map, 135
Miguel, 85–87, 94, 98
military: civilian patrol, 143n1; Denese/Dominga's story, 34; government, 44; Guatemalan civil war, 10, 44; Mateo's grandmother, 90; Miguel's grandfather, 86; Jesús Tecú Osorio's testimony, 1; recruitment, 86; Río Negro community, 44; Sepur Zarco trials, 57; violence, 129
Minh-Ha, Trinh T., 148n6
mixed methodology, 147n66
mobile archives of Indigeneity: *The Colors of Guatemala: Las aventuras de Gaby*, 82; connections among Maya women, 68, 75; cultural materials, 50, 138, 140–41; defined, 4, 30; different from traditional archives, 5, 8, 141; intergenerational impact of colonialism, 83; layered under legacies of violence, 55; migrant archives, 8; multiple generations collectively sharing information, 84, 140–141; MWLA, 114, 118, 136; normalizing the conditions of dispossession, 34; photography, 31, 114, 118; reclaiming of self-representation, 128; refusing easy incorporation into settler colonialism, 35, 80, 88, 136; sustaining ongoing social relations, 7–8; theory and conceptual framework, 21; weaving in and out of multiple identities, 15, 97, 118
mobility: collective consciousness, 7; cultural productions, 52; diaspora and Indigeneity, 140, 152n1; engaging with multiple forms of displacement and belonging, 30, 136; Indigenous migrant identity, 3; material objects, 8, 30; Maya clothing, 77; and Native subjectivity, 77; restricted, 18; socioeconomic, 152n1; transforming cultural practices, 79
Montejo, Victor, 13–14, 145n35
Mora, Mariana, 27, 147n59
"moves to innocence," 40–41. *See also* settler colonialism
Movimiento Estudiantil Chicana/o de Aztlán (MEChA), 94, 121
Movimiento Nacional de Tejedoras—Ruchajixik ri qana'ojb'äl (National Movement of Weavers), 111, 153n18

multimethodology, 25–28
museums, 5, 74

Nahuatl, 17
narco state, 13
national flag, 127–28
Native American Graves Protection and Repatriation Act (NAGPRA), 5
Native survivance, 41
naturales, 14, 63
necropolitics, 2, 25, 60
Negrón-Gonzales, Genevieve, 152n6
neoliberalism, 13, 34, 60
Nepstad, Sharon, 40, 150n18
Nguyen, Mimi Thi, 98
Nguyen, Viet, 153n24
Nicolas, Brenda, 17, 68

Oaxaca, 7, 44
objectivity, 147n59, 148n6
1.5 generation, 47, 89, 152n1, 152n6
Operation Gatekeeper, 145n33
Otzoy, Irma, 57, 72, 108

Patterson, Orlando, 145n34
peraje, 60
Pérez, Rossana, 40, 150n18
photography: challenging erasure, 112, 157n7; Las Fotos Project, 112–14; in mobile archives, 31; MWLA, 31; as a problematic medium, 31, 114, 118, 141; training, 124
Pico Union–Westlake, 17, 118–20
Picq, Manuela, 11, 151n29
Pidduck, Julianne, 88
plantation owners, 11
plátanos, 99
Pop Wuj, 81, 93, 133
po't, 20, 54–55
Prensa Comunitaria, 145n30
pueblo pedagogy, 68
Puga Ortiz, Ale, 55

Q'eqchi', 57, 155n8
queer: Black scholars, 4; excluded from notions of family, 88; and genderqueer possibilities, 83; La Comunidad Ixim, 83, 95–97, 109, 141; Mateo, 104; mobile archives of Indigeneity, 30; multiple identities and collectives to form a Maya diaspora, 15, 83; normalization of, 95; Q-Team, 94
Quetzaltenango (Xelajuj No'j): Anabel,

65; clothing from, 30, 57, 71, 92, 96; Esperanza, 62–63; Emily Grijalva, 120; location, 54; in Los Angeles, 81; Museo Ixkik', 55; María Rosario, 74; Mateo, 90, 92; photo exhibit, 8; textiles from, 55; transgender festivals, 96; Valentina, 65

Ramirez, Renya, 95
Ramos, Henry A. J., 40, 150n18
Raxche', 15
Reagan, Ronald, 40
redevelopment, 123
reina, 119
relationality: alliances with Native communities, 78; La Comunidad Ixim, 90; diasporic Maya, 21; effect on research and writing, 21, 26; mobile archives, 31, 118; MWLA, 136, 141; not linear, 95
Rifkin, Mark, 18, 37–38, 149n11. *See also* settler common sense
Rodríguez, Ana Patricia, 150n23
Rodríguez, Nestor, 144n24
Rotabi, Karen, 34

sahumador, 48–50, 52
Saldaña-Portillo, María Josefina, 154n37
Sanchez, Daina, 17, 134
Sánchez-López, Luis, 17
Santa Eulalia, 90
Schweizer, Yvonne, 5
second generation (or 2nd generation): Camila, 66–67; children's coloring book, 30, 83; clothing as archive, 68, 70, 73, 80; fragmentation and understanding, 88; learning about Guatemala, 76; Lila, 72–73; Mayas in diaspora, 65, 80–81, 98; migration as an ongoing process, 55, 88–89, 95, 98, 152n1; mobile archive of Indigeneity, 82, 109, 141; narratives, 98; organizing, 82, 95; perspective on migration, 89; racial hierarchies in Guatemala, 76, 82; terminology, 152n1; support from elders, 69–70, 75; and traditions and practices, 71, 79, 141; understanding first-generation experiences, 63, 70, 75; undocumented experiences, 65; wearing regional clothing, 28, 53–54, 68–71, 73, 79–80
Self Help Graphics and Arts, 113
Sepulveda, Charles, 139
Sepur Zarco trials, 57, 60
Sessions, Jeff, 33
settler colonialism: and Algona, Iowa, 37,

42; article about, 151n29; category of Latinidad, 4, 139; contesting, 80, 96; *Discovering Dominga*, 36, 41; erasure of the parallels that exist between the United States and Guatemala, 36; heteronormativity, 83, 97; historical use of photography, 114; imperialism, 42; Indigeneity and land, 140; Indigenous survival, 87, 96; interpersonal violence, 129; leadership of Maya women, 136; Maya identity and clothing, 78–79; mobile archives of Indigeneity, 35, 77–78; and "moves to innocence," 40–41; multiple generations confronting, 110; naturalizing, 56; patriarchy, 97; photography and technology, 114; and racial capitalism, 76, 96; scholars engaged with, 144n22, 150n18, 151n29; state violence, 129; US racial logic of Native elimination, 38; waves of, 11, 13
settler colonial theory, 10–11, 151n29
settler common sense, 18, 37–38, 149n11
settler gaze, 35, 117, 131
settler logics: anti-Indigenous, 84, 134; normalization of, 33, 38
silence: collective belonging, 129; Denese/Dominga, 43; exclusion from Latinidad, 17; and histories of displacement, 88; La Comunidad Ixim, 97; Las Fotos Project, 130; loss of older generations, 87; not showing or depicting Native sovereignty, 45; protection in response to erasure and racism, 6, 119–20, 143
Simpson, Audra, 23, 155n7
Simpson, Leanne Betasamosake, 24
Smith, Linda Tuhiwai, 23
Speed, Shannon, 151n29
social conflict, 145n28
social death: genocide, 13, 65; immigrant portrayals, 153n21; state violence, 145n34
social reproduction, 13, 57, 111, 124, 136, 145n34
Solidarity Movement, or the Central American Peace and Solidarity Movement, 39
Southern California Library, 94
South Los Angeles, 17, 21, 113, 126
sovereignty: *Discovering Dominga*, 45; Indigenous, 75, 79; Native, 45, 76; original peoples of Los Angeles, 94–95; political, 19, 85, 155n7; settler logics, 38; threats to Maya, 11

Spanish colonization, 11
Spears-Rico, Gabriela, 17
spirituality: cosmolectics, 24; cosmovision, 49; as an ethical and aesthetic framework, 30; *huipiles*, 20; identity, 70, 78; memory, 49; sense of belonging with Catholic Church or Evangelical denominations, 15
Stasiulis, Daiva, 144n22
state violence: acculturation, 16; cultural production, 143n3; and diaspora, 88; and dispossession, 9; gendered, 28, 130; in Guatemala, 9, 16; historical memory, 35, 49, 53; influence on migration, 16, 146n42; intergenerational imaginaries, 46; interpersonal, 129; Maya cultural practices, 16, 53; Maya history and great civilization, 14; personal history intertwined with, 101, 105; settler colonialism, 87, 129; as sites of belonging and collective meaning, 141; social death, 145n34; and space for joy and survival, 2, 131; transnational Indigenous adoption, 33, 35; transnational ties, 21; US role in Latin America, 144n24
Stephens, Pamela, 44
Stoll, David, 22
Stuelke, Patricia, 40, 42

TallBear, Kim, 155n7
Tataviam, 94
Teatro Frida Kahlo, 1
Tecú Osorio, Jesús, 2, 51, 143n2
Ten Years of Spring, 9
textiles: age and significance, 74; among layers of textuality, 27; appealing to a Western market and trends, 59; as archives, 30, 74, 138; collective resistance to injustices, 60; co-optation of Maya textiles by fashion designers today, 10, 134; as a critical intervention against cultural erasure, 133; IX Style, 156n1; Las Fotos Project and exhibit, 128, 132; Maya, 55–56, 58–61; Movimiento Nacional de Tejedoras—Ruchajixik ri qana'ojb'äl (National Movement of Weavers), 153n18; relationships embedded in the wearing of them, 53; relationship to particular geographic and regional areas, 152n1; as texts, 108; as vibrant Indigenous social relations, 6; and weaving, 59
Tongva, 56, 71, 94, 139
tortillas, 99
Tot, Rodrigo, 155n8
tourism, 14, 58, 112, 115, 153n17
traje, 58, 152n1
trans, 94–95
tribal citizenship, 7
T-shirt, 2
Tuck, Eve, 22, 40, 79
Turner, Dale, 19
Turtle Island, 71, 78, 144n21
Tzul Tzul, Gladys, 146n38

United Fruit Company, 9
United Nations, 145n34
Urrieta, Luis, 147n65
US Border Patrol, 19

Vásquez Ruiz, Michelle, 18
Velásquez Nimatuj, Irma Alicia, 29, 58, 145n28
Vera-Rosas, Gretel, 88
Villenas, Sophia, 150n21
Vizenor, Gerald, 75, 143n4

War on Drugs, 126
Wilson, Shawn, 21
whitemalans, 132
Wolfe, Patrick, 144n22
Wyvernwood, 122–23. *See also* gentrification

Xelajuj No'j (Quetzaltenango, Guatemala): Anabel, 65; clothing from, 30, 57, 71, 92, 96; Esperanza, 62–63; Emily Grijalva, 120; location, 54; in Los Angeles, 81; María Rosario, 74; Mateo, 90, 92; Museo Ixkik', 55; photo exhibit, 8; textiles from, 55; transgender festivals, 96; Valentina, 65
Xinachtli, 94–95
Xón Riquiac, María Jacinta, 14

Yang, K. Wayne, 22, 40, 79
Yuval-Davis, Nira, 144n22

Zapatista, 147n59
Zapotecs, 24

www.ingramcontent.com/pod-product-compliance
Lightning Source LLC
Chambersburg PA
CBHW020237170426
43202CB00008B/121